James J. Holmer

ISAAC HECKER AND HIS FRIENDS

ISAAC HECKER

and His Friends

Revised Edition

by
Joseph McSorley
of the Paulist Fathers

PAULIST PRESS
New York/Paramus/Toronto

Copyright 1952 by
B. Herder Book Co.

Copyright ©1972 by
The Missionary Society
of St. Paul the Apostle
in the State of New York

Published by Paulist Press
Editorial Office: 1865 Broadway, N.Y., N.Y. 10023
Business Office: 400 Sette Drive, Paramus, N.J. 07652

Printed and bound in the
United States of America

A Deus Books Edition of Paulist Press,
originally published under the title
Father Hecker and His Friends

Foreword

There are two dangerous, all-hungry provincialisms — space and time.

To read the story of Isaac Hecker and his friends is an antidote to the provincialism of time. We discover that a century ago men were asking questions often considered our own twentieth-century invention. We discover that aspirations of our nature and questions of our soul are so imperative that they repeat themselves, generation after generation.

Since their days, moreover, we have been shrinking space, collapsing distances, stretching the outer edges of our experience to encompass planets other than our own. Yet expanding space has not been enough to answer our deepest human needs. Wherever we go we run up against ourselves.

We read of Hecker and his companions and we are at ease with them because we feel that they would be at ease in the world we now inhabit. They challenge us still because the questions they asked are still fresh.

For over a hundred years the children of their dreams, the Paulist Fathers and others, have tried to stretch themselves for a catch of the founding spirit of these men. Not always successfully, not always easily, and for that matter not always willingly.

That such a dream persists says much. It is not easily realized. But more than this, it is worth whatever struggle is necessary to find ways for men to live with each other, seeking to fulfill visions that are bound by neither space nor time.

A community of male religious might not, in the

1970's, be the most natural place to look for men in touch with themselves, in touch with the times and in touch with the deepest yearnings of their fellows.

But it is one place. As a grateful member of the community which began with Isaac Hecker and his friends, with their sensitivity and insight, dead seriousness and good humor, I have the pleasure to recommend their story.

May you find in them men you would like as your own friends.

Conversion of St. Paul Thomas F. Stransky
January 25, 1972 President, Paulist Fathers

Contents

FOREWORD v

PART I
FIVE CONVERT REDEMPTORISTS

STUDY
- I. A Century Ago 3
- II. The First Missions 15
- III. The Southland 30
- IV. New Horizons 41
- V. Hecker in Rome 53
- (*Notes for Part I*) 69

PART II
THE PAULISTS

- VI. A "Community for Conversions" . . . 91
- VII. The Walworth Episode 106
- VIII. The First Paulist Parish 119
- IX. The First Ten Paulists 131
- X. Platform and Press 154
- XI. Hecker's Message 169
- (*Notes for Part II*) 188

CONTENTS

PART III

THE LATTER NINETEENTH CENTURY

XII.	THE AMERICAN SCENE	205
XIII.	HECKER AND BROWNSON	214
XIV.	HECKER AND ELLIOTT	237
XV.	HEWIT, GLORIFIED YANKEE	254
XVI.	DESHON, THE WEST POINTER	274
	(*Notes for Part III*)	289
	INDEX	299

PART I
Five Convert Redemptorists

I. A CENTURY AGO
II. THE FIRST MISSIONS
III. THE SOUTHLAND
IV. NEW HORIZONS
V. HECKER IN ROME

I

A Century Ago

(Notes, p. 69 ff.)

THE Paulist Fathers began to exist in 1858, just as the United States was completing an era of unique political and religious significance. In its first seven decades of history the nation had pushed its boundaries south to Mexico and west to the Pacific Ocean; the population had grown from three million to thirty million; the transcontinental railroad was helping to settle the great open spaces beyond the Rocky Mountains and to bring the gold of California back East. Education spread; the rotary printing press multiplied books and pamphlets, and provided the masses with daily newspapers. Steamboats and the magnetic telegraph helped to amalgamate the people and to deepen general confidence in the splendid destiny of the young Republic.

Inevitably in this phase the nation encountered various obstacles to peaceful, orderly development. Some trouble came from two minor wars, one with England and one with Mexico, and from sporadic conflicts with Indian tribes. More serious difficulties, occasioned by political and racial controversies over

States' rights and Negro slavery, were forecasting the Civil War. Gravest and most enduring source of disunity was religious antagonism—still a poisonous element in our life today, after more than a hundred fifty years of history. Although the spirit of enlightened toleration embodied in the Constitution had an effect upon the individual States, so that religious discrimination was gradually eliminated from their legislation, yet old prejudices were whipped up recurrently by clashing interests and intensified by misunderstanding; and sometimes deliberate calumny occasioned bitterness and even tragic violence.

The principle of universal religious equality established by the federal constitution was accepted by Rhode Island at once, and by Virginia after a short interval. Pennsylvania and Delaware extended equality to Christians only; and four States (New York, New Jersey, North Carolina and Georgia) extended it to Protestants only. Five States (Massachusetts, Connecticut, New Hampshire, Maryland, South Carolina) actually established a Protestant State Church. New Hampshire disqualified all non-Protestants for State office until 1877.[1]

Between the adoption of the Constitution and the outbreak of the Civil War the population grew ten times larger; and Catholics became a hundred times more numerous. Thus, instead of being one per cent of the total population, they formed ten per cent—a fact which of itself might give rise to a certain amount of uneasiness among Protestants. There were also other disturbing features in the religious situation.

When John Carroll—first bishop of the United States in 1789, and first archbishop in 1808—died in 1815 he had solved many complex problems happily; and the Church was in relatively good condition. But in the following years Catholic progress was checked by racial jealousies, incompetent clergy, rebellious laity. Archbishop Ambrose Maréchal, S.S., of Baltimore and his French fellow bishops, remembering the recent excesses of the French Revolution, were suspicious of such words as "liberty," and "democracy." And their attitude towards the Irish was presented frankly enough in Maréchal's memorandum which begged the Holy See not to allow the hierarchy of Ireland to nominate candidates for American sees, and not to permit Irish bishops to send unworthy priests to America. Speaking for the other side, the Irish priest, Father William V. Harold, O.P., who spent five years in America and served as vicar general in Philadelphia, while admitting the scandal given by some of his compatriots, urged the Holy See to come to the rescue of tens of thousands of Irish who were being lost to the faith in the United States for lack of priests, and also to make sure that American sees would not be filled by Frenchmen, worthy in other respects, but unable to speak intelligible English. The confusion due to this division of views was exploited in various cities by church trustees, who organized several threatening schisms. Bigots, of course, took advantage of all these troubles to publicize the harm that Catholics had inflicted and would inflict upon the community as a whole. In 1820 Rome made an effort to improve conditions in the United States by sending the courageous and able John England to fill the newly created See of Charleston. His boldness, tireless energy and tact quickly wrought improvement, although much of his work was allowed to disintegrate after his death in 1842.[2]

So far as the Germans were concerned, they were indeed involved in some of the trustee rebellions; but, on the whole, their chief defect was the failure to promote the development of a general sense of American unity transcending religious boundaries. Chief target of the Native American attack, was the largest racial group, the Irish, who had inherited a hatred of English-speaking Protestants. To place this hatred in proper perspective, one must recall that the penal code established in Ireland by the English was, in Edmund Burke's words, a machine "well fitted for the oppression, impoverishment, and degradation of a people, and the debasement in them of human nature itself." According to William Lecky, the record of its operation fills "one of the blackest pages in the history of persecution." Catholic Emancipation, conceded by the British Parliament in 1829, did not terminate frightful brutalities; and the truth of Burke's phrase was justified in the famines of the late forties when "all the roads of Ireland seemed to lead only to the graveyard, the poorhouse, or the emigrant ship."

These conditions caused huge waves of immigration to America; and the Irish brought with them, incorporated in their very proverbs, the memory of ghastly cruelties—not least the barbarities of Cromwell, forefather of the New England Puritans. The unschooled, pauperized immigrants could not forget that their sad fate was due largely to generations of mistreatment at the hands of the educated lawmakers of England; and many found themselves almost irresistibly inclined to hate culture and to resist the law.

Unfortunately, nearly two-thirds of the Irish settled in cities rather than on the land—a choice due partly to their reluctance to venture into the "open spaces," partly to their crippling poverty, partly to poor leadership. Looking back years later, Archbishop John Ireland and Bishop John L. Spalding lamented the incompetence of those who failed to direct tens of thousands of families into rural areas where they might have gained an honorable competence, "instead of going down to ruin in the fierce maelstrom of large cities." [3]

Irishmen worked strenuously in the building trades and the construction of railroads; the women took employment in domestic service and earned a reputation for faithful work. But a large percentage, forced to dwell in filthy tenements, engaged in liquor traffic; and the high rate of slum-dwelling and lawbreaking among the Irish provoked scornful criticism. Living in foul homes and paying rent to their richer fellow citizens, they seemed like malcontents to be imprisoned, beaten or even killed when they resisted injustice or violence.⁴ If the situation just described reflects little credit on the Irish, it certainly reflects no credit whatever on their neighbors—as fair-minded Protestants eventually came to see.

The reaction of the native Americans to the shortcomings of the Irish developed a hardy myth that perpetuated itself among all classes of peoples and led them to ignore the fine contributions that Ireland was making to the strength and the integrity of the young Republic. The "Nativists" overlooked the Irish Catholics whose loyalty to America and its principles were unassailable; men who were embodiments of the European tradition of culture and had received a finished education far superior to any obtainable on this side of the Atlantic; writers whose superb ability was demonstrated in the course of more than one public controversy. All this went for nothing in the minds of unreasoning anti-Catholic bigots whose shame is told in many historical accounts written by non-Catholics. Infected with suspicion, dislike, intolerance, they forgot that a large percentage of Irish Catholics, "brought with them from their native country a great knowledge of the Republic, profound admiration for its success over England." ⁵

In the thirties and forties, Catholics increased by nearly a million. Facing the obligation of providing for the urgent needs of this enormous multitude, the bishops could hardly achieve a careful screening of those priests from abroad who offered to serve on the American mission. Many of the foreign-born clergy proved to be devoted and zealous; some, however, were allergic to discipline; some scorned the idea of reading the Gospel in the vernacular to their congregations; some boasted that they had never received a convert into the Church. Yet the comparatively helpless Catholic immigrants had to depend very largely on their clergy; and this strengthened the Protestant belief that Catholics as a body were priest-ridden, incapable of self-reliance, constitutionally unable to assimilate the American tradition of personal initiative.

When we sum up the circumstances above described, we are not surprised that fear and dislike of Catholics kept deepening and spreading. Here was a tremendous horde of immigrants who, even if they did not at that moment actually form a serious economic menace, did at least threaten to grow into a mighty force hostile to Protestants and even destructive of the American way of life. A fairly general sentiment of dislike and contempt for the Irish is reflected in many of the well known writers of the time. For example, Thoreau in *Walden* calls them "a dirty, shiftless race"; he says that the "culture of an Irishman is an enterprise to be undertaken with a sort of moral bog hoe"; he makes the comment on his Irish neighbor, John Field, that neither he nor his posterity will rise in this world, "until their wading, webbed, bog-trotting feet get talaria to their heels." [6]

Two centuries had passed since the Pilgrims and Puritans disembarked on these shores to found a new

England in the western hemisphere and since the Reverend John Harvard bequeathed one-half of his estate of fifteen hundred pounds to erect a college. America had evolved a new caste, "The Brahmins," each man of whom, according to Holmes, had behind him "four or five generations of gentlemen and gentlewomen." These aristocrats would naturally look back with regret to the days of the first Bishop of Boston, John Louis Anne Magdalen Cheverus, the gracious Frenchman, who charmed Protestants with his courtly manner for fifteen years before he returned to his native land, to die there in 1836, a peer of France, a counsellor of State, a cardinal of the Roman Church. In later years, the Bishop of Boston was John Bernard Fitzpatrick, son of Irish immigrants, who battled boldly in defense of the civil rights of his flock; and in 1859—when a Catholic boy, one Tommy Wall, was whipped for refusing to read the Protestant Bible and to recite Protestant prayers in a public school—raised such a storm that for the first time Catholics had to be placed on the Boston School Committee.

From the early thirties to the middle fifties antagonism to Catholics found expression in various places and in many forms. Vicious calumnies spread by preachers, writers, editors, publishers led to violence. In many cities churches were destroyed and Catholics were killed.[7] The Ursuline convent in Charlestown, Massachusetts, was burned; and some years later in Ellsworth, Maine, a Jesuit was tarred and feathered. The celebrated inventor, Samuel F. B. Morse, published an attack on the Catholic Church entitled *A Foreign Conspiracy Against the United States*. Rebecca Reed wrote a filthy tale about nuns; and the notorious Maria Monk wrote another equally vile book which was edited by Theodore Dwight, nephew of the president of Yale, and published by Harper Brothers who marketed 80,000 copies.

As the middle of the century approached, American Catholics and American Protestants seemed to be separated by a practically impassable chasm. The less sympathetic Protestants regarded the immigration of the Catholic Irish to this country as a major national affliction. Even the better disposed were sometimes, at least temporarily, alienated; this was the case, for example, with Brownson and Hecker. Orestes Brownson, sensitive to anti-American prejudices, said that Irish Catholics had led the Americans to believe that Catholicism and Americanism are incompatible; and Hecker wrote in his diary "the R.C. Church . . . does not meet our wants, nor does it fully understand and sympathize with the experience and dispositions of our people." Fortunately, both Brownson and Hecker persevered in their search for the truth; and eventually they perceived that the Church was not and could not be racial or national, that it was and had to be global, universal, truly catholic.

The peak of the Native American outrages had passed by 1845—indeed, some of the anti-Catholic calumnies and activities backfired, moving decent-minded Protestants to denounce the behavior of their co-religionists. Thus, for example, Colonel William A. Stone, editor of the New York *Commercial Advertiser,* at much trouble and expense, personally investigated the charges made in Maria Monk's book; and his findings formed "the most effective setback that Maria Monk received."

The liberal policy inaugurated by Pius IX in 1846 seemed to forecast a democratic regime in the Papal States. America showed enthusiasm.[8] The United States sent a representative to the Vatican; a Protestant clergyman was attached to the legation there; and when Archbishop Gaetano Bedini was attacked during his visit to America in 1853, the United States despatched official regrets to the Holy See.[9]

With the passing of time Americans were beginning to see plain evidence of the integrity, the intelligence, and the loyalty of their Catholic fellow citizens. Scholarly bishops made a genuine impression by their writings and their lectures.[10] Pioneer priests and prelates played a heroic role in the settling of the West. Families like the Carrolls, and public men, such as William Gaston and Roger Brooke Taney, personified characteristics which the nation could not but admire. Meanwhile men and women converted to the Catholic faith were living demonstrations of her power to uplift and sanctify.[11] Nine converts—all but one of them native Americans—ultimately became members of the hierarchy;[12] and many converts wrote persuasive accounts of the motives which had led them into the Catholic fold.[13]

The seven provincial councils of Baltimore from 1829 to 1849 issued decrees and pastoral letters which reflect the temper of the times and the Catholic reaction. Like a series of commentaries upon religious conditions in the United States, they reveal fluctuations of hostility in the press; baseless calumnies refuted, then published again; the collecting of money to wage war upon Catholicism; the denunciation of Catholics as disloyal to the Republic; unpunished outbreaks of violence; unfair discrimination against Catholics in the public schools; attempts to proselytize Catholic children by slanted teaching and bigoted textbooks. The Third Provincial Council of 1837 answered the charge against the loyalty of American Catholics with the statement, "We acknowledge the spiritual and ecclesiastical supremacy of the chief bishop of our universal church, the pope." But "we do not detract from the allegiance to which the temporal governments are plainly entitled, and which we cheerfully give; nor do we acknowledge any civil or political supremacy, or power over us in any foreign potentate or power, though that potentate might be the chief pastor of our church."

In 1852 the First Plenary Council assembled in Baltimore. It brought together six archbishops and twenty-four prelates and gave an impressive demonstration of the Church's right to be regarded as an efficient instrument of spiritual and cultural welfare. When the council published an appeal for the faithful to affiliate themselves in an organization for the conversion of non-Catholics, it seemed as if priests and people were beginning to realize the duty of showing sympathy for, and of answering questions from, inquiring non-Catholics. It had become obvious, first that we were not placing proper emphasis on the moral virtues so highly prized in America, and also that we were failing to demonstrate the fundamental harmony between ancient Catholic truth and the spiritual aspirations of normal, modern man. A fact that stood out in bold relief was the splendid opportunity offered to writers and lecturers who would study Protestantism carefully; indicate its mistakes and shortcomings honestly, but courteously; and publish all this in simple, intelligible language.

II

The First Missions

(Notes, p. 74 ff.)

THE first "organized" parish mission to English-speaking Catholics in this country opened in St. Joseph's Church, Greenwich Village, New York City, in 1851; the first experimental mission to non-Catholics opened in St. Patrick's Church, Norfolk, Virginia, in 1856. These missions were preached by the Redemptorist Fathers; and the story behind the two events is given briefly in the following pages.

The Redemptorists came to this country in 1832, in response to an appeal from the Diocese of Cincinnati. Although originally founded by the Italian, St. Alfonso Liguori, the community at that time was composed chiefly of German-speaking members.[1] In this country the Fathers were, for the most part, occupied at first with the organizing and rehabilitating of the German parishes that had been disturbed by quarreling factions or recalcitrant trustees—in Buffalo, for example, in Rochester and in Baltimore. After an especially notable achievement in the upbuilding of the area around Pittsburgh, they were in great demand.[2]

The traditions established by St. Alphonsus and St. Clement Hofbauer favor missionary rather than parochial work. But because of the existing scarcity of diocesan clergy, these mission-minded religious at the urgent request of the bishops departed from their usual custom; they took charge of congregations and, with financial aid from mission societies in Austria and Germany, became the practical founders of many a spiritually thriving parish—the people under strict discipline, mixed marriages excluded, schools erected promptly, German customs and the German language carefully preserved. If these groups were open to criticism for their extreme race consciousness and their obvious desire to be self-contained, they were also—as any fair-minded observer would admit—conspicuously successful in preserving the Catholic faith along with their own traditions. Before long the Redemptorists were playing an important part in the Catholic life of many cities, including Baltimore, site of their provincial headquarters; Philadelphia, where the saintly (now Venerable) Bohemian, John Nepomucene Neumann, became bishop in 1852; New York, where the modest foundation on Third Street, lower Manhattan, grew into a widely recognized center of faith and zeal. Throughout the eastern United States, the members of the hierarchy came to rely heavily upon the sons of St. Alphonsus; and Archbishop Eccleston of Baltimore entertained the idea of giving the Redemptorists spiritual care of all German Catholics in the United States.

THE FIRST MISSIONS

In the year 1845, just after the American missions had been attached to the Belgian province, the "visitation" of the Redemptorists in this country was being carried out by the first Belgian provincial, Father Frederick de Held. While at Baltimore with his socius, Father Bernard Hafkenscheid, he received applications for admission to the novitiate from three recent converts to the Catholic Church—Isaac T. Hecker, Clarence A. Walworth, James A. McMaster.

Hecker, a New Yorker by birth, had gone to work at the age of thirteen after receiving rudimentary schooling. As a boy he attended a neighboring Methodist Church with his mother, but displayed less concern about external religion than about the inner life of prayer. Deeply interested from childhood in learning about God, he showed sincere sympathy for his poor neighbors and indifference to his own personal comfort; and his preoccupation with spiritual development kept him from remaining in partnership with his brothers when the family bakery grew into a big business and eventually into the plant that produced the widely advertized "Hecker's Flour." A passion for social reform led him to work for political improvement; and his youthful street speeches displayed some of the personal magnetism and capacity for leadership which distinguished him in later life. A born thinker, an eager learner, he supplemented his defective formal education by reading, particularly in the works of Kant and other German philosophers.

Important for his mental growth was the contact made with Orestes Brownson, his senior by more than sixteen years. Their friendship proved to be lifelong —Brownson going on to become one of America's foremost philosophers and publicists, and Hecker developing into a distinguished missionary. Important also was the association Hecker formed with a highly cultured group at Brook Farm where he went at Brownson's suggestion, searching for an answer to the spiritual problems that troubled him.[3]

Persuaded of the truth of Catholicism, Hecker visited Bishop Benedict J. Fenwick of Boston, who introduced him to his coadjutor bishop, John Fitzpatrick. Bishop Fitzpatrick's extremely cautious attitude taught the young inquirer a never-to-be-forgotten lesson on the need of gentleness and sympathy in dealing with outsiders approaching the Church.[4] Bishop Fitzpatrick referred him to Bishop Hughes in New York, who presented him to the coadjutor bishop (later cardinal) McCloskey, and Hecker was received into the Church by the latter on August 2, 1844. Young Hecker's preparation for his admission to the Catholic fold consisted largely of intensive study of the *Cathechism of the Council of Trent,* a volume which remained his favorite textbook for life. His first Catholic problem was to decide which of the three courses recommended to him he should follow: Brownson said he ought to devote himself to the Germans of America; Bishop Hughes counseled preparation for the secular priesthood at the Sulpician

THE FIRST MISSIONS

seminary in Paris; Bishop McCloskey advised him to become a religious. While hesitating, Hecker learned about the Redemptorist missionaries who had lately settled in Third Street; and when he visited them the atmosphere of poverty and solitude in the house touched him with admiration.

Through the Redemptorists he became acquainted with James McMaster, who later became the aggressive editor of the *Freeman's Journal* of New York, and with Clarence Walworth. Both had come into the Church from Episcopalianism. Walworth's early life had been quite different from Hecker's. Born in 1820, graduated at the age of eighteen from Union College where he had been a Phi Beta Kappa student, admitted to the bar in 1841, he abandoned his original Presbyterianism and studied for three years at the Protestant Episcopal General Theological Seminary in New York. He was received into the Catholic Church in 1845.

Late in July, 1845, having learned that Walworth and McMaster were about to enter the Redemptorist novitiate at St. Trond in Belgium, Hecker asked leave to go with them, but learned that they were to sail the next day and that he would need permission from the provincial then visiting in Baltimore. So Hecker hurried to Baltimore on the night train, presented himself at the Redemptorist house at 4:00 A.M. and—despite his unconventional approach—made a favorable impression. Frederick de Held, a Viennese aristocrat by birth, a naturalized Belgian by choice, who had changed his name from von Held to De Held, recognized in the young man some of the characteristics which seem to link Belgians and Americans. Having sent Hecker into the chapel to hear Mass and given him breakfast, De Held subjected him to a brief examination in the Latin version of the *Imitation of Christ,* and then approved his application. Hecker hastened back to New York on the morning train and sailed that evening in company with his two friends. A foreign critic of Hecker seems to regard this sudden trip to Baltimore and back as a symptom of mental disequilibrium; many of us would call it a display of American resourcefulness.[5]

The Redemptorists, two years after their first Belgian foundation at Tournai in 1831, had established themselves at St. Trond—a little town with a few thousand inhabitants, a late medieval Gothic church, and the remains of an old abbey dedicated to the patron saint, Trudo, who died about the year 698. Here the new novices found themselves in a community of some thirty Belgians, Hollanders and Germans. French was the language of the house. The spirit of the novitiate was such that the three Americans soon felt at home; and they made the most of their opportunities for solitude and prayer, taking cheerfully to the austere discipline—although in the field of conventions it took time for the Europeans and the Americans to understand each other completely. On the whole, they seem to have had less difficulty than a first group of American novices in an-

THE FIRST MISSIONS

other European community, one of whom later said with a laugh, that his band had been rather suspect for almost six months because, when addressed by the superior, they looked straight at him and gave a direct answer.

After a short time McMaster was sent home as not adapted to the religious life. The other two were admitted to their vows in 1846 and then transferred to Wittem, a town about fifteen miles from Aix-la-Chapelle, where the community had established a house of studies in 1836, and where the course in dogmatic theology had been conducted for several years by the celebrated Father Dechamps.[6] Walworth, an excellent student, was ordained in 1848. Things were more complicated in the case of Hecker whose inability to study—reminiscent of the academic inadequacy of the Curé d'Ars—made him a problem to his superiors. But as this embarrassing intellectual defect was associated with exceptional strength of character, and as he seemed to thrive on such nourishment as obedience, humility, and self-denial, the superiors decided to send him to Clapham, England, where under his old patron, Father de Held he might complete his studies, and where his friend, Father Walworth, was beginning priestly activities. De Held welcomed Hecker paternally, recognized the hidden depths of holiness and zeal in the young man, kept him under close observation and under iron discipline, and eventually presented him for ordination to the priesthood.[7] He was ordained by Bishop (later cardinal)

Nicholas Wiseman, in the bishop's private chapel on October 23, 1849; and he spent the following year in parochial duties at Clapham and neighboring places. The outbreaks of bigotry at Clapham, occasioned by the re-establishment of the Catholic hierarchy of England in 1850, gave Hecker some experience in suffering insults and threats for his Catholic faith.

In the meantime, American foundations had multiplied; and an American province was created in 1850, with Father Bernard Hafkenscheid as the first provincial. Father Bernard, as he was commonly called, was a native of Holland, a brilliant student and Roman doctor, admitted to the community after his ordination and one of their finest preachers, with a record of twenty years of mission work behind him at this time. Eloquent both in his own tongue and in German, he was also able to preach well in English, when necessity required it. According to Father Elliott, in his fervent moments he poured forth his thoughts "in a fiery torrent of oratory, whose only restraint was the inability of the human voice to express all that the heart contained." When accompanied by American-born priests, he preached only if one of them was ill, devoting himself mainly to managing the missions, dealing with local pastors, and training the missionaries in the Redemptorist tradition; and he appropriated much more than his share of the heavy work of the confessional.

Anxious to develop the missions in America, Bernard went to Europe to procure reinforcements.

THE FIRST MISSIONS

Among those he brought back were Hecker and Walworth. On shipboard, Bernard communicated to the young priests his eagerness to provide missions for English-speaking parishes; and the group had hardly landed after their fifty-four day voyage before opportunity came in the shape of an invitation from St. Joseph's Church, Washington Place, New York City. The invitation was accepted, not without some misgivings on the part of the older Fathers; and a third convert was added to the band, Augustine Francis Hewit.

Hewit, born in 1820 and baptized Nathaniel, was the son of a Congregationalist minister, and had been educated at Philips Andover Academy and at Amherst College. A licensed preacher in the Congregational Church and then a deacon in the Episcopalian Church, he finally sought admission to the Catholic Church, and was ordained priest in 1847, while living in the Diocese of Charleston. Two years later he entered the Redemptorist Order.

The mission band included also a middle-aged missionary, the Magyar, Father Alexander Czvitkovicz, usually referred to as "Father Alexander." Father Hewit describes him as "a pattern of the most perfect religious virtue," free from anything like severity or rigor and in the government of the Fathers under him a model of gentleness and consideration. He was "a most thoroughly accomplished and learned man in many branches of secular and sacred science and in the fine arts; and in the German language, which was as familiar to him as his native language, he was among the best preachers of his order." A veteran of the European mission field, particularly gifted in instructing children, he never undertook the great sermons in English.

On April 6, 1851, these men launched "the first organized mission to an English-speaking parish in this country." Misgivings were soon set at rest by Walworth's display of great oratorical power; by Hewit's dignified, impressive style; by Hecker's astonishing ability to instruct clearly and persuasively. The congregation of St. Joseph's, chiefly Irish, was aroused to so high a pitch of enthusiasm that the Fathers could hardly make their way from the house to the sanctuary. News of the mission spread in all directions. Many came who had been away from the sacraments for years; and among those who listened most eagerly to the sermons and thronged the confessionals were a good number who had been forced to borrow decent clothes in order to attend.[8]

In the following months several missions were given in the Diocese of Pittsburgh, including one at Loretto, a parish founded by the distinguished Prince Demetrius Gallitzin, second priest ordained in the United States. At Johnstown Father Hecker toured the neighborhood on horseback, inviting persons at a distance to attend the mission; group after group marched in, waiting around the church during the day and crowding it at night. Many men in their twenties made their first Communion. In September came

THE FIRST MISSIONS

a mission at St. Peter's, oldest church in New York City, at that time attended by a large congregation with a considerable proportion of rich families. An immense crowd—only temporarily awed by the tickets issued in order to keep the middle aisle reserved—practically stormed the church, filling every foot of floor space and straining against the iron railing outside. After the mission the parishioners sent Father Bernard a gift of $1,000 which he turned over to Father William Quinn, the pastor, to be used in the building of a parish school for boys. At the great mission which took place at St. Patrick's Cathedral, New York City in October, the attendance was calculated at 10,000; and at the closing exercises the archbishop addressed the congregation.

Other missions followed in New York, Michigan, Pennsylvania. In September, 1852, began a series of missions in the cathedrals of Wheeling, Cincinnati, Louisville, Albany, Richmond, Cleveland, and Baltimore. At Cincinnati the crowd was so great that Archbishop Purcell and a guest, Bishop Fitzpatrick of Boston, assisted until midnight in the hearing of confessions—evidence of the exciting conditions in these early missions. Visiting understaffed dioceses and parishes, serving vast numbers of people who had little or no chance to attend Mass or receive the sacraments for long periods, the missionaries found multitudes spiritually starving, others negligent, others almost hardened in sin. A mission was an event to be long remembered, an occasion for unbounded enthusiasm on the part of the people, but also a test of the missionary's bone and sinew. Father Hewit writes of the circumstances in which he and his companions worked:

> Another difficulty lies in the vast number of penitents, and the small number of confessors. On many missions, confined strictly to one parish, there have been from four thousand to eight thousand communions; and, of course, that number of confessions to be heard within eleven days . . . at five in the morning, each of us would see two long rows—one of men and one of women—seated on benches, flanking his confessional. At one-o'clock he would leave the same unbroken lines, to find them again at three, and to leave them in the evening still undiminished. At the end of the mission there would be still the same crowd waiting about the confessionals, and left unheard, because the missionaries were unable to continue their work any longer. . . . In a word, the nets are so full of a multitude of fishes that they break, and there are not workmen enough to drag them ashore.

After nearly two years with the American group, Father Bernard was recalled to Europe and Father Alexander succeeded him as head of the mission band. Out of the records of these early missions, an intriguing book could be fashioned easily.[9] The greatest number of confessions heard on any one mission up to October, 1853, is credited to St. Mary's in Grand Street—the parish established about thirty years earlier by the purchase of the little Seventh Presbyterian Church on Sheriff Street, where the first Catholic church bell in New York was rung. In this populous Irish neighborhood almost 8,000 persons came to confession. In that same year during a mission at the Baltimore cathedral, the group of converts received included a Lt. Kilty, U.S.N., and his eighty-year-old mother. The mission at St. Joseph's, New Orleans, in 1854, was made noteworthy by a later statement of James, Cardinal Gibbons, who said that he had been present at this mission when a youth of twenty, and a sermon by Father Walworth "created in me a desire to serve in the sacred ministry." In a mission at the Pittsburgh cathedral in 1855, twenty converts were received. In that same year, it is interesting to note, Walworth and Hecker labored together on a mission in the Church of the Annunciation, Manhattanville, which had been established two years earlier —almost exactly one mile north of a great tract of land which within three years would become the first parish of the Paulist Fathers.

The group of converts—three, when they collaborated for the first time in 1851; five after the accession of Deshon and Baker in 1856—continued as a Redemptorist band for seven years. Under the careful schooling of Fathers Bernard and Alexander—distinguished not only for their personal ability in the preaching of missions, but also for their competence to develop willing pupils into outstanding missionaries—they became adepts in the art of giving missions according to the tradition established by St. Alphonsus who, in this field, enjoys a pre-eminence similar to that of St. Ignatius in the field of retreats.

Each of the five in his own way attained excellence.

If we are to credit Elliott—no mean judge of public speakers—Walworth must have had a practically uncontested claim to be the finest pulpit orator of his day. Writing in the *Catholic World* (June, 1901) after Walworth's death, Elliott said:

> Seldom was a preacher so eloquent by his looks and bearing as was Father Walworth; and his action on the platform was a perfect match for his great themes, his ringing voice, and his well-chosen matter. If one can make the distinction, he was dramatic without being theatrical. Meanwhile his sermons were models of missionary composition. Although he was steadfast in his loyalty to the traditions of St. Alphonsus, he used the liberty kindred to that supreme missionary's spirit in preparing his discourses. . . . But he could drive the fear of God into sinners' souls with more resistless force than, perhaps, any missionary we have ever had in America. . . . His voice was the best preaching voice I ever heard. Father Walworth had a voice that could stop an army. . . . We emphasize his imperious power over his hearers, but it should be known that if he vanquished the sinner he did not fail to win him. The effect was religious fear, not slavish terror. . . . Nearly thirty years ago the present writer while serving at a mission in St. Mary's Church, Albany, had many conversations with Father Walworth on mission sermons and instructions, their matter and their delivery. . . . I adopted every one of his suggestions, and, I am not ashamed to say, I still use some of his sentences word for word. They stand the test of long experience. But one may not hope to acquire the magic of his voice, the majesty of his bearing, the force of his resistless appeal to sinners. . . . This sense of standing for God did infinitely more for his success than the noble beauty of his face and form, his splendid rhetoric, the amazing strength of action in his delivery. . . . Many were led to say that they never knew a man who had so fully assimilated the rules of the divine art of winning souls to God as Father Walworth.[10]

THE FIRST MISSIONS

As for the other four: a congregation listening to the learned Hewit, would invariably be impressed by the unconscious, almost majestic dignity of that magnificent Yankee; Baker, gracious and cultivated, had the eloquence that radiates from unaffected holiness; Deshon, military engineer turned preacher, laid down doctrinal and moral teachings in clear, pointed, practical phrases and sentences; Hecker habitually presented the Church's convincing answer to man's most critical problems and showed how effective was her method of guiding man's aspirations for holiness.

In the course of seven years the band gave more than eighty-five missions and an unrecorded number of retreats; and they aroused extraordinary enthusiasm both among the people and among the clergy, including the bishops. Father Elliott says of them: "In our judgment those men were a band of missionaries the like of whom have not served the great cause among the English-speaking races these recent generations." [11]

III

The Southland
(Notes, p. 77 f.)

FOR three years the convert Redemptorists worked chiefly in big, congested parishes of northern cities—often in cathedral towns which then, even more than now, were religious centers of cities and states. However, as time went on, the proportion of missions given in the South increased notably.

Several events made the year 1856 significant. In February, at Star of the Sea Church, in Brooklyn, New York, the missionaries welcomed a new recruit, George Deshon, aged thirty-three, who had been a lieutenant in the United States Army. He had been admitted into the Church in 1850; and had applied for admission to the Redemptorists, because he was eager to pass on to others the faith he had himself received. Accustomed to speak briefly and to the point, he proved as skillful in giving instructions on religion as he had been in teaching mathematics and ethics at the West Point Military Academy.

In March, a memorable mission was given in St. Patrick's, Norfolk, Virginia, the same church where Fathers Alexander and Walworth had conducted a

THE SOUTHLAND

mission three years earlier. In the interval between the two missions, the city had suffered from a dreadful epidemic of yellow fever which carried away half of the congregation. An air of solemnity pervaded the whole city; and the proportion of non-Catholics attending the mission was unusually large.[1] All this affected the tone of the sermons and instructions; brought the priests into an especially sympathetic relationship with the people; created many friendly contacts with Protestants. One convert, a Mrs. Higgins, admitted to the Church a few days before the mission began, was the widow of a man who had attended the previous mission; and she reported that her husband, when dying during the yellow fever epidemic, had said to her: "If you ever see Father Walworth tell him that I persevered until my death. Ask him to pray for me." Several converts were received into the Church immediately after the mission and others began their course of instruction. According to the Mission Chronicle:

> Since the last mission Norfolk had been desolated by the Yellow Fever, whole families swept off, and others much diminished by death. Among the most distinguished members of the congregation who fell victims to the plague, were Mr. Hunter Woodis, Mayor of the city and Miss Jane Herron, a lady who died with the reputation of sanctity, having remained at N. during the pestilence, merely for the sake of taking care of her slaves. Two hundred of the Catholic congregation were swept away, and in the N. cemetery, where before the fever there were only six graves, we saw more than 130 new graves, and among them seven, side by side, filled by an entire family. . . . The mission necessarily assumed a

character entirely different from that of ordinary missions. . . . Our chief object was to soothe, to console, to encourage, to instruct and to build up. Many very intelligent Protestants, whose respect for the Catholic religion had been increased by the devotion of the priests and sisters and others during the plague, attended regularly. . . . After the mission F. Hewit gave three lectures on three successive evenings on the Necessity of Faith, the Rule of Faith and the Supremacy of St. Peter. F. Hecker closed with an extremely eloquent and popular lecture on Popular Objections to Catholicity. All were well attended. This circumstance deserves to be especially noted as being apparently the commencement of a new field of labor for our Congregation, viz. the application of the system of missions to the conversion of heretics.[2]

In Hecker's career, the Norfolk lectures marked a turning point. Later in Rome, when he submitted a summary of his life to his advisers he wrote as follows:

On an occasion of public conference given by me before an audience, a great part of which was not Catholic, the matter and manner of which was taken from my second book, my fellow missionaries were present, and they as well as myself regarded this as a test whether my views and sentiments were adapted to reach and convince the understandings and hearts of this class of people, or were they mere illusions of fancy. Hitherto my fellow missionaries had shown but little sympathy with my thoughts on these points, but at the close of the conference they were of one mind that my vocation was evidently to work in the direction of non-Catholics, and they spoke of such a work with conviction and enthusiasm. "I see clearly now," said the superior (F. Walworth) of the mission, "what your vocation is, and if the subject ever comes up in my presence before our superiors I shall speak plainly to them about it." . . . Such was his language. Secular priests who were present remarked that if ever the Catholic faith were to be brought before the American people, it would have to be done in the style and way of my conference.[3]

While in Wilmington in October, the Fathers talked over possible improvements in the pattern of the missions and made this memorandum:

> We also conferred together on the long talked of project of an English House, first proposed by Father Bernard, and agreed unanimously that such a house was absolutely necessary to the prosperity of the English Missions, that the time had now arrived for establishing it, and that henceforth we would use all lawful and proper means to hasten its foundation.[4]

In November, 1856, a mission at old St. Patrick's, the original parish of Washington, attracted the interest of many citizens of the capital, including President Franklin Pierce; and the Chronicle tells that at "the festival of the Dedication of the Blessed Virgin, Mrs. Pierce sent up a bouquet of flowers, which the President assisted in arranging." Another much more important item tells that Francis Baker, convert from Episcopalianism, "most highly respected and beloved as Protestant minister in Baltimore, had been just ordained, and came for the first time to assist at this mission. He preached the opening sermon, which gave great satisfaction to all who heard it and promise that he will hereafter be a truly apostolic missionary." A truly apostolic missionary Baker proved to be.

At the conclusion of the mission in St. Patrick's, the missionaries moved on into the deep South. The two expert leaders under whom the converts won their spurs had retired, Father Bernard to be superior in Limerick, Ireland, and Father Alexander to take up the lighter duties of parish work—a well earned respite from his laborious life on the missions. The five converts were now on their own, with Father Walworth as superior. Four of them were thirty-six years old; Deshon was thirty-three. Hewit had already been named consultor of the province.

Hewit had been in the South years before. He had come to Charleston for reasons of health; and there had been received into the Catholic Church. After studying under Dr. Patrick N. Lynch, he was ordained for the Diocese of Charleston in 1847 by Bishop Ignatius Reynolds, successor of John England, and at once assigned to aid in the editing of Bishop England's works, under the direction of two able scholars, his teacher, Dr. Lynch (consecrated Bishop of Charleston in 1858) and Dr. James A. Corcoran (first editor of the *American Catholic Quarterly Review* of Philadelphia)—with both of whom he kept up a permanent friendship. Hewit therefore, at the time of the mission, possessed an intimate knowledge of Bishop England's works and projects;[5] and although in 1856—because of circumstances fully described by Guilday—England's achievements had largely disappeared, yet the diocesan clergy consisted almost entirely of men brought to this country by him or trained under his supervision. Hewit speaks of them admiringly as "men of accomplished learning and genial character, whose kindness and hospitality knew no bounds, and whose zeal made them efficient fellow laborers in the work of the missions." He mentions also that the congregation included converts

THE SOUTHLAND

from South Carolina families, and "an unusually large number of intelligent young men, trained to a great extent under the care of the clergy." We get very little information about the conversation that went on between the visiting missionaries and the diocesan priests; but we do know that within a year the five Redemptorists were embarking upon a venturesome project which would surely have delighted the late Bishop England of whom Guilday said, "No man of his times in the realm of politics or religion watched more jealously over the preservation of the ideals upon which the Republic was built." [6]

The five missionaries worked together in St. John's, Savannah, cathedral city of a new diocese—separated from the two Carolinas in 1850—which embraced the whole State of Georgia.[7] The population of Savannah, consisting largely of migrant laborers, included many careless Catholics, who lived along the waterfront amid "grog shops and dens of thieves and sinners." In the *Memoir* Father Hewit apologizes for his mention of "unpleasant and possibly shocking details," explaining that his purpose was to show that Father Baker in pursuit of his vocation to serve the most abandoned souls, had relinquished "the ease and elegance and attractive charm of his earlier position as an Episcopalian clergyman" where his chief duty was to read polished discourses to the élite of Baltimore society.

Dividing the city into five districts, and visiting "every nook and corner," the missionaries succeeded in filling the church with an earnest and responsive congregation. That the mission effected lasting improvement was made consolingly plain to Hewit two years later when he visited the city to collect offerings for the newly formed congregation of the Paulist Fathers. He tells us that he found "children clean, wives and mothers cheerful, husbands sober and kind, and everywhere encountered expressions of gratitude for what had been done by the Missionaries."

At the end of the Savannah mission, the band was invited to give missions in every parish in the diocese. They separated into two groups—Walworth and Deshon visiting Atlanta, Macon, Columbus; Hecker, Hewit, Baker going to Augusta and St. Augustine. The Chronicle puts the total attendance at the Georgia missions at nearly forty per cent of the total Catholic population.

In Atlanta the missionaries found the people responsive and the attendance good, despite bad weather, a dilapidated church, and other inconveniences. Notorious scandals were terminated; grog sellers gave up their activities. In Macon the small and lukewarm congregation, hitherto ashamed to be known as Catholics, came forward bravely and before the end of the mission were displaying pride in their faith. In response to a request from Protestants to have a sermon addressed to them, Walworth spoke to a very considerable group; and a Presbyterian minister, who undertook to reply with a lecture against

"Popery," met with an unfavorable reaction from his own people.

In Augusta the missionaries spoke in a church with a seating capacity of 500, built many years before—even before the coming of Bishop England. The Jesuit Fathers had given a retreat here two years previously; and a number of converts welcomed the missionaries. A delegation presented the thanks of the congregation and a purse of nearly $300 which was turned over to the pastor. Going on to Florida, the missionaries found that three priests were covering the whole State, with their headquarters at St. Augustine and Jacksonville. Here the piety and virtue of the inhabitants were most impressive; drunkenness was practically unknown; and Hewit comments upon the large attendance of devout Negroes as one of the edifying features of this oldest city of the United States, with its wealth of historical association and its noble monuments. He adds that the Negroes of St. Augustine, almost all Catholic, "cannot read but are admirably well-instructed, and devoted to their faith."

On January 25, 1857, all five missionaries began a mission in the cathedral of Charleston. This was the city which Bishop England had made the Catholic center of the South; and the diocese was now being administered by Hewit's former teacher, Dr. Lynch. After inviting members of the three parishes to attend the mission and scouring the lanes and alleys of the whole city, the missionaries secured an attendance of almost 6,000 persons, which filled the spacious cathedral to capacity day after day. Baker seems to have risen to a high level on this occasion, taking his full share of the principal sermons and winning a place in the first rank of mission preachers. Dr. Lynch, a good judge, pronounced one of Baker's courses "the best he had ever heard."

In his *Memoir of Father Baker,* Hewit gives a most interesting, if somewhat haphazard, account of this unusual mission tour which was to carry the group rapidly on towards the beginning of a momentous enterprise. He narrates amusing adventures; describes the various types of people encountered; notes the favorable reaction of non-Catholics to the sermons; tells that Catholics in the congested urban areas offered strong contrast to those dwelling in small cities and country towns, where the children of Catholic immigrants "were making their way upward, acquiring real and personal property, blending with the body of their fellow citizens, educating their children." He speaks also (on p. 129) of the incidental good effect of the missions upon non-Catholics when he says:

> Thousands of Protestants have come at different times to hear the mission sermons, and there have usually been several converts on each large mission, sometimes as many as twenty, and on one mission, that of Quebec, fifty. . . . Besides actual conversions, a great effect has been produced in removing the prejudices and gaining the good will of the community at large. . . . It is impossible not to see how rapidly and

generally the prejudice against the Catholic religion and the priesthood is melting away in this country. And this seems to warrant the hope that the time may soon come, when the faith may be preached to our separated brethren by means of missions especially intended for them, with rich results.

Hewit comments feelingly upon "the vast masses of people gathered in our great centers of population, exposed to a thousand demoralizing influences, and most inadequately supplied with the ordinary means of grace." According to his calculations, it would have taken about eight years of continuous work by at least 100 missionaries to supplement the work of the diocesan clergy, so that ordinary needs would be satisfied. His words provoke us to speculate as to what might have come about in this country, had a practical system of colonization been organized by Catholic leaders—at that time, unfortunately, divided on this issue; for the Irish did not view the idea of colonization as intelligently as the Germans did. The vast majority of Irish immigrants flocked to the cities; and efforts to organize immigration to rural areas ran into insuperable obstacles of apathy or open disapproval.

What might have happened had Georgia been the scene of a *well-managed* colonization project cannot, of course, be determined; but what did happen is a matter of record. When Georgia contained approximately a million people, Catholics numbered one per cent, about 10,000; a century later, in a total population of three million, they still amount to little more than one per cent. A Catholic pastor, Father Edward D. Smith, tells us that in his parish of 3,000 square miles, with a population of 100,000, there are less than 100 Catholics, and that seven-eighths of the counties of Georgia have no priest at all.[8]

The Southern campaign was significant for more reasons than one. The cities in the South were not so large as in the North; congregations were smaller; a higher proportion of the Catholics were native-born and fairly well educated; most of the time the missionaries were preaching to fellow Americans; the Protestants with whom they came in contact were on the whole uninformed rather than actually hostile; many of the converts had entered the Church in the face of most discouraging difficulties. On their way north, the missionaries were pondering on the vistas opened up by their recent experiences.

IV

New Horizons

(Notes, p. 78 ff.)

In America

THE five seasoned veterans who returned from the South in 1857 were very different from the pioneers who had begun to explore the American mission field six years earlier. Their longing to spread the faith had been intensified by visits to many widely scattered cities; by careful training at the hands of experts; by contacts with leading members of the hierarchy, various types of clergy, zealous laymen, inquiring non-Catholics. Feeling that their methods could and should be more closely adjusted to the actual circumstances, they were asking themselves what new steps might be taken to satisfy the religious hunger of their fellow countrymen. Creedless Unitarianism was spreading at the expense of old-fashioned Protestantism;[1] the great mass of the population showed eagerness to learn truth; the Constitution of the United States guaranteed religious freedom. The prospect resembled that which eighteen centuries earlier had fired the soul of St. Paul.

Walworth was busy devising a possible enlargement of the mission program. Hecker was focusing attention upon the work which he believed should have priority, the conversion of non-Catholics. Of all the group, he attained the greatest stature. Years devoted to the giving of mission instructions and to the arduous labor of the confessional had made him intimately acquainted with the common needs of the average American and the religious aspirations of many different types. He had won recognition as an efficient lecturer possessed of a style, clear, lively—often in a homely way, humorous—that carried learned and simple listeners alike along the stream of his argument. Between missions he devoted much time to the giving of retreats; and his extant notes disclose what lofty mystical ideals were imparted by this dynamic personality—the man once barely able to make the grade in his theological studies, repelled by speculative and academic niceties, never fluent in the Latin language. This was the same priest who, at the beginning of his active career, had said to Father Bernard, "Get me some place as chaplain of a prison or public institute of charity,"—thinking that he was capable of doing only this humble type of work. Fortunately, Bernard thought otherwise.

Hecker's growth was due in part to the rich variety of his youthful experiences, to his early association with gifted minds during the days spent at Brook Farm, "the greatest, noblest, bravest dream of New England," to his long meditations on contemporary

NEW HORIZONS 43

ideas and movements. His development is reflected in the pages of his Diary, begun in the year 1844; and in the summary of his inner history, submitted to his Roman advisers in 1858. Referring to his first priestly activities, he says, "Holy and important as the exercises of the missions among Catholics are, still this work did not correspond to my interior attrait, and although exhausted and frequently made ill from excessive fatigue in these duties, yet my ardent and constant desire to do something for the conversion of my fellow non-Catholic countrymen led me to take up my pen." [2]

He longed to let American non-Catholics share his own happy experience in exchanging the anguish of soul that preceded conversion for the privileges and joys that he possessed as a Catholic; and so while still a young missionary he write two books, *Questions of the Soul* (1855) and *Aspirations of Nature* (1857). One emphasized the fact that Catholic doctrine satisfies the wants of the heart; the other showed that it answers the demands of reason. Both books proved to be very effective aids to conversion; they received high commendation. Convinced that he was now on the path along which God wished him to proceed, Hecker felt highly encouraged when George Ripley—who rose to fame as literary critic of the New York *Tribune*—piloted his second book through the process of publication.

At this time the five missionaries felt like expert miners, ready to open a promising vein of ore. For a considerable period they had been permitted to act as an almost independent group, free to make their own contacts with bishops and priests and to arrange their own schedule of missions. Living apart from their brethren for long intervals, they did not feel quite at home when they returned to their convent where German was the common language and where American dreams and enthusiasm seemed rather visionary. They became more and more convinced that it would be of benefit to the missions if the order would open an English-speaking house. They failed to realize that the superiors had adopted a program into which this new idea would not easily fit.

When we bring to mind the contemporary situation in Europe, we perceive at once why it would be difficult for the superiors to sympathize with the "progressive" ideas of the Americans. Not only had the Redemptorist Congregation suffered internally from racial antagonisms; it had also in many countries been made the target of violent revolutionary outbreaks, sparked by the Communist Manifesto of 1848. Mobs had forced the old vicar general, Father Passerat, and the young Father Nicholas Mauron to flee for their lives.[3] Since the resignation of Passerat and the coming to power of Mauron, the community had been tightening things up—a policy which sometimes involved the relinquishing of posts served by the Redemptorists for years.[4]

In the United States notable changes had taken place, both among the people served by the Redemp-

NEW HORIZONS
45

torists and within the order itself. German Catholics had grown into colonies, separated from Catholics of other nationalities. Thrifty and industrious, settling sometimes in cities, sometimes in farming areas, they had built up a social order based on German conventions, using the German language in business, in school, in church. The Redemptorists were foremost in organizing and guiding them; and the personnel of the order had become more dominantly German. The first American provincial, the Hollander, Father Bernard, had been replaced by Father George Ruland.

Things stood thus when into the picture stepped Bishop James Roosevelt Bayley of Newark, himself a convert, intensely eager to spread the faith and well acquainted with the successful work of the five missionaries. He asked Father Walworth to present to the community the project of establishing an English-speaking house in the Diocese of Newark, promising to find a site and provide a building. Obviously, the proposed new foundation would differ in some respects from all existing Redemptorist houses; and it would commit the order to a plan favored by five members who had originally been American Protestants, and who cherished at least some "democratic" views not unlike those of European radicals. Moreover, the prelate who put forward the proposal was himself of American Protestant origin. So we are prepared to learn that a discouraging answer came to the bishop's offer. He was told that any such proposal would have to go direct to the superior general.[5] Thereupon Bishop Bayley wrote a long letter, outlining the plan in specific terms and emphasizing the great need for just such an establishment as the one proposed. Father Walworth also—speaking for the five—wrote to the superior general to draw attention to certain matters which he thought deserved official consideration, namely: that the American missionaries had no share in priestly activities during the intervals between their missions; that their mission work was on a precarious footing for lack of organization; that a central house to arrange a full schedule of English-speaking missions would be of great advantage to the community. Commenting on the suspicion that the Americans were being motivated by "nationalism" in their plea for greater use of the English tongue, he added that English was the language of the country, used by the people of the United States for all their ordinary affairs.

Meanwhile, rumors began to circulate to the effect that the band of five was about to be broken up; that their specific work would be discontinued; that some of them would be transferred to Canada to take charge of an English-speaking parish there.[6] Hewit and Walworth in Baltimore exchanged numerous letters with Hecker and Deshon in New York; and all four came to the conclusion that if the superior general knew all the details, he would surely approve of a project that promised such undoubted benefit to the Redemptorist Congregation and to the people of this

NEW HORIZONS

country. So they decided to send one of their number to Rome, to explain the whole matter. Baker, not near the others at the time, adhered to their decision later on.

Now came a serious problem. The decision to send a messenger to Rome had been made in view of a constitutional privilege which allowed members of the order the right of direct access to the superior general in grave and pressing issues; but this privilege had been abrogated by new constitutions adopted by the general chapter of 1855, although not yet promulgated. While awaiting approval of the new constitutions by the Holy See, the superior general had issued a circular letter prohibiting members of the society —and specifically, members living in America—from appealing directly to him. When this difficulty was referred to the provincial, Father Ruland, he replied that although personally favoring the idea of an English-speaking house, he had no authority to grant permission for the visit to Rome. Father Hewit, however, as provincial consultor, wrote and signed an official opinion to the effect that the issue in question was grave and pressing; that the constitutions in force at the time gave the right of access to the superior general; that the new constitutions not yet approved by the Holy See, were still without validity; that the superior general had no right to deny the privilege allowed by the constitution.

On the strength of this reasoning the five decided to delegate Father Hecker to represent them before the superior general; and his brother, George Hecker, agreed to pay the traveling expenses. So Hecker set forth, carrying with him various documents: a letter from Bishop Bayley, renewing the offer to establish a foundation in Newark; statements from several bishops favoring the plan of an English-speaking house; letters recommending the group in general and Hecker in particular.

As we look back, this typically American approach, direct and confident, seems rather naïve. Possibly more time and more careful planning might have brought about the opening of an English-speaking Redemptorist house in the diocese of Bishop Bayley or of some other sympathetic prelate—which was the only aim that the five had in mind when Hecker went as their representative to Rome. Whether or not such an establishment would have given them so rich an opportunity as that which they envisaged, is of course another matter. Be that as it may, the five unconsciously set in motion a chain of events complicated by earlier clashes of which they were hardly aware and leading to results wholly unforeseen; and when Father Hecker left New York on August 5, 1857, no one realized on what thin ice he was about to set foot.

In Europe

On his way to Rome, Hecker visited Dechamps in Brussels and De Held in Liège. To Dechamps, pulpit orator, old professor of theology, who had been invited to become Bishop of Liège in 1852, the matter seemed an open-and-shut issue of obedience vs. disobedience; and he told Hecker so. De Held took a different view. More Belgian than the Belgians themselves, this naturalized citizen of a most progressive little country, shared Hecker's vision of Protestant America as a land of promise. In nearby Louvain the Jesuit Bollandists had lately been reorganized to continue their work of revolutionizing the science of hagiography; and if De Held had been in authority at the time of Hecker's visit, he might well have organized a similar special group of Redemptorists to undertake the conversion of America. De Held was the type of man who would instinctively favor a promising missionary experiment; and were he of the twentieth century, he would no doubt welcome the idea of transferring special groups in various religious communities from the Latin to an Eastern Rite in order to facilitate the reunion of schismatics.[7] Twice already he had come to Hecker's aid at critical moments—twelve years earlier in Baltimore, when he accepted Hecker for the novitiate; again at Clapham when he drilled him for his final tests before ordination. Now he urged him to press his case in Rome, giving him a strong letter to Alessandro Cardinal Barnabò, Prefect of the Propaganda. De Held stood well in the esteem of the Vatican. At the peak of his career, two years previously, he had come near to being elected superior general—but at the moment he was, as he said, without influence in the community; and he briefed Hecker on the tense atmosphere in which he would find himself at headquarters. To put it briefly, the Belgians felt that the administration of the community, since the coming to power of Father Smetana, was pro-German and anti-Belgian. Now, De Held believed, the Americans were being pushed around just as the Belgians had been; and he hoped that if Hecker were well informed and acted discreetly while in Rome, affairs might come to a head and the whole order would profit thereby.[8]

Hecker arrived in the Holy City on August 26 to submit his appeal to a superior who had suffered in his own person from the excesses of "liberals"; who was sensitively aware of the recent distressing experiences of his own community; who had received from the general chapter a mandate to unify and strengthen the order on the basis of a new constitution. It was a dramatic moment when these two men, both under forty, met in the Villa Caserta.

During his two years of rule Father Mauron had guided the Congregation through serious disturbances so successfully as to win the approval of Pius IX. Now he saw new trouble in the person of an American, formerly a Protestant, an associate of four other American converts; all of them reared in a secular atmosphere; all of them eager to introduce an innovation in the form of an English-speaking house in America—even after the superior general had indicated his disapproval. Hecker, as delegate of the five, was here in Rome, presenting himself to the

NEW HORIZONS

superior general without permission—basing his right of appeal on an old privilege rescinded by the superior. Writing to his brethren early in September, Father Hecker describes what took place.

I arrived here at Rome on the 26th. The Rector Major had rec'd a few days before a letter from the Prov. announcing my departure etc.

The next day the R.M. called me to his room, and told me Father Douglas was on a Visitation and would be home in a few days and then a Consulta would be held, and I would be called upon to explain my reasons for coming here. The grounds I had for thinking I had a right to come, I could put them on paper and Fr. Douglas would translate them and give them to him.[9] This was precisely what I desired. . . . Fr. Douglas came on the 29th. . . . Fr. Douglas being the only one who understands English I begged him to come early before the Chapter was to be held, on Sunday morning, so that I could fully explain things to him, and show him such letters as were necessary to that effect. He came on Sunday, but late, and before I was half through he said that it was nine o'clock and he must go to the Chapter. The Chapter was occupied one hour and a half, then I was called, under the hope & full impression that I would be granted a full hearing. But things had all changed. The Chapter had decided I should not be heard. The fact of my coming was an act of disobedience, incurring ipso facto dismission. They did not want to hear our reasons. In foro interno all might be right.

But the Rect. Maj. began by asking my reasons. Having humbly begged their attention, I began by first citing the Cons. de voto Perseverentiae. The Rect. Maj. interrupted me, asked for the Const. read the whole passage, slurring over what regarded the right, & emphasizing the other. The Consultors silent. After having read the passage he continued & said I had no right, and gave vent to the same accusations against us in what had been done as he had to me twice or three times before. I remained in perfect silence, trusting when he got through an opportunity would be given for me to continue what I had to say in our defense. But no, while speaking he handed a paper to the secretary, & when through, he called upon him to read. And behold my dismission! . . . After it was read, I begged humbly to be heard in my defense— But no; the fact was there—no defense was worth while—no justification could be sufficient.

I went in to the Oratory & prayed before the B. Sacrament. I returned to the consulta in a few moments & begged on my knees expressly and formally to be heard, to show that the prohibitions etc. did not apply in the present case, and that they were not applicable or intended so to be applied.

My application was denied. "You condemn me then" I said, "without hearing." And the Rect. Maj. & Consultors all nodded assent.[10]

When Bishop Bayley learned what had happened, he wrote at once to several important ecclesiastics in Rome expressing great dismay at Hecker's expulsion. Bayley added that all the bishops and priests in the United States who knew Hecker would regard the formation of a band of missionaries trained under the Rule of St. Alphonsus and speaking English, as a great blessing to the country. Other American bishops too, wrote in behalf of Hecker—Hughes, Kenrick, Purcell, Spalding, Barry, and Lynch. For seven months the situation remained under discussion by the Roman officials.

V

Hecker in Rome

(Notes, p. 80 ff.)

1. AUGUST TO DECEMBER 1857

HECKER'S seven months in Rome were crowded with disappointing experiences, overshadowed by dark uncertainty about the future. In retrospect they loom up not only as a critical period for the still unborn Paulist Community, but also as a most important phase of Hecker's own spiritual development. He had come to Rome, driven by his eagerness to find the best way of carrying divine truth to men outside the Church. The shock of expulsion, an unexpected series of suspicions and accusations, and his long agonizing doubt as to the outcome effected a sort of forced growth. During this period he acquired a new resourcefulness, an increasing ability to persuade and explain and lead, a trust in God even deeper than before.

Our available sources of information include correspondence between Hecker and his colleagues in America; letters to and from high-ranking ecclesiastics; and a revealing account of his inner life, prepared for the enlightenment of the men whose counsel he followed. The correspondence with his brethren displays a general unity of purpose and a reciprocal trust. As weeks grew into months, however, the men in America grew increasingly uncomfortable in their community home and became more and more impatient for news from the battle front. Unfamiliar with the deliberate pace characteristic of Rome, they wondered what could be happening.

Hecker was still only thirty-seven years old when he had to undergo the severe test of justifying his conduct before experienced officials professionally on guard against even the appearance of resistance to authority and especially sensitive to the possibility of outbreaks by persons sympathetic with "progress." Rome knew that Protestant America had expressed violent disapproval of Catholic "authoritarianism"; and here was an American convert protesting an official decision given by tried and true European Catholics. The ex-Redemptorist therefore, began his pleading in a most disadvantageous position. He found it hard to speak persuasively, or even inoffensively. That in the end the Holy See equivalently exculpated him, is good proof of the justice of his cause.

He had come to Rome during a short interval of comparative quiet, following a tour by Pius IX which evoked demonstrations of affection and loyalty practically everywhere in his dominions. Nevertheless the pope could hardly have forgotten the assassination of

HECKER IN ROME 55

his prime minister, Count Pellegrino Rossi, in 1848, and his own forced flight from Rome. The abortive attempts of Mazzini and Garibaldi to organize revolt were quite recent; and Pius must have had some knowledge of the simmering unrest which was to boil into successful revolution a few years later, driving the Austrian troops out of the Papal States and incorporating those territories in the Kingdom of United Italy. As for Americans, the pope's notion of them was derived in part from the violence which had greeted the nuncio, Bedini, five years earlier, and from unfriendly comments on himself which had appeared in the American press. What he said to Hecker reveals his mind: "The Americans are so engrossed in worldly pursuits and in getting money and these things are not favorable. . . . In the U.S. there exists a too unrestrained liberty; all the refugees and revolutioners gather there."[1]

It was fortunate indeed that Hecker had brought with him letters of introduction to persons in high places.[2] Immediately after his dismissal, he carried his testimonial letters to Cardinal Barnabò, Prefect of Propaganda, and to Archbishop Bedini, secretary of that Congregation. These letters were written originally in order to recommend him personally and to express approval of the plan to found an English-speaking Redemptorist house in America; but the good standing they gave Hecker continued to operate in his favor, even after unforeseen issues arose.

It might seem a cruel chance that almost the first

important official to whom Hecker had to turn was the same Bedini who five years earlier had been insulted and outraged in America; but actually Bedini became a good friend. He belonged to that rare type which keeps a sense of proportion under provocation, embarrassment, injury; and he never forgot the kindness and zeal of the clergy with whom he had come in contact in the United States. As Secretary of the Congregation of the Propaganda, he was able to smooth Hecker's path considerably. Thus Hecker passed the first, and in a sense the most serious, obstacle rather quickly.

Among those who labored to have Hecker's appeal considered favorably by the Holy See, none ranks on quite the same level as Barnabò.[3] When the appellant first presented himself, Barnabò, with the caution of the trained diplomat, looked him over, listened to his story, studied his letters of recommendation. Once convinced of the reasonableness of Hecker's appeal, Barnabò advised him what to do, put him in contact with proper officials and went to the very limit of his powers. In interviews with the general of the Redemptorists and even in conversations with the Holy Father himself, he spoke out in such forthright fashion that the pope chided him with being a partisan. Barnabò answered that his seeming partiality was due to his respect for truth and justice.

There existed certain jurisdictional complications. The United States at that time, although actually larger and stronger than almost any Catholic country, was still classified as mission territory; it was canonically under the Propaganda, not under the common law of the Church formulated by the Council of Trent. On the other hand, since the Congregation of Bishops and Regulars had passed upon an earlier issue involving the unity of the Redemptorist order, it seemed proper that the same Congregation should handle the present case. De Held's charge that the administration was attempting "to establish a military despotism in place of the mild and paternal rule of St. Alphonsus," gave the pope concern lest the existing separation between Transalpines and Cisalpines should be followed by another more serious division within the Transalpine section of the community.[4] The pope therefore, despite Barnabò's advice to leave the case in the hands of the Propaganda, decided to submit it to the Congregation of Bishops and Regulars. Thereupon, Barnabò urged Hecker to set about getting strong letters from friendly American bishops; and he himself wrote to Archbishops Hughes and Kenrick and to Bishop Bayley. Answers came that were indeed strong. Of Bishop Martin J. Spalding's letter, Hecker says "It was quite perfect," and of Bayley's letter, that it was "strongly in our favor." Kenrick's letter demanded that Hecker should be restored to the congregation from which he had been dismissed. Hughes, without presuming to decide on the charge of disobedience, said to Hecker (December 30, 1857) "I shall welcome you the more heartily because, as it is stated, you have been expelled from your

Society without a hearing or trial." Letters came also from Archbishop Purcell of Cincinnati, from Bishops Lynch of Charleston and Barry of Savannah.

On seeing these letters, the pope showed signs of being disturbed.[5] And Barnabò, said: "I told Your Holiness, at first it was only a dispute between religious. It has now become a question of dealing with the American episcopate."

Meanwhile, Hecker had been making friends. Bishop Thomas Louis Connolly of St. John, New Brunswick, a privileged person at the Vatican, offered to see the pope personally and "to use all his influence in our behalf." Hecker calls this "a providential event," adding "He regards our cause as God's cause, as the cause of religion in the United States . . . he is well acquainted with our labors and our history. What gives him a status too in our matters, besides his knowledge of the wants of religion in the United States, is that part of his own diocese is within our boundaries." [6]

In the papal entourage no one was closer to the pope than Monsignor George Talbot, whose influence was so great that even the cardinals were deferential to him.[7] At first unsympathetic towards Hecker, he was converted into something approaching friendliness by Connolly's influence. This, of course, was an important gain.

Hecker had also had the advice of able counsellors whom he himself had selected after having prayed for the guidance of the Holy Spirit: Father Gregorio, the Carmelite; Father Francis, the Passionist; Father Druelle, of the Congregation of the Holy Cross. On all technical points he sought the advice of Father Bernard Smith, professor of Dogmatic theology in the College of the Propaganda.[8]

Bizzarri, Secretary of the Congregation of Bishops and Regulars (later cardinal and one of the five presidents of the Vatican Council) proved to be difficult to deal with.[9] For some inexplicable reason the case dragged on. Weeks passed in delays and postponements; yet Hecker persisted. To a minor official who seemed to be bent on trying to wear out his patience, Hecker said, pointing out of the window: "You will see those hills of Albano move before I move from my purpose to see the Holy Father."

At first Hecker's case seemed reducible to two issues: (1) Had the Americans acted in good faith when they sent a delegate to the superior general to urge the founding of a new English-speaking house? (2) Had the general and his council acted *ultra vires* in dismissing Hecker for visiting the superior general in virtue of an old constitutional privilege, rescinded by the new constitutions, which however, were not yet promulgated? Neither of these two questions was ever officially answered.

When the American Fathers received the news of Hecker's dismissal, Deshon sent a cheerful, encouraging letter (September 28, 1857) in which he said that he had already anticipated this outcome; and he predicted that "this storm will eventuate in something good for us all." Letters of the same tenor came from Hewit and Walworth; but Walworth added reproachfully, "You who are now free must try to conceive how impossible it is for us *to live* as we are now, even for a little while." Walworth seemed annoyed that Hecker was accepting the methods and adjusting himself to the tempo of the Romans, although in this Hecker was following the guidance of carefully chosen and well experienced advisers.[10]

On September 25, Hecker wrote to the Fathers that he had gone to see Father Douglas and requested him to have the whole matter settled amicably with Cardinal Barnabò as arbiter; but he met with a refusal.[11] A fortnight later he wrote to say that if the other four were prepared to accept the plan of organizing an independent band of missionaries they should send Cardinal Barnabò a memorial addressed to the Propaganda, stating their grievances, the needs of their fellow citizens, and the way in which they thought their own labors should be directed to spread the faith. In answer came a statement assuring him that the other four all felt as he felt—that they believed they had a special vocation and that if it would not be possible for the general and his consultors to recognize this vocation, they would wish to be delivered from their present painful position by whatever steps authority might devise.[12]

As time went on, the tentative plans of Hecker and his advisers underwent modifications; the idea of establishing an English-speaking Redemptorist house gave way to other possibilities. One of these was an affiliation with the Naples branch of the Redemptorists; and Hecker went with Barnabò to visit the Neapolitan Fathers at Nocera.[13] Then came the idea of a new branch of the order. Before long the idea of inaugurating a new independent community began to prevail.

By November 12, Hecker was able to report that Bizzarri had asked for a complete statement of the whole case, with a view to submitting it first to the Holy Father and then to the Congregation of Bishops and Regulars. Hecker told the Fathers that he did not think the Holy See would approve of union with the Cisalpine Fathers, or of a new division of the order in the United States. "The H. Father no doubt regrets the division which he permitted between the Neapolitan and German Fathers, and there is not the faintest hope that he will approve of another division." Hecker foresaw that in all probability "we shall have to start entirely upon our own hook. This is perhaps the best of all, all things considered. There are many things in our congregation which would hinder us to respond to the new demands and fresh wants of our country."

By this time the American Fathers were busily engaged in the composing of a memorial to be presented to Cardinal Barnabò. On November 10, Father Deshon writes to say that it will be a statement "of all our grievances," as full and clear as it can be made, and it will ask for a separation "from the jurisdiction of the Father General, and in failure of that as a dernier resort, dispensation from the vows." A postscript adds, "Fr. Baker goes with us in all things." Father Walworth writes at the same time in the same sense saying "We are all united here and hurrying on with our memorial." (November 11). Shortly after the memorial had been sent, Father Hewit wrote at great length to Cardinal Barnabò, reciting a list of grievances—among them, the practical banning of the mission program inaugurated by Father Bernard. Some of those grievances could not well be stated in the memorial, but they helped to explain the motives that prompted the sending of that document. Hewit signed the letter as secretary and consultor of the American province of the Redemptorist Congregation.

We come upon repeated manifestations of Hecker's amazing activity. At Barnabò's urging he visited Carl Cardinal von Reisach and other noted churchmen and made a very favorable impression. He also wrote a paper for the *Civiltà Cattolica* on conditions in America.[14] Cardinal Barnabò thought it would not be accepted; but, as a matter of fact, it was welcomed by the progressive-minded editor, Carlo Curci, who recognized that Hecker had something to say and the courage to say it, and who told Hecker that much important matter had been put aside to give space for this article. It was translated by one of the staff and published as two articles. The *Civiltà* at that time had

10,000 subscribers and was read by all the principal men of Italy;[15] and at Hecker's request one hundred reprints were sent to different European journals. On November 20, 1857 Hecker wrote his brethren, *"You will not find anything new in them, but they embody our hopes, views, and aspirations. They are all brand new here, and it is said that they convey a better idea of the state of things in the U.S. than anything that has been done here heretofore. . . . A member of the Holy Office told me the other day that if an Italian had written them, they would have had him up at once."*

Hecker's prestige was further enhanced by the fact that he won a convert to the Church in the person of George Loring Brown, a well known American artist then resident in Rome.[16] Brown's conversion created a sensation in the American colony. Barnabò made it his business to bring it to the attention of the Holy Father and of high-ranking churchmen.

On December 18, 1857, Hecker wrote:

> I have lived a history in a few months. . . . I have been cut and slashed at in every direction and before everybody up to His Holiness; and have lost any idea of ever having had any character at all. If these fellows don't make me a saint it will not be because they have not done their utmost to present me with opportunities. But the grace of God has guided me through it all, and thus far I am happy in having nothing to regret.

He predicts as the most probable outcome, that the five will "begin a new company of missionaries." Then he continues:

We should take our present missions as the basis of our unity and action, at the same time not to be exclusively restricted to them, leaving us the liberty to adapt ourselves to the wants which may present themselves in our country. Were the question presented to me to *restrict* myself *exclusively to Redemptorist missions, in that case,* I should feel in conscience bound to obtain from holy men a decision on the question whether God had not pointed out another field for me.

About this time, according to a letter of Hecker's (December 5, 1857), the general was complaining that Hecker had powerful friends, whereas he had none.

2. JANUARY TO MARCH
1858

During all this trying period Hecker kept strictly to his resolve to accept God's will as communicated to him by ecclesiastical authority and by the men whom he had chosen as the best available guides. A letter dated Feast of the Epiphany (January 6), 1858 tells that he had submitted a long document summarizing his whole career to his counsellors, to Bedini, to Barnabò, and to the Holy Father. In it he emphasized his attraction to the work of converting non-Catholics, and stressed the fact that a number of competent persons considered his method effective.

By January 9, he was able to report that "Mons. Bizzarri looks most favorably on our cause" and that when the pope said authority must be sustained, Bizzarri replied, "But if the authority has committed an injustice?" Hecker comments, "From the mouth of Mons. B. this was of weight and importance, and it was then the H. Father replied, 'In that case the matter must be examined.' Now I am told, the mauvais impressions made upon the pope have gone, and he is now disposed to be in our favor." Hecker adds, Bizzarri "has pluck, and won't give up if he knows he is right, even to His Holiness."

A few days after Hecker had submitted his document, he wrote to the American Fathers (January 10) that Bishop Connolly had reported the Holy Father as saying: "Why do they not form themselves into a new company of missionaries?" When told they were ready, the pope said: "They cannot expect me to take the initiatory step; this would be putting the cart before the horse. Let them present their plan to me, and if I find it good it shall have my consent."

On February 1, 1858, Hecker wrote: "Bedini goes tonight to see the Pope with his hands full of letters from Abps. and Bps. of the U.S., and these of the right stamp, and with the express authority of Cardinal Barnabò to inform His Holiness that the matter was become most serious, and to insist upon something being done immediately. The Pope knows Abp. Kenrick and his Letter . . . will have the greatest weight with him . . ."

When Bedini "proposed reading the letters in his possession" to the pope, he was told that this was not necessary. Bedini then sent them to Bizzarri with a request for a report on the following Friday.

On February 13, Hecker wrote to his brother: "The pope seems to think now that we are good fellows, and by and by he may regard us as zealous missionaries, devoted to God and His Church, and called to a special and providential work, and hence take a special interest in our regard. . . . My views on these subjects are becoming daily more clear, just and practical."

The pope had by now received a great sheaf of testimonials, reports, and suggestions. It was time, thought Barnabò, to press for an audience; and finally Hecker was received. Pius made a few rather mild animadversions on the shortcomings of Americans in general, but seemed to like Hecker's forthright replies, his wholehearted zeal, and his complete readiness to accept whatever decision the Pope might make. At the end of the audience, Hecker says, "He gave me a blessing and repeated in a loud voice as I knelt, 'Bravo! Bravo!'"

On February 19, Hecker reported that, despite the tangled course of events which had caused him more anxiety and pain than he had experienced in all his Catholic life, he had finished a "large scale novitiate." His painful experiences, he thought would leave him more entirely devoted to the work of God. When it began to be plain that he and his companions would be liberated for the apostolate to non-Catholics, he multiplied his prayers and called upon his friends to join him in the request for divine assistance. On March 9, he was able to write:

The Pope has spoken, and the American fathers, including myself, are dispensed from their vows. The decree is not in my hands, but Cardinal Barnabo read it to me last evening.[17] The General is not mentioned in it, and no attention whatever is paid to his action in my regard. The other Fathers are dispensed in view of the petition they made, as the demand for separation as Redemptorists would destroy the unity of the Congregation, and in the dispensation I am associated with them. The Cardinal is wholly content; says that I must ask immediately for an audience to thank the Pope.

On March 16, reports Hecker, the Pope received him and blessed him "in order that I might become a great missionary in the United States." The final decision, ignoring the question of who was right and who was wrong in "the Hecker case," created a totally new situation by separating the two parties.

Observers acquainted with the ins and outs of ecclesiastical administration, thought it really amazing that a man who had approached the Holy See under the stigma of religious disobedience was able seven months later to leave Rome with what amounted to an equivalent permission to organize a new congregation. No doubt the true significance of this may be found in a friend's comment: "Hecker fell on his feet, because he had first fallen on his knees in prayer."

Writing on March 27th, Hecker told his colleagues: "Our first location I would have far from a church, & in a place where we would not be called upon to exercise parish duties. Any offer on location which involves parish duties, however favorable, would prove the grave of our little band & the death of our hopes."

To his brother George, he communicated some of his ideas about the projected community, saying among other things: "My suggestion is for a house with a garden outside of New York City. No parish."

On April 3, 1858, he wrote, "I saw the General on Tuesday of this week to take leave of him. After some conversation we left in good feeling, promising to pray *pro invicem*."

Early in May Hecker landed in New York and he and his companions at once set about the work of organizing the Paulist Fathers. The little boat with its crew of five had cut loose from the great mother ship and was about to venture upon perilous, uncharted seas.

NOTES FOR PART I

For source material the present book depends chiefly on the Paulist Fathers' Archives, referred to here as PFA.

STUDY I (Text, pages 3–14)

1. See Sanford H. Cobb, *The Rise of Religious Liberty in America.* (New York, 1902), 507. The New Hampshire constitutional convention in 1912 discussed the question of dropping two discriminatory words, "evangelical" and "Protestant," from the Bill of Rights, and George W. Stone of Andover urged that the phrases should be eliminated as they constituted "a disgrace to the intelligence of the people of New Hampshire." When submitted to the people at the election, the proposal to eliminate the two phrases was defeated by a margin of more than 2,000 votes. The same result took place when the proposal was again submitted to the people after the constitutional convention of 1918–1922, this time by a margin of more than 7,000 votes. See Joseph F. Thorning, S.J., *Religious Liberty in Transition.* (New York, 1931) ch. V. The word, "Protestant," still remained in the Bill of Rights in 1952, according to a letter from the Attorney General of the State of New Hampshire in the possession of the present writer.

2. Brilliant intellect, courageous temperament, experience in organizing fitted John England well for the post to which he was called in 1820, when he was named Bishop of Charleston, the social and political center of the South. In the difficult period which followed Carroll's death, he had to rule over a diocese embracing Georgia and the Carolinas; and his see was at that time the center of perhaps the most serious of the various schisms threatening the American Catholic Church. Born in Cork in 1786, he had witnessed, as a boy, the brutalities inflicted upon the people after the abortive insurrection against English rule in 1798. Ordained in 1808, he taught in and presided over the diocesan College of Cork; battled alongside Daniel O'Connell to keep the English gov-

ernment from obtaining the right of veto over the Catholic bishops; advocated vigorously the humanizing of conditions on the transports which carried Irish political prisoners into exile.

Almost immediately after arriving in Charleston, he opened a classical school which attained top rank, and also a diocesan seminary. He founded the *United States Catholic Miscellany,* the best Catholic weekly in the country; and within two years he gave more than two hundred lectures in courthouses, non-Catholic homes, Presbyterian, Methodist, Baptist, and Episcopalian churches. Despite the reluctance of the Archbishop of Baltimore, he succeeded by incessant pressure in having the American bishops adopt the practice of holding provincial councils periodically. He made four trips to Europe to bring back financial aid and priests and nuns to assist in serving the diocese. He recommended repeatedly that Rome should nominate none but American citizens to American sees. He spoke before the state legislature in behalf of Catholic rights; and in January, 1826, he addressed the Congress of the United States in the presence of President John Quincy Adams, answering criticisms that had been leveled against the Church by Adams several years before, when he was Secretary of State. England was on good terms with his fellow citizens of all classes and beliefs; and, in the early years of his administration, he gave a week of lectures in a Protestant church, then at the request of the minister, occupied the pulpit on Sunday, on condition that he would be in sole charge of the service.

At the request of Pope Gregory XVI he spent four years in heart-breaking, fruitless efforts to effect a concordat between the Vatican and the Republic of Haiti. Although, mainly through the opposition of Maréchal and his French colleagues, England's plans were blocked and he himself was denied promotion to a more important see such as Philadelphia or New York, he was, according to Archbishop Francis P. Kenrick, the outstanding figure in the hierarchy of his day. In 1842, as he lay dying, at the age of fifty-six, worn out by almost superhuman labors, we are told that prayers were offered for him in the Protestant Episcopal Churches in the city and in the Hebrew Synagogues. *United States Miscellany* (April 2, 1842). See Peter Guilday, *The*

NOTES FOR PART I

Life and Times of John England, 1786–1842 (New York, 1927), II, 538.

3. Sister Mary Gilbert Kelly, *Catholic Immigrant Colonization Projects in the United States, 1815–1860.* (New York, 1939), 269 n.

4. Official documents give a detailed description of a pesthole in Boston—Half Moon Place, near Fort Hill, inhabited chiefly by Irish—inspected in 1849, when the city authorities were frightened at the spread of cholera. As evidence of the propensity of the Irish for law-breaking, Oscar Handlin cites the records of the Boston Police Department which gives "Nativity of Arrests for the year 1864: Germany, 138; England, 426; Ireland, 9,791." *Boston's Immigrants, 1790–1865.* (Cambridge, 1941), 244.

5. John Talbot Smith, *History of the Catholic Church in New York* (New York and Boston, 1905), I, 127. The author continues:

> Free labor, good wages, the right to vote, the privilege of buying or taking up land, decent treatment as human beings, flattering treatment as citizens, were theirs without question or hindrance. They had suffered incredibly from the absence of these blessings in Ireland, where they were mere slaves of the soil, persecuted, harrassed, and kept in desperate poverty. These people became more American than the Americans, and knew how to appreciate the blessings of civil freedom far better than the natives, who had always enjoyed such blessings. They looked up to the Fathers of the Republic as to the saints, kept the national holidays with a fervor that surprised all, and took the oath of allegiance to the United States with a fervor the deeper that they were asked to foreswear allegiance to King George, for whom they had no loyalty, no feeling except hate.

As Guilday says, "The historian of the United States can no longer pass over in silence Ireland's part in the making of America or allow his pen to copy the misstatements of his predecessors." *op. cit.*, II, 2.

6. Henry D. Thoreau, *Walden* (Boston, 1854), 222, 225.

7. In Philadelphia in 1844 the Native Americans caused the death of at least a dozen persons and burned the valuable library of the Augustinian Fathers. Prominent individuals who attained notoriety in the anti-Catholic "war" were: Reverend George Bourne, editor of the first violent anti-

Catholic weekly, *The Protestant,* in 1830; Reverend John Breckenridge, whose attack on Catholics in 1832 was answered by John Hughes, later Archbishop of New York; Dr. Lyman Beecher, father of Harriet Beecher Stowe, and preacher at the Park Street church, Boston (on Brimstone Corner, today within a stone's throw of the Paulist Information Center), who helped to instigate the burning of the Charlestown convent in 1834. For testimony concerning the outrages of this period, see Gustavus Myers, *History of Bigotry in the United States* (New York, 1943); Ray Allen Billington, *The Protestant Crusade, 1800–1860* (New York, 1938).

8. Horace Greeley of the New York *Tribune* eulogized the pope. At a meeting of approval held in the Broadway Tabernacle in November, 1846, Bishop John Hughes was surrounded by clergymen of different faiths and other persons prominent in political and civil life. In 1847 the legislature of Louisiana urged the inaugurating of diplomatic relations with Rome. In 1848, the United States sent Jacob L. Martin to the Vatican as *chargé d'affaires,* to cultivate friendly civil relations between the two governments and to promote commerce. Dr. Martin died soon after his arrival in Rome; but his successor, Lewis Cass, presented his credentials in November, 1849.

9. Bedini, papal nuncio to Brazil, who carried a letter from Pius IX to President Pierce, had been the pope's representative in Bologna when an unrising there was suppressed by Austrian troops, and a Barnabite monk, Ugo Bassi, was executed. Exploiting this tragedy, an apostate Barnabite priest, Alessandro Gavazzi, friend of Bassi, inflamed anti-Catholic sentiment in Boston; and in various cities Orangemen and members of Italian secret societies—political kindred of the fanatic Orsini, who five years later tried to assassinate Louis Napoleon—organized riots during the nuncio's visit. In Cincinnati several persons were killed; in New York a conscience-stricken conspirator who disclosed a plot to assassinate Bedini, was himself assassinated. The spread of the campaign against Bedini will be understood better, if we realize that, until the Atlantic cable began to function in 1866, people in this country did not get prompt information about events in Europe. When Bedini was leaving America, friends took him secretly to Staten Island, and thence by tugboat

to a steamer—to the annoyance of Archbishop Hughes, at that time absent from the city, who said later that had he been at home he would have driven to the wharf in an open carriage, alongside Bedini. Despite his unpleasant adventures, Bedini retained a friendly feeling for America; kept up his friendship with the bishops here; and later on, as Secretary of the Congregation of the Propaganda, gave much help to Father Hecker during the latter's troubled days in Rome. Bedini was appointed to the See of Viterbo, named cardinal in 1861, and died in 1864 at the age of fifty-eight.

10. Archbishop John Carroll, so helpful during the nation's infancy, had been followed by other worthy prelates. John England revived classical learning in South Carolina; John Baptist Purcell, Bishop of Cincinnati in 1833 and archbishop in 1850, gave prestige to the Church by his scholarship; Francis Patrick Kenrick native of Dublin, Archbishop of Baltimore in 1851, a man familiar with the original texts of Sacred Scripture, translated the Bible into English. Two other outstanding prelates were John Hughes, native of Ireland, Archbishop of New York in 1850, who lectured before Congress on "Christianity, the Source of Regeneration," and visited Europe as President Lincoln's agent during the Civil War; and Martin J. Spalding, Kentucky-born, Archbishop of Baltimore in 1864, who by writing and lecturing corrected many erroneous notions of Catholicism, aided the Negroes after the Civil War, gave loyal support to Father Hecker.

The people paid tribute to such intrepid bishops as Flaget, Du Bourg, Edward Fenwick, Rosati, Bruté, Blanchet; and to missionary priests such as the Russian prince, Demetrius Gallitzin in Pennsylvania and, farther west, Badin, Nerinckx, and De Smet, the Jesuit to whom the United States looked repeatedly for help in dealing with the Indians. The distinguished Father Gabriel Richard, a newspaper editor, was a member of Congress from Michigan.

11. The Carrolls produced Archbishop John Carroll and his distant cousin, Charles Carroll of Carrollton, signer of the Declaration of Independence. Then there were the Ewings whose father, Thomas, baptized on his deathbed in 1871, had been Secretary of the Treasury and senator of the United States. His three sons were Philemon, justice of the supreme court of Ohio, Hugh and Charles, both generals in the Civil

War. His daughter Eleanor married General William T. Sherman.

Among the nation's most respected citizens were William Gaston, Princeton graduate in 1796, an outstanding justice of the supreme court of North Carolina; and Roger Taney (brother-in-law of Francis Scott Key), state senator in 1816, fifth chief justice of the supreme court of the United States in 1855.

12. Three were archbishops: Samuel Eccleston of Maryland, a Catholic in 1819, Archbishop of Baltimore in 1834; James Frederick Wood of Philadelphia, a Catholic in 1836, Bishop of Philadelphia in 1860, and later archbishop; James Roosevelt Bayley, born in Rye, New York, a Catholic in 1842, first Bishop of Newark in 1853, and Archbishop of Baltimore in 1872. Bayley's great great grandfather, Isaac Roosevelt, was also an ancestor of Theodore Roosevelt and of Franklin Delano Roosevelt. Bayley became President of St. John's Seminary, Fordham, in 1846. Six days after his ordination in 1844, his paternal grandfather, James Roosevelt, disinherited him, thus depriving him of a bequest that amounted to some $70,000.

Six were bishops: William Tyler of Vermont, a Catholic in 1821 and first Bishop of Hartford in 1843; Josue Maria Moody Young of Maine, a Catholic in 1828 and second Bishop of Erie in 1854; Sylvester Rosecrans of Ohio, a Catholic in 1845 and first Bishop of Columbus in 1868; Thomas Albert Becker of Pittsburgh, a Catholic in 1853, and first Bishop of Wilmington in 1868; Richard Gilmour of Glasgow, Scotland, a Catholic in 1848, and Bishop of Cleveland in 1872; Edgar P. Wadhams of Essex County, New York, a Catholic in 1846 and first Bishop of Ogdensburg in 1872.

13. Convert authors who wrote before the Civil War numbered more than fifty. See Brother David, C.S.C., *American Catholic Convert Authors* (Grosse Pointe, Michigan, 1934).

Study II (Text, pages 15–19)

1. Soon after the establishment of the community at Scala, near Amalfi, in 1732, Alphonsus, abandoned by all his priests save one, made new foundations; but the Neapolitan government acquired practical control of them. In consequence, the Holy See ruled that only the houses outside the kingdom of

the Two Sicilies would be regarded as the Redemptorist Congregation; and thus the saint died in 1793 outside the order he had founded. The order however, was extended into many countries by Clement Hofbauer (canonized in 1909), "Apostle of Vienna," and his companions; and soon it had spread into Germany, Austria, Poland, Switzerland, Belgium, Holland, England and America.

In its original pattern, the Redemptorist order was not divided into provinces. Each house had a rector; and the head of the whole Congregation was a rector major, residing at Nocera near Naples, and assisted by a (practically independent) vicar general who ruled the "Transalpine" houses. In the nineteenth century these latter increased so fast that the vicar general was soon ruling over many more houses than the rector major; and to correct this anomaly the Holy See proposed to divide the community into provinces, with the rector major residing in Rome. As the Neapolitan Fathers did not like this departure from the original plan of St. Alphonsus, the matter was referred to the Congregation of Bishops and Regulars; and in 1841 a commission of seven cardinals, headed by the papal Secretary of State, Luigi Cardinal Lambruschini, decreed that the community should be separated into two mutually independent congregations —the houses in the Two Sicilies and the houses outside that area. The commission further decreed the creation of six provinces, two in the kingdom of the Two Sicilies, and four outside the kingdom, including the new Roman province.

2. John F. Byrne, C.SS.R. *The Redemptorist Centenaries.* (Philadelphia, 1932) Ch. III.

3. Father Vincent Holden, C.S.P., who has pieced together all available clues, dates the beginning of the intimacy between Hecker and Brownson in the early days of 1842, while Brownson was in New York delivering a course of four lectures on Civilization and Human Progress. *The Early Years of Isaac Thomas Hecker (1819–1844).* (Washington, 1939), 54–59.

In *Brook Farm* (New York, 1900), Lindsay Swift describes the faculty, including George and Sophia Ripley, John S. Dwight, Nathaniel Hawthorne, Charles Anderson Dana; among members and visitors were Margaret Fuller, William H. Channing, Ralph Waldo Emerson, Orestes A. Brownson, Theodore Parker, Elizabeth Palmer Peabody, and George

William Curtis. Much information about Hecker's reaction to this group is conveyed by Father Elliott in his *Life of Father Hecker* (New York, 1891) and by Holden *op. cit.* After leaving Brook Farm, Hecker spent some months at Concord, boarding with Henry Thoreau's mother and taking Latin lessons from the scholarly George Bradford.

4. Father Hecker described Bishop Fitzpatrick as a man of high mental endowments, and added:

> He carried into the domain of speculative philosophy and theology certain traditional methods peculiar to the theologians and philosophers of his day, and he was impatient with one who would not prefer these methods to all others. He had little sympathy with any one who could not find a solution of all difficulties in the historical argument of the church or in the external marks of the church's Oneness, Holiness, Catholicity, and Apostolicity. *Catholic World*, XLV (April, 1887), 1.

5. Maurice De Meulemeester, C.SS.R., *Le Père Frédéric von Held Rédemptoriste, 1799–1881*. (Jette, 1911), 179, 206.

6. Victor Dechamps (1810–1883), a brilliant young abbé of Tournai, had entered the Society in 1835. He became rector of Liège in 1842; Bishop of Namur in 1865; Cardinal Archbishop of Malines in 1875. His works are published in ten volumes, *Oeuvres de S. E. Le Cardinal Dechamps* (Malines, n.d. The author's foreword is dated June 29, 1874.)

7. While provincial of Belgium, De Held had made an official visitation of the English missions, taking with him as socius, his trusted fellow Belgian, Father Dechamps; and, at the end of his second term, he was sent to England to build up the Redemptorists there. In 1848 he founded a house at Clapham in suburban London, where a large number of Catholics were practically without religious ministrations. He made important contacts with the Duke of Norfolk and other influential laymen and with the Honorable and Reverend George Talbot (fifth son of the third Baron de Malahide, educated at Eton and Oxford, received into the Catholic Church in 1842 by Wiseman, and made canon of St. Peter's by the pope), who functioned for some twenty years as the Roman agent, first of Wiseman and then of Manning—their "henchman," Shane Leslie calls him. De Held received several valuable recruits for the order, including the Oratorian, Robert Coffin (later first provincial of the English province and eventually Bishop of Southwark);

and Father Edward Douglas, already six years in the Church, ordained a priest in Italy, and member of a wealthy Scottish family whose funds helped to build a church and convent at Clapham.

8. Rev. A. F. Hewit, *Memoir and Sermons of Rev. F. A. Baker* (New York, 1865), 124–5.

9. The (unpublished) *Chronicle of the English Missions given by the Redemptorist Fathers in the United States of N. America* (commenced April 6, 1851) covers eighty-six missions preached before the founding of the Paulist Fathers in 1858. The record is continued thereafter in the *Chronicle of the Missions given by the Congregation of Missionary Priests of St. Paul the Apostle* (commenced April 18, 1858), PFA.

10. The *Catholic World*, LXXIII (June 1901), 320 ff.

11. *op. cit.*, 244.

Study III (Text, pages 30–40)

1. In those mosquito-ridden days, cities along the seaboard were visited with tragic regularity by epidemics.

2. The *Chronicle*, I, 91.

3. PFA, Hecker Papers.

4. The *Chronicle*, I, 106.

5. One of Bishop England's projects (which continued to impress and influence men long after it had been discontinued) was his extraordinary device for keeping in touch with his people by a system of annual conventions, which brought together the clergy and laity, first of a whole state, later of the whole diocese. An account of this can be read in Peter Guilday's biography. *op. cit.*, II, XXXIII.

6. *op. cit.*, I, viii.

7. Francis Gartland, born in Dublin, vicar general of Philadelphia, consecrated first Bishop of Savannah in 1850, died within four years, during a cholera epidemic. That same epidemic brought death also to a visiting bishop, the heroic Edward Barron, native of Ireland, educated in Rome, president of the diocesan seminary of Philadelphia, who had worked as a missionary in Liberia until the territory was taken over by a religious order. He then devoted himself to mission work in Philadelphia, St. Louis, and throughout Alabama and Florida. At the time of the Redemptorist mis-

sion, Savannah was under an administrator, the Irish-born John Barry, who became Bishop of Savannah in 1857, only to die two years later.
8. The *Paulist News* (New York, June 1951).

STUDY IV (Text, pages 41–52)

1. Unitarianism, which required no creed even from its ministers, was organized in 1825 shortly after the celebrated sermon of William Ellery Channing. It received great impetus from Theodore Parker, radical pastor of the First Unitarian Church of West Roxbury, Massachusetts, and from Ralph Waldo Emerson, popular poet, essayist, and lecturer. By the end of the Civil War, the movement was large enough to justify the holding of a national convention.
2. PFA, Hecker Papers.
3. St. Clement Hofbauer's companion, Father Joseph Passerat, became vicar general in 1820, and held office until his resignation in 1848, dying two years later. During his rule the community expanded swiftly.
4. In 1854 the vicar general, Father Rudolf Smetana, ordered the Fathers to withdraw from Monroe and Detroit; and Bishop Peter P. Lefevre appealed to the Holy See. The Congregation of the Propaganda sanctioned the withdrawal from Monroe, but directed that Detroit should be retained for the time being; and the Fathers remained there until after the death of Bishop Lefevre. With the permission of the next bishop, Caspar H. Borgess, they left in 1872. Byrne, *op. cit.,* 213.
5. The highest official in the Redemptorist Congregation was called the "Rector Major" until the Chapter of 1855, which elected the first superior general. The change of titles seems not to have passed into general usage for some years however.
6. Invitations to found houses in Canada had come from Toronto in 1852 and from Quebec in 1856. Both requests were urged repeatedly; but the acceptance was postponed for some years. St. Thomas, Virgin Islands, which had been assigned to the Redemptorists by the Holy See, was waiting for a priest to take care of the people there, ninety per cent colored. Father Louis Dold, temporarily detached from the house of studies in Cumberland, was sent to St. Thomas in

1858. The following year the Belgian province took over and Father Louis de Buggenoms succeeded Father Dold. Byrne, *op. cit.*, 511.

7. The Jesuit, Benedictine, Redemptorist and other orders have adopted the novel missionary device referred to in the text.

8. After Passerat's resignation in 1848, the Holy See decided to appoint a temporary vicar general to effect the consolidation of the two sections of the order. All forecasts pointed to the nomination of De Held, an old disciple of Clement Hofbauer, founder of the whole western section of the Congregation. Contrary to expectation, the man appointed was Father Rudolf Smetana; and almost from the beginning of his term of office he and De Held were separated by a diversity of views.

When the attempted consolidation failed, chiefly because the King of Naples would not consent to have the head of the order live outside the Kingdom of Naples, the Holy See decreed that the houses in the Two Sicilies should remain under a special rule; and that all the other houses should be under a superior general, resident in Rome, to be elected by a general chapter. De Held believed that Smetana, in arranging the convocation of the chapter, had been guilty of grave canonical irregularities, notably in naming superiors who were his own docile followers, although they lacked the required age. At the chapter of 1855 the Belgians, under the leadership of Dechamps tried to elect as first superior general, De Held, "Father of the Belgian province," the man who in Passerat's opinion was best fitted for the office. But, after a morning of fruitless ballotting, they could muster only enough votes to prevent Smetana from gaining the requisite two-thirds majority; and they accepted a compromise candidate, Father Nicholas Mauron, who, as Dechamps observed, at least was able to speak both French and German. The new superior general, according to the Belgians, proved to be under the influence of Smetana, who remained in Rome although he held no general office. Moreover, many of the general consultors were ineligible according to the constitution. Dechamps and De Held soon found themselves local rectors instead of provincials. De Held said to Hecker, "Perhaps Divine Providence has permitted these things to happen in order that Rome may see in what way we are governed and that the Holy See in its wisdom may find a way to remedy this sort of thing without allowing too much suffering to be endured by the body of the congregation, which is sound and promising." De Meulemeester (*op. cit.*, 266–275) describes the election of the superior general in 1855 in considerable detail. De Held's views are given in sixteen letters he sent to Hecker in Rome, especially the letter of October 14; and also in Hecker's letters of late 1857 and early 1858. PFA, Hecker Letters.

9. Father Douglas—who had entered the novitiate while Hecker was a student—was now Roman provincial and a member of the general council. The *Verdesi Guide-Book* (198) states that on the Via Merulana, "is a modern church, with its adjoining convent, built in Gothic style by the English architect G. Wieley for the Scottish convert Father Edward Douglas of the Redemptorist Congregation. Here is venerated a very ancient and world famous picture of Our Lady of Perpetual Succour, saved from the old church of St. Matthew that once stood in the neighborhood but which was destroyed during the French occupation in 1798."

10. See letter (written apparently in early September, 1857) from Hecker to Fathers Walworth, Hewit, and Deshon. This letter was not received until after the whole affair had been settled by the Holy See in a decree dated March 6, 1858.

Study V (Text, pages 53–68)

1. PFA, Hecker Letters, December 22, 1857.

2. Hecker carried with him a letter from Archbishop Hughes to Cardinal Barnabò, recommending Hecker as a "laborious, edifying, zealous, and truly apostolic priest"; another from Hughes to Hecker himself, asking Hecker to tell Mauron that Hughes was desirous to have an English-speaking house. A letter from Bishop Bayley to Barnabò states that Hecker "with the approbation of the provincial goes to Rome to confer with the superior general," and to present a plan of which Bayley approves heartily. In another letter to Mauron, Bayley urges the establishment and promises to promote it by every means in his power. He adds: "Rev. Father Hecker, well known to all the bishops and priests in this region for his eminent qualities, and the zeal with which he labors for the salvation of souls, is entirely cognizant of my whole

mind in this matter and he will be able to explain the business to your Reverence by word of mouth better than I could in even lengthy letters." To Archbishop Bedini, Bayley writes: "Father Hecker, as you already know, is one of the most distinguished converts of whom our religion can boast in this country, and he has already rendered the greatest service to religion by his writing and by his apostolic activities. . . . I do not doubt that you will aid him with all your power in the important undertaking which determined him to visit Rome." There was also a letter from Ruland, the American provincial; and a letter from Hewit presenting Hecker as the delegate of the Americans. In addition, Hecker had letters from McMaster, widely known journalist; from Dr. Brownson, the celebrated philosopher; from Dr. Silliman Ives, the honored convert who had been an Episcopal bishop. *Ibid.* For Bishop Bayley's letters see Sister M. Hildegarde Yeager, C.S.C., *The Life of James Roosevelt Bayley, First Bishop of Newark and Eighth Archbishop of Baltimore, 1814–1877.* (Washington, D.C., 1947), 174–179.

3. Alessandro Barnabò (1801–1874), Prefect of the Congregation of the Propaganda, exercised jurisdiction over the United States, the British Isles and other missionary countries; and he was doubly important in all ecclesiastical affairs because Giacomo Cardinal Antonelli, papal Secretary of State, was a deacon, not a priest. In addition to being Prefect of the Congregation of Oriental Affairs, Barnabò belonged to several other important congregations—of the Council, of the Holy Office, of Rites, of Ceremonies, and of Extraordinary Ecclesiastical Affairs. When he was created cardinal in 1856, he took as his titular church, Santa Susanna, which strangely enough, in 1922, was entrusted to the Paulist Fathers who had recognized Barnabò as a sort of godfather, preserved his name in the constitution of their Society, and after his death, assumed the obligation of offering a Mass annually for the repose of his soul.

4. On October 24, 1857, Hecker wrote to the Fathers that "De Held stands high with His Holiness;" that his letter made "a complete refutation of the calumnious charges of the general against me"; that it described the arbitrary government of the general's predecessor, Father Smetana; that it aroused the hope of "a change of the rule." Two weeks later Hecker reported Smetana's departure from Rome, but

added, "There is no prospect of any change; he has bent them all his way." To Hecker's suggestion of a visit to Rome by De Held, the latter replied that "It would be a dangerous enterprise;" and Hecker made the comment: "The Belgians are in as bad a fix as we are. They are afraid to appeal to Rome and hope our case will throw light on theirs." PFA, Hecker Letters.

The following year, in his visitation of Belgium, Mauron announced to the local rectors that he wished the dispute about the observance of poverty to be settled by the Holy See. De Held's biographer says that the old rector's "filial respect and touching docility towards the general, removed from the latter's heart the uneasiness occasioned by the unfortunate intervention in the Hecker case." The biographer notes however, that on the next list of new superiors, the name of De Held—for the first time since 1832—did not appear. He ceased to be rector of Liège; Dechamps ceased to be rector of Brussels; and neither of them ever became superior again. Writing to a friend, Dechamps said "You ask if it is true that I am no longer rector? Yes. Have I then been appointed provincial again? No. Neither general, nor provincial, nor local consultor. Am I then now just nothing? Oh! Nothing would be too little. What then? By God's grace, a Christian; by God's grace a priest; by a greater grace, a religious. Is that not enough? Father De Held like me, is no more than a Christian, a priest and a religious. May we render a good account of these dignities." De Held died in 1881; Dechamps, Cardinal Archbishop of Malines died in 1883. After a stroke of apoplexy in 1882, Mauron began a slow decline, but he remained superior general until his death in 1893. Meulemeester, *op. cit.*, 267, 344.

5. PFA, Hecker Letters, March 5, 1858. Pius was fearful lest the outcome might work injury to the Redemptorist Congregation in whose reorganization he had personally participated. It was typical of the Holy Father to wish to do justice to everybody without hurting anyone. This was well illustrated in the Errington case, a few years later. Forced to discredit either Cardinal Wiseman or the cardinal's coadjutor, Archbishop George Errington, Pius begged the latter as a favor to resign his coadjutorship. Errington, former Bishop of Plymouth, had shown strong disapproval of Manning who had replaced him in the councils of the cardinal.

Errington refused to resign and the pope dismissed him from office most reluctantly. Wilfrid Ward, *Life and Times of Cardinal Wiseman* (New York, 1897) II, 369.

6. The American side of St. John's River was in the Diocese of St. John until 1870. Thomas Louis Connolly (1815–1876), born in Cork, educated at Rome, joined the Capuchins and was ordained in France. He went to Nova Scotia as secretary to Archbishop William Walsh and in 1845 became vicar general of the Diocese of Halifax. He was consecrated bishop in 1852 and succeeded to the See of Halifax in 1859. He gained a reputation for great tact in his dealings with Protestants, and according to a prominent Protestant clergyman, was "a sagacious, far-seeing, large-hearted man, superior to all littleness, who practically eliminated ill feeling between Catholics and Protestants in Nova Scotia." He was an outstanding orator. To Hecker he said: "I am ready to die for your cause, and I am going to tell the Pope so." He even offered to assist in paying Hecker's personal expenses in Rome.

7. Talbot had formed a friendly association with the Redemptorists when they first came to Clapham. His hold on Pius was explained neither by character nor by intellect. Manning called him the most imprudent of men; Bishop Ullathrone said he was notoriously lacking in judgment; Newman described him as "the most dangerous man in England." Talbot passed his last years in a mental asylum in Passy and died there in 1886. See Fergal McGrath, S.J., *Newman's University Idea and Reality* (New York, 1951), 110 n.

8. Of Father Gregorio we have little information except that he was definitor of the Carmelites, that is, an official elected by the chapter to assist the superior in the government of the community. Father Francis of St. Lawrence, Hecker's director, had the reputation of being one of the most spiritually enlightened men in Rome. The Necrology Register of the Passionists, gives the following account:

> Father Francis of St. Lawrence having lived in the world and in the married state until middle age, acquired general esteem by his spirit of fervor and self-denial during his novitiate. After ordination, he labored first in the retreat of San Salvatore, which was later given up by the Passionists; and he then discharged various offices in the motherhouse at Rome. The last years of his life

were spent in unremitting physical weakness, endured with admirable patience and tranquility. He died in 1864 at the age of 74. He spent thirty years as a Passionist.

Father Druelle was at that time procurator general of the Fathers of the Holy Cross—a fact which reminds us that some sixty years later another procurator general of the same congregation was of enormous help to the Paulist Fathers when they were negotiating with the Holy See, preparatory to receiving charge of the church of Santa Susanna in Rome. Druelle was born in France in 1812, ordained in 1838, and before coming to Rome had served as superior of a seminary in Algiers, also as visitor to the Holy Cross houses in America, also as Prefect Apostolic of Guadeloupe. He died in Paris in 1875, shortly after finishing a nine-year term of office as head of the French province. His winning manner, extraordinary tact, ability to mix successfully with all types of people made him a man of great value to his community; he was one of the solid pillars of the congregation in its early days. His great influence in Rome and his intimate friendship with Barnabò was not only a precious asset for the congregation of the Holy Cross—it gave great support to Hecker also.

Bernard Smith, an Irish-born Benedictine of Monte Cassino—separated for a time from his community because of difficulty with the Italian government—was Roman agent of many American, Irish, English, Canadian and Australian bishops. He became acting head of the North American College when it opened in 1859; he died as Abbot of St. Paul's Outside the Walls. Smith took an unfriendly attitude toward Newman during the discussion about the establishment of an oratory at Oxford; and Ambrose St. John, writing to Newman, May, 1867, speaks of Smith as "a great big mouthing, good-natured (so they say) Irishman who blusters about . . ." Wilfrid Ward, *The Life of John Henry Cardinal Newman* (London, 1912), II, 164.

9. Giuseppe-Andrea Bizzarri (1802–1877), titular archbishop and Secretary of the Congregation of Bishops and Regulars in 1854, visited the King of the Two Sicilies in 1855 to negotiate diplomatic difficulties about the marriage laws. He became cardinal in 1862.

10. In an endeavor to explain the situation, Hecker wrote on November 20, 1857:

You are under the impression it seems, that my time is employed in a private affair of honor. This is a mistake. Every document presented by me embodies all our aims in globo. And there is no other way of obtaining what we desire than by making the decree against me as the basis of all our operations. . . . First our innocence must be established, before any ulterior steps can be taken. I say our, for all through you are identified in my expulsion, though you were not thus served.

11. The American provincial, Father Ruland, wrote to Hewit, stating that Father Douglas, writing in the name of the general who was ill, had rejected the provincial's petition for the reinstatement of Father Hecker; that Douglas had said the general "would prefer to abandon the whole American province and to be obliged to withdraw his subjects from the U. States, rather than to admit among us principles subversive of the very essence of the religious life." Douglas had answered the charge that Hecker was dismissed without being heard, by saying "The Father General assures Your Reverence that such an accusation is utterly false." Douglas added that, after Hecker had stated his case to Propaganda and the Congregation had openly espoused his cause, the Holy Father had given orders for Hecker's statement and Father General's answer to be laid before him personally. PFA, Hecker Letters, December 14, 1857.

12. *Ibid.*, October 20, 1857.

13. Writing on October 26, 1857, Hecker said:

Could you have been with me on my visit to Naples and Nocera you would have seen the congregation as established by its H. founder, the very spirit of St. Alphonsus pervading those communities. The German Fathers have lost the spirit and traditions of the Cong. if they ever had it? . . . All that we want is that the congregation should not depart from the Rules and customs of its Founders, which have been preserved by the Italian Fathers. What you say about a rector provincialis is word for word what their rector major expressed to me. I wish you could have seen him, he is so unaffectedly kind, humble, sincere, wise, and prudent. He said that I would be sure to attain success if I would have patience to remain long enough in Rome.

Hecker speaks again of his visit to Nocera, in a letter dated October 31. According to Walworth (November 17) the sentiment of the American Fathers was against affiliation with the Neapolitans, and he suggested the possibility of organizing as Religious Missionaries of the Propaganda with the rule of St. Alphonsus and the same missionary privileges as before.

14. Hecker's first idea had been to get Dr. Brownson's "Mission of America" translated into Italian; but on second thought he decided that would be too hazardous. So he substituted two articles in the *Civiltà Cattolica* on "The present and future prospects of the Catholic Faith in the U.S. of North America." The aim of the articles was to show that America had been prepared for conversion to the Catholic faith by the Transcendental movement, the Beecher movement, the Know-Nothing movement, and by the character of American institutions in general. All these things are "by the Providence of God so many ways of leading our people to the Catholic truth, provided we do our duty." *Ibid.*, October 24, 1857.

15. The *Civiltà Cattolica* had been founded in 1850 by the Neapolitan, Carlo Maria Curci, and his three fellow Jesuits, Taparelli, Bresciani and Liberatore, all of them well-known men, for the purpose of defending Catholic teaching and papal policy against attacks. Curci, one of the most influential speakers and writers in all Italy, gained distinction in the first years of his meteoric career by his refutation of the philosophical and political teaching of Gioberti. In later years, criticism of the clergy, opposition to papal policy and favoring of the plan for a United Italy, was followed by his dismissal from the Society of Jesus and the placing of his books on the *Index*. Shortly before his death he retracted everything contrary to Catholic faith, morals or discipline and was readmitted to the Jesuits. *Dictionnaire de Théologie Catholique* (Paris, 1908), t. 3, *s.v.* Curci.

16. George Loring Brown, born in Boston in 1814, pupil of Jean Baptiste Isabey, portrait painter and miniaturist, spent many years in Europe. He is best known for his paintings of Italian scenes, including *The Doge's Palace at Sunset*, and *The Doge's Palace at Sunrise*. His *Bay of New York*, painted in 1860, was presented to the Prince of Wales, and his *Crown of New England* was purchased by the prince. He met Hecker by chance and the two men developed a close friendship. The Paulist Father Theodore Petersen recently unearthed in the Library room of the Museum of Fine Arts in Boston a notebook in which Brown recorded various items

of daily expenditures for meals and carriage rides taken in company with Father Hecker. Brown passed his last years in Malden, Massachusetts, and died there in June, 1889, leaving a wife and daughter. He was buried from the Baptist church. See the *Boston Daily Globe*, June 26, 1889.

17. The text of the decree follows:

> Certain priests of the Congregation of the Most Holy Redeemer in the United States of North America recently presented their most humble petition to our Most Holy Lord Pope Pius IX, that in view of certain special reasons he would grant that they might be withdrawn from the authority and jurisdiction of the Rector Major and be governed by a superior of their own, immediately subject to the Apostolic See, and according to the (Redemptorist) Rule approved by Benedict XIV, of holy memory. If, however, this should not be granted to them, they most humbly asked for dispensation from their vows in the said Congregation. After having carefully considered the matter, it appeared to His Holiness that a separation of this kind would be prejudicial to the unity of the Congregation and by no means accord with the Institute of St. Alphonsus, and therefore should not be permitted. Since, however, it was presented to His Holiness that the petitioners spare no labor in the prosecution of the holy missions, in the conversion of souls, and in the dissemination of Christian doctrine, and are for this reason commended by many bishops, it seemed more expedient to His Holiness to withdraw them from the said Congregation, that they might apply themselves to the prosecution of the works of the sacred ministry under the direction of the local bishops. Wherefore His Holiness by the tenor of this decree, and by his Apostolic authority, does dispense from their simple vows and from that of permanence in the Congregation the said priests, viz.: Clarence Walworth, Augustine Hewit, George Deshon, and Francis Baker, together with the priest Isaac Hecker, who has joined himself to their petition in respect to dispensation from vows, and declares them to be dispensed and entirely released, so that they no longer belong to the said Congregation. And His Holiness confidently trusts that under the direction and jurisdiction of the local bishops, according to the prescription of the sacred Canons, the above-mentioned priests will labor by work, example, and word in the vineyard of the Lord, and give themselves with alacrity to the eternal salvation of souls, and promote with all their power the sanctification of their neighbor.
>
> Given at Rome, in the office of the Sacred Congregation of Bishops and Regulars, the 6th day of March, 1858.
>
> (L.S.)   G. Cardinal Della Genga, *Prefect*,
>   A., Archbishop of Philippi, *Secretary*

PART II
The Paulists

VI. A "COMMUNITY FOR CONVERSIONS"
VII. THE WALWORTH EPISODE
VIII. THE FIRST PAULIST PARISH
IX. THE FIRST TEN PAULISTS
X. PLATFORM AND PRESS
XI. HECKER'S MESSAGE

VI

A "Community for Conversions"

(Notes, p. 188 ff.)

FATHER HECKER knew that the movement to convert Americans would require a society of priests carefully selected, highly trained. Once he wrote, "the controlling thought in my mind for many years has been that a body of free men who love God with all their might and yet know how to cling together, could conquer this modern world of ours." Elliott quotes these words as a brief description of the community Hecker would like to see established.

On many occasions Hecker gave his notions of the most desirable pattern. First, he believed it should have a definite, specialized aim; for "a new religious community, unless its activity is directed chiefly to supplying the special needs of its time, wears itself out at the expense of its true mission and will decline and fall . . ." He knew that every community as a rule chooses some particular field of work, different from that in which the diocesan priesthood as a whole is regularly engaged; and he felt that the general principle would apply with particular force to a community hoping to win the non-Catholics of America.

Such a group must ordinarily be free of the obligation of conducting schools, serving parishes, preaching the usual type of missions to the faithful; and if any of these duties are to be undertaken by way of exception, they should be discharged in a spirit and with a technique appropriate to the grand purpose of the community. Missions to the faithful, for example, should be "slanted" toward non-Catholics and should inspire Catholics to undertake apostolic work among their neighbors.

Hecker believed further that the community in question would function best if it were small in size. For it would need to be very adaptable; and adaptability becomes more difficult as size increases. The "Community for Conversions" would not resemble one of the older religious orders with tens of thousands of members co-ordinated into a closely knit, worldwide force, with everybody's energies synchronized. It would be externally distinguished less by humility, poverty, obedience, than by zeal for conversions—the kind of zeal which St. Paul symbolizes. Indeed, Pius IX mentioned St. Paul as an appropriate patron for the community to which he and Hecker were looking forward.

It might be advisable for a single house to serve a whole country; missionaries residing in a given locality often possess less prestige and exercise less influence among their neighbors than missionaries from afar. Multiplication of houses, said Hecker, would necessarily involve increased expense, complicated

A "COMMUNITY FOR CONVERSIONS" 93

organization, wasted energy. Moreover, in the nineteenth century the whole continent was easier to cover than a single country in earlier days; and the telegraph was making it possible to send messages in a few seconds to distant places which once would have required months to reach.

Discussing the routine of life for this ideal community, Hecker once wrote:

> You ask me which I would prefer: to have a rule and manner of life adapted to a large number of men, embracing many of a common type, with men good enough for an average work, intended to include and seeking to retain men of mediocre spirit and dim understanding of our institute; or would you prefer the rule to be made for only a select body, made up of such men as Bishop Keane, Father Rosecrans and the like? I should prefer the rule to be for the smaller and more select body of men.[1]

The chief motives of each member, Hecker held, should be desire for his own salvation and perfection and zeal to meet the pressing needs of the Church and his fellowmen. The first qualification for membership therefore, was to be whole-hearted consecration to the ideal of holiness presented in the New Testament —the ideal elaborated in the lives and teachings of the saints and spiritual masters of the Catholic Church, the ideal that includes the mutually complementary habits of prayer and self-denial. Lack of spiritual vision would be a disqualification; mediocre men would slow the progress of the common undertaking. Hecker insisted on the primary importance of spiritual insight. He frequently drew attention to the need of that unreserved dedication to the will of God, which is depicted as fundamental in the New Testament, in the *Imitation of Christ,* in the writings of St. John of the Cross, St. Teresa of Avila, St. Philip Neri, and in the books of the Benedictine, Augustine Baker, and the Jesuits, Caussade and Lallemant. Years after Hecker's death, one of his associates told a younger priest that Father Hecker loved to repeat those words of the *Imitation,* "Unless a man be lifted up in spirit and set at freedom from all creatures and wholly united to God, whatever he knows and whatever he does is of no great weight."

It is obvious that liberty and adaptability, useful and desirable as they are, may in certain circumstances entail the risk of developing individualism to a point where it becomes incompatible with the common good; that authority and freedom are related in inverse ratio. If tyranny lies at one extreme, anarchy lies at the other. Both are dangerous. Hecker felt convinced that the great need of the day was men with a spirit like that of the early martyrs, men who placed more emphasis on conscience and the guidance of the Holy Spirit than on rules and discipline; and he believed that this type of man multiplies in proportion as Catholics cultivate the spirit of lawful independence and learn how to use the liberty of the children of God. Hecker held that men of good will more easily slip into the fault of abusing authority (which leads to despotism), than into the fault of abusing liberty (which leads to lawlessness.)

A "COMMUNITY FOR CONVERSIONS" 95

With regard to the bond holding the members together, Hecker preferred an agreement rather than a vow. He reasoned that the community should facilitate the exit of dissatisfied members, since in a small group such men seriously hamper the activities of their companions. This preference implied no lack of respect for vows, nor did it leave the members free from the obligation to pursue holiness; and Hecker assumed that every right-spirited member of the community "would be ready and willing to take vows at any time." At the beginning of the community's existence he stated its aim thus: "We shall, in brief, practice all the religious virtues in the same manner and perfection as those under vows, on the voluntary principle. Similar in this respect to the Congregation of the Oratory founded by St. Philip Neri."

According to Hecker, the crusade for conversions called for a central headquarters, not only in the United States, but in every European country. He said he would like to see a community for conversions established in London, Paris, Madrid, Berlin, Florence, Rome. He discussed this idea "with the most experienced and best minds in the church and found them in agreement." When in Rome attending the Vatican Council he wrote, Europe too, "needs men who from a fresh view and contemplation of truth, and a deeper love springing therefrom, would consecrate themselves to the propagation of the faith and the good of humanity." They would, in the spiritual order, correspond to the Zouave troops who from every part of the world rallied to the defense of the rights of the Holy See.²

From what has just been said it is clear that Hecker wished the "Community for Conversions" to possess certain features characteristic of already existing orders. Conspicuous in the United States, for example, were the Sulpicians, a community of priests without special vows, founded 200 years earlier to train candidates for the priesthood, and offering an impressive example of holy living and unflagging zeal.³ Even a more suggestive pattern was the Oratory, established in the sixteenth century by St. Philip Neri, who insisted that the members should not assume the obligation of vows and that each house should be completely independent of the others, to stand on its own feet and to survive or pass out of existence as circumstances might determine. The Oratory lent itself easily to modification, as could be seen from its history in France and England.⁴

Hecker, who regarded St. Philip as the saint of the future and as one of his special patrons, wrote from Rome to the other Fathers about the possibility of affiliating with the Oratory. After saying (October 3, 1857) it would be best to form an organization under Bishop Bayley or some other friendly bishop, who would allow the group "full liberty to work for the conversion of the country," he added that Bedini had specified the Oratory as the congregation best adapted for their purpose. Significantly enough, the Oratorian form of life was urged on Hecker's attention by

A "COMMUNITY FOR CONVERSIONS" 97

Bishop Spalding of Louisville, who later, as Archbishop of Baltimore, became Hecker's most powerful friend.

Walworth, however, on October 23, declared "We feel no vocation to be Oratorians."

* * *

During Hecker's absence in Rome his companions were working steadily in the mission field. They gave their last Lenten mission of 1858 at Little Falls, New York. At its close, Father Baker went back to Annapolis. The other three returned to the Redemptorist convent on Third Street, New York; and here on April 6, the Tuesday after Easter, they received a certified copy of the papal decree dispensing them from their vows as Redemptorists. On that same day they left the convent for George Hecker's residence at 23 Rutgers Place, where they occupied the entire third floor as a community house, with Father Walworth acting as temporary superior. All four Fathers participated in the two closing missions of the season at St. Patrick's, Watertown, in April, and at St. Bridget's, New York City, in May; and on April 17, the Saturday before the Watertown mission began, "A letter came with the rescript of the Pope giving us the necessary faculties."

Hecker landed in New York on May 10; and, at the close of the mission on May 16, the five took lodgings in a boarding house on East 13th Street, near churches and chapels where they could say Mass. A little later, having been invited to occupy George Hecker's whole house during the summer, the Fathers returned there to continue their discussions. These were serious days; yet the Fathers were able to derive amusement from an episode related by Father Hewit, who in his *Memoir*, tells that late one night two sneak thieves "came into the room occupied by F. Baker and one of his companions, and robbed them of their watches, which were fortunately of small value, some articles of clothing likewise not very costly, and a trifling amount of loose change." [5]

Before going further, we may take a glance at the leaders of the group. Hewit, with better theological training than the others, had profited greatly by his experience in editing the works of Bishop England; and he enjoyed the prestige attached to the office of provincial consultor. Walworth, close to Bishop Bayley and other prelates, head of the mission band for several years, took the chair by right of seniority when the first meeting opened. Hecker, back from Rome after having received much counsel from experts on the matters to be discussed, focused attention on the main point—survival; and his gift for distinguishing between essential and secondary issues gave him increasing ascendancy over his colleagues. Deshon and Baker seem to have followed him readily; and Hewit once said he had faith in Hecker, even when he did not understand him.

In order to give a definite form to the proposed organization it was necessary to select one of several

A "COMMUNITY FOR CONVERSIONS"

possibilities. It had been the common desire of all to remain Redemptorists. But the two plans first proposed had proved to be impractical. Affiliation with the Neapolitan Fathers had little to commend it; and the idea of establishing an English-speaking province within the congregation was not acceptable to the Holy See. The new group must therefore, affiliate with an existing community or start afresh. They chose the latter alternative; and—apparently without paying much attention to the possibility of placing themselves under the immediate jurisdiction of the Holy See—they decided to become a diocesan community. They were sure of a welcome from a number of bishops. Bishop Bayley had promised to secure them a place in Newark; Bishop Lynch of Charleston had offered them a house and some 600 acres of land in his diocese, all ready for them. But Bayley thought that New York on the whole, would be preferable; Barnabò had suggested New York; Hecker's general policy favored headquarters in an important center.

So they resolved to draw up a program of rule and then to apply to Archbishop Hughes; and Hecker was chosen superior by secret ballot.

On the agenda were three questions of importance:
1. What common order of life should they adopt?
2. Should they announce the community aim in general, or in specific, terms?
3. Should they unite on the basis of a vow or of an agreement?

The first question was answered with comparative

ease by the adoption of an order of life, "in all essential respects similar to that which is commonly observed by religious congregations."

To understand the significance of the second question, we must recall certain facts that suggested caution. If the Fathers were to declare that they were dedicated to the service of souls outside the Catholic fold and would be therefore inevitably less concerned with those inside the fold, they might easily arouse criticism. Catholics in general were sensitively aware that these five converts had inherited Protestant family traditions; that, after having been converted to Catholicism, they had first sought admission to, and later had requested separation from, an old, highly respected, extremely efficient missionary order; that, in addition to being of Protestant birth, they were enthusiastically American; that they were planning to bring into the Church a multitude of converts from American Protestantism.

Now the vast majority of Catholics, lay and clerical, were Europeans by birth and training; the whole northeastern United States lay within the provinces of the Archbishops of New York and Baltimore, both of whom had suffered grievously—as had their brother bishops—from the violence of American Nativists; both prelates had been forced to deal sternly with rebellious Catholic church trustees whose aggressiveness apparently stemmed from an exaggerated American idea of independence. At the time of which we speak, a large proportion of Catholics, for one reason or another, became uneasy when they saw that American-born Catholics had as much affection for America as European-born Catholics had for their own homelands. The Latins and the Irish came from Catholic countries or from countries which had once been Catholic, whereas the United States had never been Catholic and was dominantly, even at times offensively, Protestant.

Moreover, priests were too few to give adequate service to Catholics. A phrase often heard on Catholic lips was, "Why all this excitement about the Protestants? We have enough to do to take care of our own." This "anti-American" attitude gave great concern to thoughtful Catholic leaders; but it was a sentiment "bred in the bone." It could not successfully be argued against; it had to die out. And it died out so slowly that a generation later it was still a target of Archbishop Ireland's wit when he wrote his preface to the *Life of Father Hecker;* and it was rebuked by Cardinal Gibbons in a famous address at Milwaukee in 1891. Surely then in 1858 that sentiment would have to be taken into account by a group of American converts planning to win other Americans to Catholicism. Even within the group of five there was already a difference of opinion with regard to the aim. Hecker favored specific dedication to the work of conversion; and this indeed, seemed to be in line with what Pope Pius and Cardinal Barnabò expected. On the other hand, Walworth had expressed definite, strong disapproval. Writing to Hecker in January, 1858, he said,

"Many are displeased with your peculiar ideas in regard to the means of converting America. . . . Remember—the rest of us do not altogether sympathize with you in some of these things, and would be sorry to have our cause identified with them."

Of course, to dedicate a community to the work of conversion would not be quite the same as to *announce* this dedication. There is no record of detailed discussion on this point. When eventually announced, the aim of the community was presented in non-committal terms—"to carry on the missions in the spirit of St. Alphonsus."

The third question, "Vow or Agreement," was a thorny one. If they were to form a new community without vows, it would be the first procedure of this kind in the history of the American Church. To the average Catholic this would convey at most only a slightly disturbing suggestion of novelty. But to some observers it might recall "old unhappy far-off things and battles long ago." These persons might remember the thirteenth and fourteenth century feuds between the secular clergy and the religious orders—when the Universities of Paris and Oxford warred upon the mendicants; when William of St. Amour, opponent of St. Albert the Great, drew upon himself a censure from the Holy See for his attack upon the vow of poverty; when Richard Fitzralph, Chancellor of Oxford and later Archbishop of Armagh, was summoned to the papal court at Avignon to explain his denunciation of the friars.

To be sure, those were ancient scandals; but they seemed to re-echo in the recent debates provoked by the English convert, Henry Edward Manning, future cardinal, whose aggressive tactics toward religious orders occasioned much resentment. For the man who later wrote that spiritual classic, *The Eternal Priesthood,* in order to lift the diocesan clergy to a proper appreciation of their vocation, had already used harsh words in his comments on the comparative perfection of the priesthood and the religious life.[6]

The discussions about the constitution of the new community therefore, involved issues which were likely to stir up deep feelings and provoke antagonisms. Hecker took a balanced view; he had definitely expressed his preference for the voluntary principle, but he also believed "that a true Paulist should be ready to take the vows at any moment." In the debate Hewit and Walworth seem to have been most articulate. Hewit declared himself strongly opposed to vows, because he was unwilling to make another venture in the kind of life which had occasioned him so much disturbance and unhappiness. Walworth's dissent from Hewit was emphatic and final; he would accept no compromise. He rejected the suggested alternative of taking annual vows on the ground that, theologically speaking, the very essence of the religious life consists in perpetual vows; and to the religious life, he said, he felt he had a true vocation—although he found no existing order that suited him. As the discussion proceeded, Walworth grew more and more dissatisfied; and eventually he withdrew.

After his departure, the others continued their discussions; and, having agreed upon "a programme of rule," they submitted it to the archbishop on July 7.[7] When he accepted it, the four men became a diocesan community; and on July 10, an agreement was signed between John Hughes, Archbishop of New York, and the Congregation of Missionary Priests of St. Paul the Apostle. In this agreement the four members of the Congregation (in their own names and in the names of those thereafter to be admitted to the Congregation) "bind themselves to observe the Rules, which they have presented to his Grace, the Archbishop and which have been approved by him." They agreed also to take charge of a parish extending from West 52nd Street on the south to 109th Street on the north.[8]

Thus the duty of building and serving a parish in the outskirts of the rapidly growing city was officially laid upon the shoulders of the infant community. A fortnight later Hecker reported to a friend that the society had been canonically instituted on the basis of "a strict religious life in community, starting with the voluntary principle; leaving the question of vows to further experience, counsel, and indications of divine Providence. Our principal work is the missions, such as we have hitherto given, but we are not excluded from other apostolic labors as the wants of the Church may demand or develop."

But "not excluded from other apostolic works" is a far cry from "specifically dedicated to the work of

A "COMMUNITY FOR CONVERSIONS"

converting non-Catholic Americans." The new community was not to be a body of strictly limited membership, a *corps d'élite,* ordinarily resident in one central headquarters, and professing conversion of the United States as its primary vocation. These perhaps were the missing characteristics that Hecker had in mind when in a letter from Ragatz, Switzerland, on August 4, 1875, he wrote: "The idea of the Paulists is one which God's grace inspired my soul for the U.S. Its form is not so much mine, as those who associated with the idea." [9]

It was a battered little craft that had made port, but at least the four survivors were raising the flag of a new community.

VII

The Walworth Episode
(Notes, p. 193 ff.)

CLARENCE WALWORTH stood in a unique relationship to the first Paulists. He was a distant cousin to Father Hewit, and he was, except Brownson, the oldest friend of Hecker, although never particularly close to him. A leader in the movement to separate from the Redemptorists, he withdrew on the very eve of the new community's birth and entered the ranks of the secular clergy in Albany. Two years later he asked to become a Paulist. He was received; but after working four years alongside his old comrades, he withdrew again to Albany.

According to Father Elliott, when the five American converts undertook to organize a new community, "Nothing was done hurriedly; a fair and full consideration of all questions from every point of view, which lasted until early in the month of July, enabled each one clearly to understand his new relation in its every aspect. Father Walworth not being entirely in agreement with the others, withdrew to the diocese of Albany and took charge of a parish."

These quiet words give a very inadequate idea of

the blow that startled and shook the little group planning to work together for life. It was hard enough to have one member withdraw at this critical point—especially so important a member as Walworth; but the circumstances of the withdrawal gave a disastrous setback to the hopes of the other four. Paulist history might have been very different if, during these early discussions, Walworth had been ready to do what he did do two years later when he asked to be admitted to the community.

Unfortunately, in addition to separating from the others, Walworth took steps that could hardly have been expected. He built a barrier between the little company and two prelates who otherwise might have been their strongest patrons, Bayley the future Archbishop of Baltimore, and McCloskey the future Cardinal Archbishop of New York. Approaching these bishops unilaterally, Walworth told them that his companions were making plans to which he could not in conscience subscribe; and later he reported to his companions: Bishop McCloskey's "judgment in the matter coincides with that of Bishop Bayley, and my own deep convictions, that if you adhere to the course of policy which you have lately adopted, I cannot in prudence and good conscience continue with you." Up to this point Bayley had been one of the most enthusiastic patrons of the project in which the five were engaged. He was never the same again. Only with great reluctance did he, a few years afterwards, permit one of his clergy, Father Alfred Young, to join the

Paulists; and Bayley's biographer records no later letters between him and any of the Paulists, except when he enlisted Father Deshon's aid in winning President Grant's sympathetic attention to the plight of the Catholic Indians. Bishop McCloskey, who was Hecker's first spiritual director, also experienced a change of heart. In a biography of the bishop, Cardinal Farley stated that McCloskey began to evince "the born Catholic's fear of the reforming element so strong sometimes in the newly converted."

We have no actual record of what Walworth said to the two bishops; but he himself summarized his statements in a letter, dated July 19. It was written to the newly consecrated Bishop McFarland, who had been pastor of St. John's, Utica, New York, in the preceding November when Walworth and two companions conducted an extremely successful mission there. The letter was sent in reply to a request from the bishop for a mission in the cathedral of Providence—at that time a part of the Diocese of Hartford. After having stated that he has withdrawn from his former colleagues and that he has forwarded the request for a mission to Hecker, Walworth adds that "a desire not to be misunderstood by one whose regard I prize so highly" prompts him to explain matters to the bishop. With what seems to be a departure from the usual conventions of privacy, Walworth speaks of the "great surprise and shock" he experienced when he discovered that his companions did not share his high esteem of the vows of religion and contemplated the abandoning of the position to which they had previously committed themselves before the people, the bishops and the Holy See. He adds that the spirit they manifested was so destructive of all his confidence in the affair that he finally decided to withdraw. His chief motive for so doing was that he felt his "vocation to be of the Religious state and the vows"; and he says that, although for a time he endeavored to reconcile his mind to the compromise of annual vows, he found himself unable to do this. His late associates however, are "estimable, talented and energetic Priests." "We have parted as brothers part, without the least breach of charity, and they are to me personally the same dear friends as ever." He has taken this step, "after long consultation with the bishops of Albany and Newark, and with their full approbation." [1]

When Walworth withdrew from the discussions, it was not clear for the moment whether or not he meant his separation to be final. Both Hewit and Deshon wrote to him—Hewit to apologize for strong words spoken during the debate that might have caused offense, and Deshon to say that, having interviewed Bishop Bayley (whom Walworth had quoted as approving his withdrawal), he received the impression that Bayley had not given the unqualified approval of Walworth's action that Walworth claimed. Walworth replied that Deshon was completely wrong; Bishop Bayley in his "first and in every interview with me condemned most unequivocally the dropping of the vows." In any event, after having conferred more than once with Bayley, Walworth was in Albany on June 17, seeking advice from Bishop McCloskey. On June 28, in reply to a request from his companions for a definite decision, he answered that he would like to speak with Bayley once again before giving the last word; but, if they needed an immediate decision from him, they could regard it as negative. "Negative" it remained; and ten days later his old companions, as already related, sent the result of their deliberations to Archbishop Hughes.

There is little to show that Walworth ever realized the obstacles he was creating for his late companions. Apart from the tremendous difficulties inherent in the task of organizing a community, they now found themselves confronted with a calamitous lack of sympathy in high ecclesiastical quarters—not only from the bishops just named, but also from Archbishop Hughes of New York and Archbishop Kenrick of Baltimore, the two most important prelates in the country, whose provinces included all the states along the entire Atlantic seaboard. Hughes was troubled by the fact that there was "too much of the spirit of accommodation among some of the American converts of his flock." Kenrick, at first friendly toward Hecker and his companions, after Walworth's communications to the bishops, expressed his lack of confidence in the Paulists, and wrote to Hecker (November 26, 1858): "I see no guarantee of the permanent success of your undertaking." Incidentally, it may be noted that one of Baltimore's suffragan sees, Philadelphia,

THE WALWORTH EPISODE

was in 1858 ruled by the saintly Redemptorist bishop, Neumann; and that Baltimore itself was the provincial headquarters of the Redemptorists.

These then were some of the obstacles faced by the little community as it began to exist. Barely a year later, new distrust of convert priests in general was stirred up by a shocking incident, the apostasy of Dr. John Murray Forbes, convert pastor of St. Ann's Church, New York City.[2]

* * *

There is no satisfactory explanation of the Walworth episode. He displayed strange inconsistencies, notably in his shifts: out of the Redemptorists; into the secular clergy; then into the Paulists; then back to the secular clergy.

From a merely human point of view, one might regard his conduct as not quite "sporting"; for twice he withdrew from his companions at an extremely critical moment—first when they were launching out on their dangerous adventure, and again when they were almost swamped for lack of manpower by Baker's death, the founding of the *Catholic World* and the swiftly increasing burden of parish responsibilities.

Looking at the episode from a supernatural standpoint, we are, to say the least, puzzled that, while stating his conviction that he was called to a life under vows, Walworth remained unwilling to apply for admission to any existing religious Order on the ground that, "The experience I have of religious orders makes me afraid to throw myself among strangers whatever the rule may be." Further, it seemed inconsistent to separate from his companions on the ground that they were planning a rule of life "that might indeed sanctify them, but would not make them canonically religious"; whereas he himself withdrew to a much easier life concerning which he had once said, "God forbid!" [3] After his second withdrawal, Walworth lived for thirty-five years an active, highly respected, successful pastor, tied down by no religious rule, free of the heavy burden which his former companions continued to carry in virtue of their "mere voluntary promise."

A psychologist analyzing Walworth's inconsistencies would probably draw attention to his manifestations of emotional temperament. This characteristic was displayed in his style of preaching. Gifted with a matchless voice and a flair for the dramatic, he would sometimes, during impassioned moments, throw his arms about the mission cross, tear down the white cloth and throw it over his shoulders. He was able, almost at will, to reduce a congregation to tears. In fact, the record of the mission at St. Patrick's, Utica, in March, 1855, laments the lack of enthusiasm of the congregation, and gives this description: "Father Walworth did his best to get them to shed a tear and could not even get them to kneel, after waving the crucifix over them and commanding them to do so. . . . Not a tear had been shed scarcely during the

THE WALWORTH EPISODE

mission. . . . But the renewal of the vows made up for all. Never did I hear such answers from men's throats, and at the word 'Farewell!' there was such a burst of grief as I never heard."

Walworth's sketch, *Early Ritualism in America* (written in 1893), reveals his edifying, but highly fanciful and short-lived, enthusiasm for the establishing of an Episcopal monastic community in the north woods in company with Edgar Wadhams, later Catholic bishop of Ogdensburg. Walworth's poems would engage the interest of a psychologist because of their emotional coloring. A manifestation of emotion is discernible also in his reaction to the trial of the Episcopalian Bishop, Benjamin T. Onderdonk, by a court of twenty-three brother bishops, including Bishop Silliman Ives of North Carolina, later a convert to the Catholic Church; for all Walworth's disapproval was directed not against the offenses which caused the trial, but against the court of bishops for their willingness "to bring such a scandalous matter to so public an exhibition." [4]

The psychologist might also point to indications of an inner conflict in Walworth, springing from unconscious rivalry with Hecker. During the first period of their friendship—or more exactly their acquaintance—the relationship between them was on the whole, external and superficial, with Walworth obviously occupying the higher level. He was the son of the chancellor of New York State; he could, as he demonstrated in a book on the Walworth family, trace his genealogy back to the fourteenth century; he was a Phi Beta Kappa alumnus of Union College, at that time larger than Harvard; he was a member of the New York State Bar. He had been officially superior of the mission band of the Redemptorists for several years; and he was probably as forceful a speaker as any man in this country. By contrast, Hecker was self-educated; he had experienced great difficulty in obtaining a passing mark in the studies preparatory to ordination; and his power over men came mainly from his original ideas, his honesty, his habit of presenting truth in clear and simple terms, his manifestation of a magnetic power commonly associated with personal holiness. Thus, during the years of study and of mission preaching, Hecker had been on the plain solid earth, on the same level as the people with whom he came in contact; Walworth was a first magnitude star.

It would hardly be possible for a man of Walworth's temperament to accept a reversal of these roles without some inner turmoil. He had never manifested much appreciation of Hecker. In fact, his nearest approach to praise seems to have been the comment made in Norfolk, in March, 1856, when Hecker for the first time showed a flash of genius for the expounding of Catholic doctrine to Protestants; and Walworth rather condescendingly said:

I see clearly now what your vocation is, and if the subject ever comes up in my presence before our superiors, I shall speak plainly to them about it. And nothing would give me greater consolation and would be productive of greater effects than if you would devote yourself to the work of the non-Catholic community. You should advance, and after you had opened the way, my vocation would be to follow up and complete your work. You would remove prejudices and excite an interest and desire to become better acquainted with the doctrines of the Catholic faith, and I would come and offer this knowledge.

On other occasions too, Walworth implied that he did not have an exalted opinion of Hecker; definitely he did not share Elliott's esteem for Hecker as "a great teacher of men." [5]

* * *

Less than three years after separating from his four companions, Walworth changed his mind. Lonely in his new position, he opened up the question of entering the Paulist community, by writing to the Fathers on December 15, 1860:

I have often thought of joining you again. . . . I cannot find in my present life that which looks like my vocation. . . . My element is not here. Where is it? The experience I have of religious orders makes me afraid to throw myself among strangers whatever the rule may be. The members are the real constituents of an order, and live men are better than a dead rule. Your rule was not what my soul craved when the Redemptorist plank broke under me, but it has a great advantage in being made to fit yourselves and I think now that I can make myself fit to it. You have, besides the missions, your regular hours and religious exercises, and that is more than I can well have alone. Besides my heart and all my sympathies are with my old companions. Their place to me can never be filled by any other. If you think the old horse can be of any service, I offer him. . . . I have said nothing as yet to the Bishop. . . . He can scarcely make any difficulty, for I stipulated with him on entering his diocese, that he should put no obstacle in the way of my entering any religious order, and he is not the man to cavil about an honorable promise . . ."

Walworth returned to the Paulists on Easter Monday 1861, and received an affectionate welcome. He was given rank immediately after the superior. For the next four years he preached on some twenty-five missions and in the intervals took his share of parish work and wrote a book, *The Gentle Skeptic*,[6] which presents a geologist's rebuttal of religious difficulties drawn from the biblical account of creation. His last mission given in company with Hecker, Hewit and Young, at St. Mary's Church, Clifton, Staten Island, ended on April 4, 1865—the very day that Baker died. Exhausting work and the shock of Baker's death were followed by serious illness. Ellen Walworth writes:

. . . even his strong frame quivered at last under the long strain and brain fever resulted. . . . He lay in the rectory of what was then a raw, up-town New York parish. The region was indented here and there with neglected malarial pools. Its newly opened streets were but partially graded and drained. They ended abruptly in a rocky, shantytown of squatters and goats. Close by were the unkempt southern confines of a newly planned park. Many laughed at its name, Central Park, for it was as far as it could well be from the center of the city.

His father came down to visit him; Walworth was given sick leave and then escorted to Saratoga, where he "was slowly coaxed back into life and strength

THE WALWORTH EPISODE

amid the comforts of a long-established home."[7]

In July he wrote to Father Hecker expressing a desire to resign from the community. Having been assured he was free to go, he wrote again to say,

> I have been sick since receiving your kind letter, and much of the time in bed. I cannot tell you how much I have been relieved by the sweetness and charity of your language. I thank you and the other Fathers also for taking away the bitterest pang to me of our separation. My heart will always go with you in all your labors. . . . For myself I scarcely know what to look forward to. Sometimes I think my time is up . . . I take all the means that I know of to improve my health while at the same time in the quiet and repose which surrounds me here, I find the thought of death less startling than it has been for years before. Although I am completely satisfied of the wisdom and necessity of the step which I have taken my thought and sympathies are so much with you that I feel anxious to know as much as possible what is going on. . . . I shall be stationed for the present at the Cathedral in Albany. It suits me well just now, for except preaching there is little work to do, and in case of necessity I am always near this place of retreat, which is the best place to be sick in I have ever found . . .

Friendly intercourse with his former associates was never interrupted. He usually visited the Paulist house when he came to New York; he wrote frequently for the *Catholic World*. Appointed pastor of St. Mary's Church, Albany, the building that occupied the site of the earliest Catholic place of worship in that city, Walworth invited the Paulists as well as the Redemptorists to give missions in his church. Under his supervision St. Mary's became an important religious center; and he himself was recognized far and wide as a civic and religious leader of high rank. The Episcopal Bishop of Albany, William C. Doane, closely associated with him in public movements, described him as "the most aristocratic of democrats and the most democratic of aristocrats."

It is edifying to know and pleasant to record that the later relationship of Walworth and the Paulists remained always gracious. Not one word of blame or resentment came from his old colleagues, no evidence to show that they felt he had been partly responsible for the limited success of their venture. This kind of experience is not uncommon in the lives of pioneers, crusaders, missionaries; and what God's providence permitted, the first four Paulists accepted uncomplainingly.

VIII

The First Paulist Parish

(Notes, p. 196 f.)

JOHN HUGHES, named archbishop in 1850, lived on Mulberry Street, with his cathedral on Mott Street between Prince and Houston. Highly intelligent, a forceful administrator and bold along conventional lines, he was more concerned with the immediate needs of his diocese than with long-range, nationwide possibilities. His flock on Manhattan Island numbered about one quarter million. The Germans had five churches; but the English-speaking Catholics had no church on the east side, north of St. John the Evangelist (then at 50th Street and Fifth Avenue), except St. Paul's, Harlem; and none on the west side, north of St. Columba's on West 25th Street. Postponing the plan for a new cathedral, the archbishop opened several parishes; and, when the four missionaries became a community under his jurisdiction, he added them to his diocesan force and directed them to form a parish in a sparsely settled area alongside the Hudson River, about three miles long and a half mile wide. Perhaps some future historian will study the effect of this decision on the history of the Paulist community.

New York had adopted the "gridiron" plan in 1810

—with twelve avenues running north and south, and cross streets running east and west, twenty to a mile; and in 1857 the city fathers began to landscape the rectangle destined for Central Park, which was bounded by Fifth Avenue, Eighth Avenue, 59th Street and 110th Street. The territory assigned to the Paulists ran from Central Park to the Hudson River. On its northern edge rose Morningside Heights, where Bloomingdale Asylum stood for seventy years, until it yielded its site to Columbia University in the early nineties. Farther north lay the village of Manhattanville, on the level road connecting the Hudson and the Harlem rivers (the Old Hollow Way, now 125th Street). Beyond on the first rise of Washington Heights stood a convent, founded in 1847, which later developed into Manhattanville College of the Sacred Heart; and nearby was the Christian Brothers' School which became Manhattan College.

The Paulist parish contained small farms, market gardens, stretches of rocky land; and numerous squatters lived in nondescript buildings they themselves had constructed. The typical shanty, on top of a great rock, with dogs, goats and children roaming about, was approached by wooden stairs; and it would stand out in the evening a quaint silhouette against the background of the lordly Hudson, the Jersey hills, the sunset in the far distance. The parish embraced the Dutch Village of Bloemingdale (Vale of flowers), which Washington Irving found so pleasant; and Bloomingdale Road, which yielded its name to

Broadway forty years later, ran diagonally to the northwest. Near the center of the parish was the Brennan farmhouse, where Poe, after leaving Fordham cottage, came to board, and where he wrote *The Raven*—as recorded on a tablet at the northwest corner of Broadway and 84th Street. The poet used to sit and look out over the Hudson from the huge rock at the foot of 83rd Street—still known as Mt. Tom.

The cornerstone of St. Patrick's Cathedral was laid in August, 1858. About the same time the Paulists began to solicit funds for the new parish church and community house. Their appeals brought gifts from many quarters, the first from Father Early, S.J., of Georgetown and the largest from Father Hecker's brother George. Charles O'Conor, the distinguished lawyer, sent an offering with an apology for not making it larger.[1] At a cost of some $63,000 land was bought on Sixtieth Street, west of Ninth Avenue—streets which at that time existed chiefly on the map—and a combination church and convent was erected, fifty feet wide, nearly 140 feet deep, and set back from Ninth Avenue far enough to allow space for a large garden of vegetables, flowers, and fruit trees. The edifice was three stories high, but the chapel which extended two-thirds of the length rose only two stories. The convent occupied the rest of the building.

The cornerstone was laid on June 19, 1859. Stages were still running on Broadway and Bloomingdale Road, and horsecars had been introduced on Sixth and Eighth Avenues as far north as 59th Street. The

New York *Freeman's Journal* notified visitors to the ceremony that the clergy were to assemble at the residence of the priests, "on 60th Street, first house west of Broadway, near the terminus of the 8th Avenue Railroad." The New York *Times* (June 20, 1859) calculated the attendance at about 15,000.

House and church were completed in the following November. By that time the Paulists had acquired their first recruit, Father Robert Tillotson. He assisted the others on a mission lasting from December 18 to December 25, planned to give a start to the new congregation. The Mission *Chronicle* states, "The success was all that we could desire. There was scarcely any person present in the parish capable of receiving the sacraments who did not receive them. A great many young men received Communion for the first time, during the mission." The attendance was 725 adults and seventy-five children. Because "the congregation was composed principally of the poorest class," the city, in 1860, gave the parish $1,226.40 to help pay an assessment.[2]

During the draft riots of 1863, Father Hewit received a severe wound in the head when he tried to check a mob that gathered at 59th Street and marched down 11th Avenue tearing up railroad tracks, burning houses, including the ferry house in West 42nd Street. Another crowd of rioters was menacing St. Luke's Hospital at Fifth Avenue and 54th Street; and a call for help which came to the Paulist rectory was answered by Father Deshon, who hurried over to the scene and dispersed the mob in good West Point style.

After the Civil War the territory of the parish built up rapidly and at one time was served by nine churches. The present writer remembers hearing a traction magnate regret his refusal to give a small sum for a good-sized farm, which was worth a fortune a few years later. In 1871 Roosevelt Hospital opened on 59th Street, opposite the rectory. As the "manpower" of the diocesan clergy increased, the Paulists relinquished more and more of their original territory. In the northern part costly residences were built, and Riverside Drive bordering the Hudson became one of the city's splendid avenues.[3] The Paulist parish was eventually restricted to the lower sixties and the upper fifties, where the shore was lined with docks, slaughterhouses, railroad yards. Along "Death Avenue" a "cowboy" used to ride a white horse, waving a red flag to warn pedestrians and vehicles of approaching freight trains. To the west, the immediate neighborhood of the church became a congested section, with a single block housing more than 4,000 people. In 1888 several flimsy tenements on West 62nd Street—not yet occupied—collapsed, killing a number of workmen.[4] Within a stone's throw of the church, there developed a Negro slum, San Juan Hill —almost as notorious as Hell's Kitchen, the white slum a mile to the south; and about the end of the century policemen patrolled their beats in twos, not daring to walk alone. All this is reflected in the remark of a supercilious lady of the east side, who stunned one of the Paulist Fathers not long ago by "giving thanks to God that she had never been west of Eighth Avenue!" But for years to many an underprivileged family in these drab surroundings, the services in St. Paul's brought the one touch of beauty and dignity that they could really appropriate as their own.

To meet the needs of the growing congregation the original church was enlarged twice—once in 1861 and again in 1865. When the parishioners numbered approximately 6,000 in 1877, the Paulists opened a temporary wooden church facing on 60th Street, with a spacious sanctuary of twenty-five by one hundred feet, with pews for a thousand people, and with broad aisles giving space for an additional thousand to stand. The old building continued to serve as headquarters of the community, parish rectory, house of studies and novitiate. The construction of an abattoir not far from the Paulist house in the early seventies, caused Hecker to hesitate about going on with plans to make 59th Street the permanent headquarters of the community; but other counsels prevailed. After a public official had predicted that "the elevated railroad will never run this far north," the cornerstone of the new St. Paul's was laid close to Ninth Avenue. The railroad did come a few years later, and, although it helped to bring visitors to the services, it was not only an eyesore but also a nuisance, by reason of noise and dirt from the steam engines that drew the trains.

The present church was opened in 1885. It stands

a majestic monument to the vision and courage of the early Paulists who poured energy, intelligence, community resources, family legacies into it—making it their own true monument, although as a parish church it belongs legally not to the community, but to the Archdiocese of New York.

* * *

As superior, Father Hecker was ex-officio pastor; he therefore had to direct the parochial activities and at times share in them—responsibilities which he accepted joyously. The records note his baptizing of ten babies in one crowded day. He established exact liturgical standards and strict observance in everything relating to public worship; he introduced congregational singing; he supervised the model Sunday school; he took the lead in collecting, planning, building. His rule against the taking of "seat money" had to be cancelled in order to keep the ship afloat; and the ordinary meagre income was supplemented by mission stipends and by the considerable fees which Hecker received on his frequent lecture tours.

The first years of parish history tell of strenuous labor and much hardship. Many interesting stories have been handed down from the early days, some of them confirmed by records, some preserved in tradition. For example, the baptismal register shows that the first baptisms took place in "the chapel in Mr. Scanlan's house." By the end of the year, the new baptistry was ready; and on January 1, 1860, Father

Hecker baptized Matthew Clark, born on Christmas day, son of "a County Cavan father and a County Tipperary mother." Three days later, Father Tillotson baptized the first convert, Mary Welch, wife of Thomas Welch. Several years later, August 29, 1873, Father Thomas Robinson baptized little "Mary Rose," a two-weeks old infant, quietly deposited in the convent garden one August night and discovered there in the morning.

In addition to discharging their parish duties, the Paulists conducted missions, delivered lectures, wrote books. The "open door" policy established in the rectory extended a welcome to parishioners and visitors, the poor and the rich, Catholics and non-Catholics. So many of the Fathers had lived for years in Protestant surroundings and then enlarged their experience by work on the missions, that the general atmosphere of the convent was one of sympathy for the difficulties of both non-Catholics and Catholics. The record of converts received into the Church makes a long and impressive list. Moreover, the influence of the Paulists was greatly heightened by numerous friendly contacts with the diocesan clergy, not only in the immediate vicinity of the Paulist parish but throughout the country; and gradually the Catholic laity realized their obligation to spread the faith.

As for preaching, it is no exaggeration to say that the Paulist pulpit made a splendid contribution to the spiritual development of the city and the nation.

It was usually occupied by men who were trained public speakers and experienced teachers of religion. Few congregations had opportunities to hear sermons and instructions such as those given by Hecker, the popular lecturer; Hewit, scholar and theologian; Deshon, master of the art of instruction; Baker, Tillotson, and Rosecrans, noted for their eloquence; Walworth, a true orator; Young, a musician of great ability and a superb preacher; Elliott, one of the outstanding missionaries of the century. In addition to the more elaborate discourses delivered at high Mass, the Paulists gave a five minute instruction at each low Mass on Sunday; and these were printed in the current Catholic weekly paper. Many of the longer sermons were published in a series of volumes entitled *Sermons by the Paulist Fathers.* All this activity was the more important because the office of preaching had been so minimized and neglected in some quarters that Archbishop Hughes made it mandatory for pastors to have sermons preached every Sunday, threatening in his rough and ready way that any who disobeyed his orders would be sent "back to their native bogs."

Visitors, many of them non-Catholics, came from far and wide to this church where the solemn service —strictly liturgical and therefore leaning to the austere—was always impressively beautiful and where the congregation enjoyed the privilege, unusual at the time, of singing hymns at non-liturgical services. There was no stressing of any particular devotional practice, unless that name be applied to the literally universal devotion to the Holy Ghost, which consists in constantly remembering, adoring and obeying the indwelling Spirit of God—a practice embedded in the tradition established by Hecker.

No one attentive to the Paulist preaching could remain unaware that the Catholic ideal regards all religious externals as means to an end; that ecclesiastical authority aims not to suppress but to guide, develop, and enrich personality; that the rights of reason, the dignity of the individual, the freedom of the will are to be cultivated as precious gifts of God; that to become holy one needs strong character in addition to divine grace. Listeners would quickly learn that the Catholic Church is universal and supernatural, not merely racial, not narrowly patriotic; and that in her eyes all nations, all peoples, belong to God —Americans no less than Irish, French, Germans, Italians. What was spoken from this pulpit provided no excuse for the notion that Catholicism is a European institution; it gave no encouragement to the lurking disloyalty of native, or foreign-born, Catholics who thought of the Protestant Church as "the American" Church. And the lessons given to the eager and attentive crowds that frequented the Paulist church fitted into the pattern established by Hecker, the pattern which magnetized men like Archbishop Ireland and Father Elliott, the pattern which helped to create in the American Catholic a new mental attitude towards his fellow citizen.

Special mention must be made of the care given to the children and young people. From the first days, the Sunday school was a matter of particular concern to Father Hecker, who visited it faithfully each week when at home. It came to be regarded as a model of its kind. According to the historian of the archdiocese, the Paulist Fathers were the first to give the study of religion its proper place in the curriculum "grading the course from childhood to manhood, securing proper methods, text-books, and teachers, winning the regular attendance of the children, and graduating them in due form with proper honors. . . . Despite the criticism which the young society received, the spirit of their work and the success of their methods influenced all the other communities, and had a beneficial effect on parish work everywhere. Their methods were copied, which was a natural tribute to American ingenuity." [5]

Father Young was fortunate enough to secure the services of a very gifted organist, Edmund Hurley. In addition to directing the ordinary services for many years, he trained the young people of the parish in the presentation of several Gilbert and Sullivan operettas, which won general acclaim. When the parish school was organized the teaching staff consisted at first of laywomen, some of them veterans of the public school system. It was confided to the efficient sisters of the Holy Cross in 1904.

In addition to the "Ten First Paulists" (described in the following chapter), a number of other priests served the parish in its early days. Some were permanent members of the community: Edward Brady, first Irish-born Paulist Father; two Englishmen, Algernon Brown and his brother Louis, conspicuous in their zeal for liturgical exactness, who had been received into the Church at the London Oratory; Henry Wyman, so typically Yankee in appearance that he was nicknamed "Uncle Sam," who derived his first sympathetic notions of Catholicism from Professor Diman of Brown College, father of Hugh Diman, the late Benedictine prior of Portsmouth. Among the priests who were members of the community for a limited time only, were Thomas O'Gorman, friend of Archbishop Ireland and later Bishop of Sioux Falls, James Kent Stone and Francis Spencer.[6] Other priests who served at times were: John L. Spalding, later Bishop of Peoria, who lived with the Paulists while writing the life of his uncle, Archbishop Martin Spalding; and two scholarly priests who assisted in the teaching of the Paulist students—Henry A. Brann, later pastor of St. Agnes Church, New York City; and Louis A. Lambert, founder of the *Catholic Times* of Buffalo, famous for his controversial *Notes on Ingersoll*.[7]

IX

The First Ten Paulists

(Notes, p. 197 ff.)

AT their foundation the Paulist Fathers numbered four. Ten years later the community possessed five permanent members—that is, members who remained in the community until death. In 1872 they ordained their tenth permanent member—the first to come from Catholic stock. All the others were converts, except Rosecrans whose father was a convert. In religion they represented Lutheran, Calvinistic, Unitarian, Episcopalian, Methodist strains; and they exhibited an interesting variety of academic and racial origins—a good symbol of the Catholic Church. Two were Princeton men; one each came from Amherst, West Point, Harvard, Notre Dame, Virginia Military Institute; one had taught in the United States Military Academy, and one had taught in the United States Naval Academy during the Civil War. In their family trees were several Mayflower pilgrims, a colonial governor, members of the Continental Congress, officers in the armed forces of the United States in the Revolution, the War of 1812 and the Mexican War, and a Governor of Virginia.

Father Baker

Our knowledge of Father Baker comes chiefly from Father Hewit's *Memoir*. Born in Baltimore in 1820, Francis Asbury Baker was given his middle name in honor of the well known Methodist bishop who had died in the neighboring State of Virginia four years earlier. Later in life he changed it to "Aloysius." His paternal grandfather, William Baker, a German immigrant who married a young woman of Irish origin, had been a successful merchant; his maternal grandfather, John Dickens—an English Methodist preacher who died in Philadelphia during a yellow fever epidemic—had a son, the Honorable Asbury Dickens, secretary of the United States Senate for almost fifty years, and a daughter, Sarah, who married Dr. Samuel Baker, professor of medicine in the University of Maryland, member of the Methodist Church, and father of the future Paulist.

Young Baker was graduated from Princeton College in 1839. Attracted neither by the Methodist religion of his relatives nor by the Calvinistic atmosphere of Princeton, he received baptism in the Episcopal Church two or three years after graduation; and soon thereafter he took orders in the Episcopal Church in company with his friend, Dwight Lyman, ardent disciple of John Henry Newman.

In 1843 Baker developed a friendship with Nathaniel Hewit (later Augustine Hewit, second supe-

THE FIRST TEN PAULISTS

rior of the Paulists), who at this time was studying for ordination in the residence of the Episcopal Bishop of Maryland, Dr. William Rollinson Whittingham. The two friends acquired a knowledge of Catholicism from observing the Tractarian Movement in England and from visiting the Catholic churches in Baltimore—never during services, however, because such visits were prohibited by Bishop Whittingham, a professed antagonist of the "schismatical and all but formally heretical Roman Church." Baker and Hewit did not sympathize with the bishop's dislike of the Roman communion. They were members of the "Church Reading Society" which prayed for Catholic unity; and they received from England "sermons and spiritual instructions, borrowed or imitated from treasures of Catholic sacred literature."

Ordained deacon in the Episcopal Church in February, 1845, Baker occupied the pulpit for the first time in the following August, preaching a splendid sermon, "perfectly Catholic in its doctrine and tone." "Universally and warmly loved and admired" in a diocese containing a number of excellent preachers, he attained and kept first rank and grew steadily in general esteem. But he was distressed because, although he believed himself to be a priest, he had to act as a Protestant minister, and was not free to bestow on the sick and dying the sacraments of which he felt they had serious need.

He discontinued correspondence with Hewit when the latter became a Catholic; and on the rare occasions when they met Baker was extremely guarded in speech. As if trying to quiet his own misgivings, he displayed hostility to the Catholic Church and increased his zeal for the Catholicizing of his own church. Meanwhile, in letters to his friend, Dwight Lyman, he revealed his torment over the unanswerable question, "How can I be a true Catholic without becoming a Roman Catholic?" Appointed rector of St. Luke's, Baltimore, in 1851, Baker two years later ended his period of indecision, resigned his pastorate, and asked Archbishop Kenrick to admit him to the Catholic Church. His original baptism was judged valid; the baptismal ceremonies were supplied; and he made his first confession to Father Hewit. His conversion caused a sensation in Baltimore; among the converts received into the Church soon afterwards, were several of his former parishioners and also his friend, Dwight Lyman.

Impressed by what he had seen of the Congregation of the Most Holy Redeemer, Baker sought admission to the community and was at once accepted as a candidate. Father Hewit notes that his library was given to the Redemptorists, "by whom it was afterward kindly restored to him and is now in the possession of the Paulists in New York." Baker was ordained September, 1856. Within two months he was associated with the other four convert Redemptorists, preaching his first mission sermon in St. Patrick's Church, Washington.

Baker then returned to Annapolis to prepare him-

THE FIRST TEN PAULISTS

self with great enthusiasm for the missions; and soon afterward the five converts toured the southern States in what proved to be one of the most pleasant experiences in Baker's whole priestly career. He became a most effective missionary; and his deeply spiritual sermons were long remembered both by the simple people and by the cultured. Work in the South was succeeded by more strenuous labor in the North, which entailed far heavier duties than were justified by Baker's delicate constitution. Father Hewit described a typical day during this period of his life:

> He usually said Mass at five o'clock, after which he went to the confessional, rarely leaving it even for a moment. At half-past seven on those evenings when he was not to preach he gave the instruction and recited the prayers which preceded the principal sermon. A considerable part of the remaining time was taken up by reciting his office and other private religious duties, leaving but very little for relaxation, and none whatever for exercise, unless it was snatched at some brief interval, or required by the distance of the church from the pastor's residence. During the first few days of each mission, the confessionals were not opened, and the preacher of the evening sermon was always freed from its labors in the afternoon. Frequently, however, those first days were devoted to a special mission given to the children of the congregation; and Father Baker was always prompt and ready to fulfill this duty, which he did in the most admirable manner, adapting himself with a charming and winning grace and simplicity to the tender age and understanding of the little ones, and reciting with them beautiful forms of meditation and prayer . . . composed by himself, during the whole time of the Mass at which they received Communion. The hardest part of the work of the mission, after the confessions began, was continued during from five to eleven successive days, according to the size of the congrega-

tion, and requiring from ten to twelve hours of constant mental application each day. Besides this necessary and ordinary work, performed with the most patient and unflagging assiduity, F. Baker often employed all the remaining interval of time—not taken up by meals and sleep—in instructing and receiving converts. Wherever there was any work of charity to be done, he undertook it quietly, promptly, and cheerfully, always ready to spare others, and willing to relieve them by assuming their duties when they were exhausted or unwell, seldom asking to be relieved himself. It was never necessary to remind F. Baker of his duty, much less to give him any positive command. During a long course of missions, in which I was superior, with F. Baker as my constant companion and my associate in preaching the mission sermons, and one other long-tried companion as the preacher of the catechetical instruction, I remember, with peculiar satisfaction how perfect was the harmony with which we cooperated with one another, without the least necessity of any exercise of authority or any disagreement of moment.

When the question of separating from the Redemptorists came up, Baker went along with his four companions. He was taken aback and confused by Archbishop Kenrick's claim that Baker properly belonged to the Archdiocese of Baltimore; and he wrote a letter which annoyed the archbishop. The difficulty was soon smoothed out and he continued to labor alongside his old comrades.

Baker developed an impassioned type of eloquence well fitted to his imaginative style of writing. According to Hewit, he preached even better in the parish pulpit than on the mission platform. Readers may judge for themselves by comparing the four mission sermons with the twenty-five parish sermons—all printed in the *Memoir*. In a notable sermon on

"Mortal Sin," he likened the corruption of the soul by sin to "canonical degradation." This ceremony, which deprives a cleric of all his priestly powers, symbolizes the degradation by taking away the chalice, by desecrating the anointed hands, by removing each of the sacred vestments, chasuble, stole, cincture, alb. At a retreat given to the members of the St. Vincent de Paul Society in the New York cathedral in October, 1858, Baker aroused intense enthusiasm by what was described as "a magnificent sermon in the happier vein on the characteristics of Christian perfection for men in the world."

Not now hampered in his pastoral ministrations as during his Episcopalian days, he worked incessantly among the parishioners, finding great joy in his visits to the sick and dying, in giving advice and comfort to confused and unhappy souls, in helping outsiders into the fold of the Church. But parish work, unlike the scheduled activities of a mission, never ends; and one important element of a balanced life was lacking —relaxation. "During the summer months" wrote Hewit, "he would never go into the country, even for the sake of recruiting his health." He began to show indications of failing health. He gave his last mission in Birmingham, Connecticut, in February, 1865; and he preached his last parish sermon in the Paulist church at a Lenten service. By a strange coincidence he was replacing another preacher in an emergency on this occasion and, having neither time nor strength to prepare a new sermon, he used his old sermon on

"The Necessity of Salvation"—the very one that had made so good an impression when he appeared on the mission platform for the first time in Washington, nine years earlier.

Typhus fever was creeping through the parish; Baker contracted the disease; pneumonia supervened; and not even the devoted and skillful attention of his physician, Father Hewit's brother, assisted by two specialists, could save him. He died on Tuesday in Passion week, 1865, leaving his companions with a sense of irreparable loss. Hewit (on p. 5 of the *Memoir*) relates that a priest noted for calm judgment and discretion made the comment: "The best priest in New York is dead." This verdict recalled another tribute to Baker made by a Protestant clergyman when speaking to a Catholic friend: "You have one perfect man among your converts."

Father Tillotson

First recruit to enter the community and first Paulist to die was Robert Beverly Tillotson. A native of New York, he studied at the General Theological Seminary, made a visit to John Henry Newman in England, was received into the Church and became a member of the Oratory. He was ordained in 1856, in his thirty-first year. After being an Oratorian for almost nine years, he visited America on sick leave and while here decided to apply for admission to the Paulists—much to the distress of Dr. Newman who

THE FIRST TEN PAULISTS

seems to have held "Father Robert" in high esteem. But Tillotson argued that if the Paulists had been in existence at the time of his conversion, he would have applied to them then.[1]

He was admitted to the Paulist community shortly before the opening of the motherhouse and church in November, 1859. He proved to be a sterling character and an able preacher—coming just in time to set free three Fathers for missionary duty, while two remained in the parish. The records show him to have been a tireless worker with a particular zeal for the winning and instructing of non-Catholics; and he was the first to receive a convert after the opening of St. Paul's parish church. Although far from robust, he gave valuable service to the community for nine years, taking part in the missions until they were suspended in 1865; and he may well have worked himself to death like others of his brethren. Elliott who entered the novitiate just while Tillotson lay dying, wrote a moving account of the circumstances.[2]

Father Young

Alfred Young, second recruit to the community and the only non-American in the first ten Paulists, was born in Bristol, England, in 1831, but came to the United States as a child. He was graduated at Princeton in 1848, took his degree in medicine at New York University four years later, and practiced for a short period. Having become a Catholic in 1850, he studied theology at the Sulpician Seminary in Paris; and he was ordained in 1856 by Bishop Bayley. After ordination he served as vice-president of Seton Hall College for a year and then spent three years as pastor of St. Paul's Church, Princeton. Before his ordination he had been in touch with Father Hecker at the Redemptorist convent in Third Street; and in July, 1858, he wrote to Hecker, asking the Paulists to conduct a retreat for his parish:

> The good Providence has placed me the pastor here, and this dreary domain of Calvin has been for so many years under his strict surveillance that I fear even Catholicity has become slightly Calvinized, so as to obscure the beauty of the pure metal.
> There has never been a retreat here and I am very anxious that both Catholics and Protestants should have the benefit of one. There are several whom I suspect to be wavering among the Protestants and I feel assured that it would be attended with the most happy results.
> My church holds about 400 people. The congregation numbers about 1000 scattered. Now I am entirely ignorant of the expenses etc. of a mission, and in case you could arrange to give one for us, will you be kind enough to tell me all about that.

Hecker answered at once, promising the mission; and Young expressed his delight, adding, "I look upon the noble effort of your devoted little band as an epoch in the history of Catholicity on the Western Continent, and you have all my sympathy and all my poor prayers and you will not wonder at that when I shall tell you how it is the fulfillment in a higher sphere of a long, dormant unexpressed wish of my own."

The mission was opened in January 23, 1859, by Fathers Hecker, Deshon, and Baker. It created unusual enthusiasm; and despite the inclement weather the church was crowded morning and night.

The following year Father Young applied to be admitted to the Paulists; but Bishop Bayley, handicapped by the small number of priests in the Diocese of Newark, would not grant permission until July, 1861. Young was delayed also by his obligation to make some provision for his two nephews, aged seven and eight, bequeathed to him by his brother. When eventually Young moved to the Paulist house, he forewarned Hecker that he would wish to return for a day "to inspect the erection of a tombstone over my Father's and Mother's remains in Princeton." He added that he "had bought that copy of the English Chant Manual, dear as it was. It is just such a book, except its arrangement of parts, as I myself had proposed to publish."

The last reference reminds us that Father Young gained fame as a pioneer in the restoration of Gregorian chant. He astonished the people of St. Paul's in 1870 by introducing a chancel choir of men and boys in cassock and surplice to sing the complete service at the solemn Mass and at Vespers. His lectures, articles and correspondence aroused such wide support for the restoration of old traditions that surpliced choirs using Gregorian music and congregations singing hymns ceased to be unfamiliar in the United States. Young expressed the early Paulist view of liturgical music and of congregational singing in numerous articles, one of which, "Let All the People Sing," provides exceptionally good reading even today.[3] He published several hymn books containing many of his own compositions; and to hear a thousand voices singing Young's "Slain for My Soul," at the end of a mission sermon on the Passion, is an experience not quickly forgotten. The same may be said of the Eucharistic hymn, "My Soul Doth Long for Thee," when sung by fifty or a hundred stalwart young men at Benediction services in a seminary or novitiate.

A forceful, finished speaker, Father Young did fine work in the parish pulpit and on the mission platform. He published numerous articles in the *Catholic World,* taking on several formidable opponents, among them John Jay and Robert Ingersoll. In his most serious controversial work, *Catholic and Protestant Countries Compared*,[4] he presented official statistics to correct the prevalent notion that crime was more common in Catholic than in non-Catholic countries. When the great Paulist church was in process of construction, he offered valuable, practical suggestions including the recommendation to build a step outside the sanctuary rail so that communicants might kneel on a higher level than the floor on which the priest is standing.

A long, painful illness terminated his quarter cen-

THE FIRST TEN PAULISTS 143

tury of devoted service, and he spent almost three years in a wheel chair. One of the present writer's earliest priestly duties was to take Holy Communion to Father Young during his last days. He died on April 4, 1900.

Father Rosecrans

Adrian Rosecrans lived an even shorter life than Tillotston, dying in 1876, just before his twenty-seventh birthday. He was the son of General William Stark Rosecrans, U.S.A., whose defeat at the Battle of Chickamauga has long been a matter of controversy.[5] The Rosecrans family, immigrants to Pennsylvania in the eighteenth century, had an interesting history and a memorable record of public service. Their earliest known forebear, Erik, after having received a rosary (rosenkrantz) from the pope in 1325, added this emblem to his coat of arms. The general's family came from Holland, settled in Pennsylvania, and then migrated to Ohio. His paternal grandfather, Daniel Rosecrans, fought in the American Revolution; his maternal grandfather, Stephen Hopkins, signed the Declaration of Independence; his father, Crandall Rosecrans, served as United States minister to Mexico, then as a member of Congress for two terms, then as an official of the Treasury Department. In 1845, while teaching at the United States Military Academy, William Rosecrans became a Catholic; and he helped to win all his family to the faith, including his brother Sylvester—who was ordained priest in 1852, consecrated bishop in 1862, appointed first Bishop of Columbus in 1868.

The general's first son, who died in infancy, was born at West Point and buried there. Louis—later called Adrian, presumably after his uncle, Adrian Hegeman—was born at Newport in 1849; attended Mount Saint Mary's College, Cincinnati, and Notre Dame, Indiana; and from the latter institution wrote to ask his mother's permission to smoke, because "it is a great pleasure at college—the only one here." At the age of seventeen Adrian could not obtain his father's approval to enter the army; so father and son sailed around the Horn to California, where Adrian worked first on a mining project and then in the Customs House. The reading of a life of the Curé d'Ars helped to decide his vocation; and he applied for admission to the Paulists in 1867. He was ordained by his uncle in May, 1872; and a few months later he wrote to his sister: "I returned from Wilmington last night, where I assisted for the first time in what is to be the work of my life. . . . Father Deshon, Elliott and myself gave the mission."

His letters to his family throw side lights on his character. A love of music is reflected in his letter from the Paulist motherhouse, which says "Mr. Hurley, the organist, wonders why I always get him to play Strauss waltzes when I come to see him in the choir hall. I tell him it sounds differently with a fiddle and piano." From Lake George he sent his sister a little poem written on a piece of birch bark, for her fifteenth birthday. One letter tells of a trip with Father Searle to give a boat to a poor old hunter living at the foot of one of the mountains, about twenty miles from the Paulist summer home: "We . . . lashed the boat to one of our new ones and set all sail we could in both. I steered one, and Fr. Searle the other. We fairly shot thru the water and made the twenty miles inside three hours. I spent the night in a barn where I made a comfortable bed with some quilts and a pillow." [6]

From the time of his ordination until the summer of 1875, he preached missions with only brief periods of rest; and, although he suffered a severe attack of malaria in the summer of 1874, he returned to mission work the following fall—probably too soon. Early in 1875 he traveled to the West coast to take part in an exhausting series of missions, in company with Deshon, Elliott and two others. The series was undertaken at the urgent and repeated invitation of Joseph S. Allemany, O.P., Archbishop of San Francisco, and his vicar general, Father John Prendergast; and the first mission opened in St. Mary's Cathedral, San Francisco, February 14, 1875.

The Mission Chronicle notes that the people "expressed the greatest joy on our arrival, and joined in the common sentiment of high and low that the Paulists ought to have a community in San Francisco." At St. Mary's, Oakland, Father Elliott gave a lecture to raise funds for a new bell which was to be called "St.

Paul," in honor of the missionaries. At St. Peter's Church, San Francisco, they received an application for the community from Alexander P. Doyle, a graduate of St. Mary's College; and he was ordained in 1880, the first English-speaking native Californian to enter the priesthood.

The particularly heavy work in this new field told on the missionaries. Two were nearly prostrated early in the series; Elliott was taken ill with diphtheria at St. Patrick's Church, San Francisco, in March; Rosecrans had to curtail, and at times entirely forego, his share of the work. In March Rosecrans preached at San Rafael, the residence of his father, but he was not able to take part in the mission at Sacramento; and at San Jose he preached only once. In May he went to Virginia City, Nevada, and at Salt Lake City in June, he preached his last mission.

Back in New York, he rested without, however, regaining health; and in May, 1876, two weeks before the fourth anniversary of his ordination, he died. Elliott, closely associated with him during all his life as a Paulist, sent the sad news to his family and many years later made the comment: "It is unfortunate we had so little medical knowledge at the time, or his life might have been saved." In reply to a message with regard to the family's wishes concerning the place of interment, General Rosecrans wired: "Bury him beside his Paulist brethren to await the great resurrection day, and God bless all who have been kind to him."

FATHER SEARLE

George Searle was born in London in June, 1839, while his parents, both Americans, were visiting England. He was a descendant of Thomas Dudley, colonial governor of Massachusetts—who entertained the visiting Jesuit missionary, Gabriel Druillettes in 1650—and of Anne Hutchinson, co-founder of Rhode Island. A precocious child, Searle astonished observers by his mental acumen at the age of five, took his degree at Harvard in 1857, and on that occasion received a prize of $200 for a paper in astronomy. Quickly recognized as a highly gifted mathematician, he was assigned to a post in the Dudley Observatory at once; and he won a place in astronomical records by his discovery of the asteroid, Pandora, in 1858. In 1859 he entered the United States Coast Survey; he acted as assistant professor of mathematics at the United States Naval Academy during the Civil War, and he returned to Harvard as assistant astronomer in 1866. In 1877 he wrote *Elements of Geometry*.[7]

His parents, presumably Episcopalians, had died in his early childhood and he was brought up as a Unitarian by his foster-parents. He never displayed any interest in Unitarianism, believed in God but not in revelation, and looked upon Catholicism as an ancient, outmoded system of unverified doctrines and foolish practices.

A sermon in an Episcopal church, on the text, "You

cannot serve God and Mammon," aroused in him a desire to study the Scripture, and he began to consider Episcopalianism. But the dispute between the "High" party and the "Low" party deterred him; and he was disturbed by the failure of the Episcopal Church to give any definite, official interpretation to our Lord's words in the sixth chapter of St. John: "I will give you my flesh to eat." After reading the *Catechism of the Council of Trent,* he became convinced of the inadequacy of Protestantism; and a year of study led him to visit a Catholic rectory, ring the bell and say to the priest who answered his ring, "I want to become a Catholic." He was received into the Church in 1862; applied for admission to the Paulists; and became a priest on March 25, 1871.

For forty years, he contributed articles to the *Catholic World* and to scientific journals. His paper on "Molecular Mechanics" appeared in 1870, and one on the Great Comet in 1882. He discussed the possibility of other inhabited worlds; he wrote on Darwinism, on the sun's place in the universe, on the discovery of the North Pole; and he earned wide acclaim by his extraordinary accuracy in computing the precise time for the reappearance of Halley's comet in June, 1908.

At the Catholic University of America he had his own little observatory which helped give the University good standing in scientific circles; and persons still alive remember the bearded figure, cowled and cloaked, with lantern in hand, striding over the fields, to watch the stars on a wintry night through the big telescope.

A pioneer in modern aeronautics, Searle constructed a small workshop on the campus of the University where he carried on experiments. To wondering inquirers, he would reply, "Yes, indeed, he did believe the time would come when men would fly." Being an old friend of Langley's, he was enormously interested in the experiments of 1903; and we still remember Searle's unhappy mood when, with all Washington assembled to see the first flight of Langley's high-powered light-weight machine, it splashed into the Potomac (actually because of defective launching apparatus), bringing ridicule on the inventor and withdrawal of the War Department's financial support.

Searle was a mathematician to his fingertips. He thought in straight lines; he took little account of the imponderables and intangibles which affect the normal man's assent to a proposition. In many characteristics he bore a definite resemblance to William G. Ward. Like Ward, he would have been glad to find an infallible decision served up to him every morning with his coffee and his newspapers—and to welcome the dogma with Ward's comment, "We cannot have too much truth." As he made clear in an article entitled "The Margin of Faith," in the *Catholic World*, of April, 1906, the attitude of mind which he regarded as proper for a Catholic is that which "pays more attention by far to the devotions and practices authorized by the Holy Roman Church, to the beliefs which she encourages, and to the common belief of the faithful, than to the objections of learned critics."

The endless anecdotes which cluster about Searle reflect kindliness, honesty and the semi-serious naïveté which often goes with scientific ability. His gentleness and courtesy, even under intense provocation, won universal enduring respect. He could be very impatient superficially; but he never showed real anger.

Often he gave expression to his playfulness of mind by writing jingles, more than a few of which still dwell in the memory or are enshrined in community traditions. The present writer—never quite forgiven for having a last name which did not lend itself easily to rhyme—was properly punished, when appointed assistant (or *Socius*) to the master of novices; for Searle promptly rhymed "socius" with "ferocious". Developing into a baseball fan in middle age, Searle insisted on computing the daily batting averages himself. He could hardly believe that some people were really unable to add three columns of figures simultaneously. He carried a watch which was really a chronometer and he used to look mournful if it lost a second a month. Once having synchronized this watch with the clock of the Lick Observatory on the Pacific Coast, he carried it east all the way to Lake George, and then asked a student to compare it with the old clock in the railroad station. When the student reported that the difference was considerable and that he had set Father Searle's watch by the station clock, Searle, not trusting himself to speak, took the watch and turned away.

Searle was the author of a clear exposition of Catholic doctrine, *Plain Facts for Fair Minds*—being half amused and half annoyed when through a misprint, it was advertised as *Plain Facts for Fair Maids*. He published also a book of instructions, *How to Become a Catholic*. These volumes have remained in constant use.[8] His script was so regular and legible as to arouse the envy of his colleagues—whose peace of mind was restored however, by the discovery that Searle's easy-to-read manuscripts were usually handed over to the least expert type-setter in the printing shop, and therefore, his work often appeared with errors.

Of the first ten Paulists Searle offered the most definite contrast to Hecker. The precise nature of the contrast is not easy to describe; but it resembled the contrast between Ward and Newman. Inevitably therefore, after Searle had attained the position to which years and scientific eminence entitled him, members of the community who did not see eye to eye with Hecker would look to Searle for leadership. But no great trouble resulted, for Searle was a man of superlative integrity who played every game strictly according to the rules.

Following Father Deshon in 1903 in the office of superior general, Father Searle was the last survivor of the seven converts who headed the list of the Paulist Fathers, the last convert Superior General, and almost the last of the converts in the Community. He died July 7, 1918. Thirty years later the Paulist Fathers had not one native American convert in their ranks.

Father Robinson

Thomas Verney Robinson was born on July 16, 1840, probably in Petersburg, Virginia. He entered Virginia Military Institute in August, 1857, but was dropped the following April. Tradition attaches him to a Confederate battery which, at the Battle of Chancellorsville, had Walter Elliott's old Fifth Ohio Regiment under fire.

He was ordained with Rosecrans and Elliott on May 25, 1872. He never enjoyed good health and served for the most part in routine parish duties, dying on February 16, 1903.

The following sketch of Father Robinson appeared in the *Confederate Veteran:*

The late Rev. Thomas Verney Robinson, of the Paulist Fathers, New York City, was a Confederate veteran. On his mother's side he was a descendant of Pocahontas, and paternally of a prominent Irish physician, who was a distinguished member of the United Irishmen, forced to flee for his life after the execution of Robert Emmet.

When the war broke out Father Robinson, who was of an intensely religious nature, was a theological student in the Episcopal Seminary at Alexandria, Va. He had entered there a short time before, having made part of the course of the Virginia Military Institute. Previous to that he had reached his graduating year at William and Mary College.

THE FIRST TEN PAULISTS

His parents were very wealthy, and young Robinson was brought up in affluence, having his own body servant, and his early life surrounded with every luxury. When Virginia seceded he left the seminary and enlisted as a private soldier in the Richmond Howitzers. With them he remained till after the battle of Chancellorsville, partaking of the wonderful experiences of the war in Virginia. Though offered a commission, he refused it, and remained in the ranks by preference. In the early summer of 1863 his health broke down, and he was induced to accept the place of ordnance sergeant. At the surrender of Richmond and Petersberg he remained too long at his post, and was captured. After a short imprisonment on Ward's Island, New York harbor, he was released by the termination of the war.

His family was made penniless by the war, and he was for several months in great straits for the necessities of life in New York City. He obtained employment as a school-teacher and private tutor. Meanwhile his mind had been working anxiously upon religious questions. Finally he was received into the Catholic Church by the late Monsignor Preston, of New York City, and soon after that joined the Paulist Fathers.

After he had made his studies he was, in 1872, ordained priest. His career as a priest was greatly distinguished by his love for the poor and the sick, whom for many years he visited, assisted, consoled, and in every way loved. Some ten years ago his health, weakened by the hardships of the war, was much enfeebled.

His allegiance to the Confederate cause was something wonderful. He never faltered in it. To him, as to so many other heroic souls of the South, there was no "lost cause." Wholly devoid of bitterness, he was yet steadfast and outspoken in his loyalty to the great movement for Southern independence.[9]

The remaining four of the First Ten Paulists—Fathers Hecker, Hewit, Deshon and Elliott—are discussed in other chapters of this book.

X

Platform and Press

(Notes, p. 200 f.)

SENSITIVE to the strong contemporary trend away from Christian and Catholic principles, Hecker felt the need of a modern crusade to overcome the foes of true progress. He said once, "The language of the opponents of Christianity makes it plain that these are not ordinary times. Their aim is no less than the entire overthrow of Christianity, and with it the destruction of all religion whatever. Men are needed, who, devoted to the same good old cause, will go forth in their full strength, aided with new light and fresh love from on high, to battle against the enemies of the Church of God, society, and of all true progress. The champions in this new arena, must be equipped with the weapons of their enemies, arms suitable to their age, and skilled in their tactics if they are going to win." [1]

During the early years of the community Hecker's activity was literally prodigious. As speaker, writer, editor, publisher, he produced or helped to produce an enormous number of lectures, sermons, articles, pamphlets, books; and his sound practical judgment, his persuasive earnestness, his gift of lucid exposition made this output amazingly effective.

Platform

No more concerned with oratory in his speaking than with rhetoric in his writing, Hecker yet became a distinguished lecturer. Crowds flocked to hear him; and hundreds of applications for lectures came from different parts of the country, especially from New England and the western states. The income from the lectures formed a large part of the revenue upon which the little community lived; but far more important than income was the splendid opening for advertising the Church by means of the lecture platform. Hecker was among the earliest to recognize this opportunity. Encouraged by Thoreau, Emerson and Wendell Philips in earlier days, the United States had established a vast number of lyceums. The time was at hand when Henry Ward Beecher would receive $1,000 for one appearance, and when Henry Stanley, freshly back from the sources of the Nile, would be offered a contract for $100,000 to deliver 100 lectures. A few years later the British Ambassador, James Bryce, called Chautauqua "uniquely American." President Theodore Roosevelt regarded it as "the most American thing in America."

Writing to Cardinal Barnabò in 1862, Father Hecker described the way in which he went about securing the attendance and the interest of Protestants: "In three different cities I gave, in a large public hall, a course of conferences on religion, one every evening from Sunday to Sunday inclusive. The expense of the hall was paid by the priest of the place, the lectures were all free, and addressed exclusively to Protestants. The halls were crowded at each place and that my audience might be such as I desired to address, I begged Catholics to stay away. At the close of one of my lectures there were present 2,500 persons, chiefly Protestants."

Despite the invitation to stay away, a sprinkling of Catholics would usually be found in the audience; and on a certain occasion in Detroit in 1868, Walter Elliott, a young lawyer, veteran of the Civil War, was among Hecker's hearers. He describes the impression made upon him when for the first time he saw Hecker on the lecture platform:

He was then in the full tide of success, conscious of his opportunity and of his power to profit by it. We never can forget how distinctly American was the impression of his personality. We had heard the nation's greatest men then living, and their type was too familiar to be successfully counterfeited. Father Hecker was so plainly a great man of that type, so evidently an outgrowth of our institutions, that he stamped American on every Catholic argument he proposed. Nor was the force of this peculiar impression lessened by the whispered grumblings of a few minds among Catholics themselves, to whom this apostolic trait was cause for suspicion. Never was a man more Catholic than Father Hecker, simply, calmly, joyfully, entirely Catholic. What better proof of this than the rage into which his lectures and writings threw the outright enemies of the Church? Grave ministers lost their balance and foamed at him as a trickster and a hypocrite, all the worse because double-dyed with pretence of love of country.[2]

In developing a theme, Hecker always tried to let his audience see that Catholicism was much more sympathetic with the instincts of the unspoiled human soul than Protestantism—a method not wholly novel, yet as a rule new to his hearers. He began by assuming the good faith of those with whom he was dealing; next he corrected errors and misunderstandings, pointing out difficulties patiently and kindly; finally he proceeded to outline the arguments supporting the Catholic position. This was the kind of treatment which in his own case he had desired, but sought in vain for a long period. An instance of the effectiveness of his method occurred at Ann Arbor where, in the Methodist meeting house, Hecker lectured to an audience that included almost the entire student body of the University of Michigan, about 700 in number. He spoke on "Luther and the Reformation." At the first mention of Luther's name, the listeners gave half-defiant cheers; but as the speaker progressed a change could be observed, and they listened to the rest of the lecture in thoughtful silence.

According to Elliott—our chief source of information with regard to this matter—Hecker's lectures covered the entire ground from skepticism to Catholicism. Among the most popular were those aimed at humanitarians, rationalists, indifferentists, atheists. Several dealt with materialistic philosophy and with the movement known as "Spiritualism." Favored subjects were: The Church and the Republic; The State of Religion in the United States; How and Why I became a Catholic. He also spoke often on the Church as a society; on the invocation of saints; and on the sacraments of penance and holy Communion.

A good outline of the main trend of Hecker's thought may be discovered in his first two books, *Questions of the Soul* and *Aspirations of Nature;* and a sample of his style may be found in the short preface to the first of these volumes, which had attained a fifth edition by the year 1864:

> The age is out of joint. Men run to and fro to find the truth. The future lies hid in obscurity and thick darkness. The wide world seems afloat. The question, Has man a destiny, and what is it? agitates the souls of all men. It would seem that God had never made known to man his destiny, or that man had missed the way that leads to it. Who will bring the light of truth once more to dawn upon the soul? Truth that will give to man life, energy, and a purpose worthy of his noble and Godlike capacities? One thing we can truly say of the following sheets; they are not idle speculations. Our heart is in them, and our life's results. That they may be a means to answer life's problem to earnest souls, is our only ambition. With this, knowing that truth is never spoken in vain, we send them forth.

As a lecturer, Hecker attracted the sharp attention of Protestant preachers, some of whom used his statements as texts for Sunday sermons, week after week. Usually instead of discussing the issues presented by Hecker's arguments, they dilated on ancient calumnies and dusted off the same old fables which Newman called "the basis of the Protestant views." Elliott reports that the tone of Hecker's antagonists contrasted strongly with his "frankness, good humor and courtesy." The lectures got good coverage from the secular press which as a rule was sympathetic towards Hecker's new approach to old controversies. The Catholics—people, priests and bishops—developed great admiration for him; many were deeply stirred by his bold yet reverent handling of profound truths, and by his skillful opening up of spiritual vistas. Often one of the faithful would say, "That is the kind of Catholic I am, and the only kind it is easy for me to be." And some non-Catholics declared, "If I were quite sure that Hecker is a genuine Roman Catholic, I think that I could be one myself." [3]

At the beginning of his missionary career, Father Hecker had shown so little promise of becoming an eloquent preacher that he was usually assigned to give instructions and to hear confessions, while his colleagues preached the sermons. But diligent labor under the direction of competent superiors brought about vast improvement; and, although it was on the lecture platform rather than in the pulpit that he achieved his greatest distinction, he did become a magnetic and impressive preacher.

He showed marked individuality in the choice and treatment of topics; and many of his sermons were long remembered. Examples of his varied approach in dealing with different topics may be seen in the contrast between a sermon preached in the Paulist Church, New York, on the eve of his departure for the Vatican Council and a sermon preached in the same church on St. Joseph, "The Saint of Our Day." [4] The last named sermon gives a good notion of Hecker's simple, winning style, free of dramatic flights and rhythmic periods. Dealing with a saint great enough to be officially declared patron of the universal Church, the preacher chose to present St. Joseph as a model for all who live by manual labor. Delivered three-quarters of a century ago, this sermon could be preached effectively again today, practically without change. One of Father Hecker's favorite themes was the obligation of Catholics to give spiritual aid to neighbors outside the fold. He also repeatedly reminded the laity that each individual soul is called to holiness—a topic less frequently touched on in that day than at present. His retreats, too, should be mentioned; for Hecker loved to conduct them and his habitual encouragement of all who longed to make progress in the life of prayer planted fruitful seed in the hearts of countless priests and brothers and nuns.

Hecker's influence was exercised also within the Paulist walls. Often he addressed his brethren on what was for him the justification of their corporate existence, namely the cultivating of a distinctive way of life that united American spirit and methods with timeless religious ideals and the undiluted Catholic faith. That he was not wholly ineffectual may be gathered from the words in which he reports a visitor's comment on the little community in its early days: "Father Sherwood Healy took dinner with us after he got home from Rome, and he said to me afterwards: 'There is something singular about your men. You have a Community, and you live and work together in harmony; but I notice that every man holds his own individuality of view and of character generally.' I told him that I was glad he had noticed that, because it was just what ought to be." [5]

In the parish church of the early Paulists, liturgical correctness, ceremonial dignity, fine music and good preaching, drew numerous visitors from a wide area; and as already mentioned the Fathers were pioneers in the preaching and printing of weekly five minute sermons. Trained on the missions to speak with simplicity and with professional ease on the practical problems of life, the speakers dealt often with the occasions of sin; and one "occasion" which received particular emphasis was intemperance. Missionary experience had made the priests so painfully aware of the deadly effects of this widespread vice that they spared no effort to warn their people against it.

Archbishop Ireland wrote that "The Paulist pulpit opened death-dealing batteries upon the saloon, when the saloon keeper was the hero in state and Church." [6] Although Fathers Elliott and Doyle are the better remembered champions of total abstinence, the C.T.U. of A. convention of 1880 recorded Hecker's own summary of his views upon this practice:

> For a man to say I am strongly in favor of total abstinence for those who need it, is only saying I am a Catholic.
> For a man to say, I am strongly in favor of total abstinence

for those who need it, and I am willing to encourage and strengthen them by means of taking the pledge, is only saying, I am a sincere and earnest Catholic.

For a man to labor to create a public opinion against intemperance and all that leads to it, is only saying, I am a well wisher of my race.[7]

The Press

In his report to the Propaganda in 1833, the great Bishop England stated that he had been led to publish his weekly paper by the realization of the enormous power of the press in America. Two decades later Hecker was proclaiming his belief in the printed word as an effective instrument for checking anti-Christian trends and diffusing Catholic principles. Whether or not he invented the phrase "the Apostolate of the Press," he certainly was ready to devote his own strength and the resources of the Paulist community to this apostolate. For he considered the press to be a divinely fashioned natural aid for the building up of religion, a kind of mental sunlight or oxygen. As his biographer puts it,

No man of his time was better aware of the power of the spoken word, and few were more competent to use it. . . . But he also felt that the providence of God, in making the Press of our day an artificial medium of human intercourse more universal than the living voice itself, had pointed it out as a necessary adjunct to the oral preaching of the truth. He was convinced that religion should make the Press its own. He would not look upon it as an extraordinary aid, but maintained that the ordinary provision of Christian instruction for the people should ever be two-fold, by speech

PLATFORM AND PRESS

and by print; neither the Preacher without the Press nor the Press without the Preacher.[8]

In the spring of 1870, on his way home from the Vatican Council, Hecker wrote to Father Deshon from Assisi, "I felt as if I would have liked to have peopled that grand and empty convent with inspired men and printing presses. For evidently the special battle-field of attack and defence of truth for half a century to come is the printing-press!"[9] To him the Apostolate of the Press meant the largest amount of truth to the greatest number of people. By its means a small band of powerful men could reach an entire nation and elevate its religious life.

Although busily engaged in active mission work, he found time to write the two books which moved an historian of Catholic apologetics to speak as follows: "These books certainly struck a new note in American apologetics. Their appearance was a sign that a new period, or rather interlude, had already commenced, the chief characteristic of which was the attempt to attain the ideal which Hecker had conceived and which found a place not only in literature but in the organization he founded."[10] That ideal was to win the sympathy of the man in the street by letting him feel that his difficulties were understood, to explain the significance of Catholic teaching in such a way that it could be grasped even by persons with confused religious ideas, who were hungry for truth.

According to Hecker, an exposition of Christianity showing the union of its internal with its external notes of credibility, is calculated to produce a more enlightened and intense conviction of its divine truth in the faithful, to stimulate them to a more energetic personal action; and, what is more, it would open the door to many straying children for their return to the fold of the church. He held that an apostolic vocation practically consists in demonstrating the synthesis between the truths of divine revelation and those already held by the class addressed, be these truths few or many, immediate or remote.[11]

Not only did he feel the personal obligation to write, but he also persuaded others to write; and because of the disadvantage under which Catholics were laboring for lack of an adequate medium of free expression, he took the bold step of founding a first-class monthly magazine—a step more daring than we can realize at this distance of time. Not satisfied with this, he even undertook to establish a publication society which would enable Catholic writers to reach the public and would effectively counteract anti-Christian propaganda by refuting accusations, explaining mistakes and proving or illustrating Catholic beliefs.

At the time in question, conditions in the publishing world were such that any promoter of Catholic literature on a large scale might well have been daunted. No less than 400 periodicals came into existence between 1850 and 1857; and of magazines that did not last long, Catholics had a good share.[12] But the reading public was increasing rapidly. Books poured

PLATFORM AND PRESS

from the secular press in ever growing volume. The "required sale" for entry in the best-seller class was a quarter of a million copies in 1860 and a half million in 1890. The *Atlantic Monthly,* which appeared in 1865 under the editorship of James Russell Lowell, and *Harper's Magazine* were stimulating and shaping the American mentality. It became more imperative than ever that the Church should have a voice.

Against this background we can best appraise Hecker's activities as founder, organizer, editor, contributor, publisher. The first great venture came with the launching of the *Catholic World* in April 1865, which Hewit described as Hecker's most important and most successful enterprise in the field of literature. Its effectiveness, said Hewit, was "chiefly due to Father Hecker," head of a battalion of about one hundred writers who contributed the greater part of its first fifty volumes. A glance at the early issues reveals the wide field the magazine covered, and the reason, of its steady increase in prestige and power. It has rightly been called "the most complete record we have of the growth of Catholic letters." In addition to original articles there were many translations and reprints. A good idea of the range of interest envisaged by the editor may be gathered from an article on "Catholic Literature and the Catholic Public" in the issue of December, 1870, and another on "The Church and the Press" in June, 1872.

Most frequent of the contributors were Father Hewit and Dr. Brownson, the last named being the author of no less than seventy articles. One example of Father Hecker's editorial instinct was his advice to the young Agnes Repplier, to leave the field of the short story, where she was no better than commonplace, and venture into the field of the essay, in which as the world knows, she won enduring fame.

Children's periodicals were multiplying; and in 1870, three years before *St. Nicholas* appeared, Father Hecker introduced *The Young Catholic*. It was not the first periodical for Catholic children—four had preceded it and two were still feebly struggling. But it was by far the most successful. Within a year it had attained a circulation of 50,000; and Father Hecker's own opinion was that it could safely aim at a circulation of half a million. But having demonstrated the possibilities in its field, it was soon forced to compete with a score of rivals and it never reached those ambitious heights. Hecker usually wrote the "Uncle Ned Letters" and his sister-in-law, Mrs. George V. Hecker, acted as editor. Father Hecker delivered the rather surprising verdict that *"The Young Catholic* is doing more for the future of our religion than any other work in which I am engaged." [13]

There was also need of organized production of good books and pamphlets. Novel and ominous theories, especially with regard to education, were widespread; the public was being misinformed on a large scale; secularists advanced the startling opinion that religion was banned from the schools by the First Amendment to the Constitution, which enjoined

Congress "to make no law respecting an establishment of religion." Both Catholics and non-Catholics needed warnings with regard to the dangerous theory that the State has the right to exercise complete control over education. With this and other issues in mind, Hecker undertook to establish a publication society, for the printing and distributing of books and tracts on a national scale. His idea was endorsed heartily by Archbishop Martin Spalding and many other members of the hierarchy, and by the clergy. Numerous books, tracts and leaflets were issued, Archbishop Spalding himself writing one of the pamphlets.

By invitation of the Archbishop of Baltimore, Father Hecker addressed the assembled hierarchy at the second Plenary Council of Baltimore, on Tuesday, October 16, 1866. According to Archbishop Ireland's testimony, one of the bishops present at the council affirmed that, "When Father Hecker appeared before the assembled prelates and theologians in the advocacy of Catholic literature as a missionary force, the picture was inspiring and that the hearers, receiving a pentecostal fire within their bosoms, felt as if America were at once to be converted. So would it have been if there had been in America a sufficient number of Heckers." [14] Guilday writes "Considerable interest was aroused at the time by the strong approbation given in the *Pastoral* to the project of the Paulist Fathers who, under Father Hecker's leadership, had established a Catholic Publication Society (for the distribution of tracts and books on Catholic doctrine) which the Fathers called 'second to none in importance among the subsidiary aids . . . for the diffusion of Catholic Truth.' " [15]

The Catholic Publication Society had a short although impressive career; only a small proportion of the clergy promoted the plan; the financial panic of the seventies gave a serious blow to the project. Hecker's health was failing and, despite the large contributions made by George V. Hecker, the Society never attained full growth. It was taken over by the Paulist Fathers, who later established their own printing press next door to the motherhouse; and gradually it was transformed into the Paulist Press which today distributes pamphlets at the rate of some six million annually.

Before leaving the subject of the Catholic press, it seems worth while to mention here another project that failed to mature. Father Hecker conceived the idea of founding a Catholic daily newspaper and actually began to collect funds for it. The same reasons that militated against the development of the Catholic Publication Society made this plan impossible. Walsh alludes to the project of the Catholic daily as "the greatest of Father Hecker's plans." [16]

XI

Hecker's Message

(Notes, p. 201)

THE reader already has a general notion of Hecker's background and of the world in which he lived and developed. We have his own record of his youthful eagerness to help that world towards truth and peace. At first the remedy for existing evils seemed to be political reform; later he realized that the imperative need was an adjusting of all human relations to Christian principles. How to effect this adjustment however, remained a problem until he perceived that the fundamental difficulties were personal; that the basic need was religion; that peace would come only when individuals were ready to co-operate with God's will. Once convinced that both the national welfare and his neighbor's spiritual growth depended on religion, he set forth on his crusade. As a remedy for the contemporary confusion he offered a system of principles and a program of action forged during years of patient thinking, observing, praying, suffering—a pattern of life approved by a divinely commissioned Church. His message might be likened to a symphony with these dominant themes: human nature; Catholicity; political freedom.

When Hecker returned from Rome in the spring of 1858, he had still thirty years to live. Prolonged and recurrent illness cut his active life down to less than twenty years; but, during this comparatively short career, he displayed prodigious energy, planning, directing, writing, speaking, traveling; and his sturdy faith, clear vision, bold courage revealed a personality which looms large even today.

Hecker, who had received little formal education, was an eager reader, a keen observer, a tireless thinker. The two books published early in his Catholic life—*Questions of the Soul* and *Aspirations of Nature*—show his readiness to recognize whatever was good and true in any school or in any man. It was characteristic of him to assume the sincerity of the person or party to whose opinion he was opposed. It was equally characteristic of him to urge that an honest mistake sometimes spoils one's opportunity to arrive at truth, goodness, happiness—that an error, even if sincere, may entail disaster in philosophy, in morals, in religion, just as surely as in physics, or medicine, or industry.

* * *

In his own endeavor to solve spiritual puzzles he had found organized Protestantism practically useless. Sooner than most of his contemporaries, Hecker perceived that the Church's chief battle had to be waged not with Protestant orthodoxy, but with undogmatic Christianity which slipped so easily into the Unitarianism of Channing or the Transcendentalism of Emerson. When he discovered in the *Catechism of the Council of Trent* answers to all the questions that really needed answers, he at once made this book his daily manual. The Church became the keystone of his intellectual and spiritual arch.

Hecker had no new doctrine to offer—only a clearer display and a more orderly arrangement of truth, and a shifting of emphasis. He insisted it is important: (1) to accept all truth; (2) to prize most what matters most. God had given him a synthetic mind, a balanced judgment, a dislike of extremes; he was instinctively Catholic, not exclusive. His ability to see the partial truth on both sides of a dispute and the justice in each of two conflicting claims is most impressive when he approaches problems that involve the relationship of nature and grace, of freedom and authority, of the outer and inner elements of religion. He could appraise both what was fine and what was defective in America and in Europe; in Latin, in Celt, in Anglo-Saxon, in German, in Semite; in old institutions and in new. Men of this kind who see both sides, often offend neighbors who, while focusing attention on one aspect of truth, quite unconsciously ignore another.

When instructing men in the relationship between liberty and authority, Hecker always presented the Church as divinely commissioned to command; but he also emphasized the fact that man's obedience is that of a free spirit, not of a slave or a machine. It is harder to balance two complementary truths than to concentrate on one; and Hecker's declaration that "Man is created to give free service" annoyed two types of person—those who exaggerate human freedom, and those who underrate it. The one class imagine themselves independent of all authority; the other class overlook man's inalienable freedom to make an individual choice between good and evil.

Three hundred years earlier Protestantism had discredited reason and free will; in the nineteenth century it was exaggerating them. Some Catholics, when opposing this modern trend, were disposed to suspect everyone who stressed the importance of reason and will; and Hecker came under fire at times for maintaining the balanced Catholic doctrine which teaches that spiritual progress is not exclusively the result of the infused virtues given by grace; that it needs also the exercise of the natural virtues acquired by repeated acts. For man must be not merely receptive; he must be active—energetically using the powers of mind and will bestowed on him by the Creator; and Hecker consistently stressed the value of the individual's own contribution to the building up of character. He kept repeating that supernatural grace does not substitute for truth and justice, but lifts them to a higher level.

In appealing to the non-Catholic mind dissatisfied with Protestantism and tempted by a liberalism that professed to be honest and noble, Hecker took his stand on rational philosophy and on the moral code accepted by the normal, well-disposed American. But since these, sound as far as they went, are demonstrably insufficient, it was necessary to go on to consider the possibility of getting help from "revealed religion." Having shown that no form of Protestantism, orthodox or liberal, was able to answer the mind's legitimate questions or to satisfy the soul's finest aspirations, he proceeded to weigh the claims of Catholicism. Many an earnest seeker, persuaded thus to contemplate the logically coherent and sublimely spiritual ideals presented by the Church, soon arrived at an awareness of the Church's divine origin and submitted to her authority.

* * *

Probably the most formidable obstacle to the acceptance of the Church by high-minded non-Catholics is their misunderstanding of her doctrine about the inner life of the soul. They often feel a deep instinctive dislike for the elaborate external system of Catholicism. Their insistence upon the primacy of inner worship seems to contrast violently with Catholic insistence upon the importance of ecclesiastical organization. They compare Christ's proclamation of the law of love with the Church's "promulgation of codes of Christian behavior." The American Founding Fathers and most of the early English-speaking immigrants to this country inherited a Protestant tradition which placed comparatively little emphasis on the external ecclesiastical system, much emphasis on the internal, subjective element. To them Catholics seemed extravagantly, if not exclusively, concerned with outward forms—liturgy, ceremonies, sacraments, priesthood, hierarchy. Where, they asked, is the emphasis on the inner life that dominates the pages of the New Testament—those pages which say so much in favor of secret prayer and personal consecration, so much in dispraise of rites and laws and ceremonies?

Now Catholics themselves sometimes cherish a distorted idea of the Church's doctrine. In their eagerness to urge the necessity of submitting to the Church, they may over-emphasize the external and belittle the inner element. Naturally enough, Protestants are misled when they find a professed Catholic acting as if outer observance could completely take the place of that adoration in spirit and in truth which is essential to the proper relationship between the soul and its Creator. Protestants may thus come to imagine that we Catholics think we are saved by mere membership in an organization; and they will, therefore, assume that they are attacking a Catholic principle when they proclaim that "religion is a personal matter between self and God." But of course the Catholic Church teaches and has always taught that the individual conscience is an inviolable sanctuary in which the soul communes with the Holy Ghost. Any well-informed Catholic should be able to prove that a virtuous non-

Catholic owes his happy spiritual condition to principles that have been carefully preserved through the ages by the Church—principles that defend reason and free will, principles that foster the sense of personal relationship with Christ. The official doctrine of the Church, the teaching of the theologians, the writings of the masters of the spiritual life, all present the same view—that the outer element of religion is related to the inner as means to an end, that externals are a help to effect the soul's union with God.

Hecker laid strong emphasis upon the ability of Catholicism to satisfy the spiritual hunger of aspiring but bewildered men. He realized that the earnest seeker for true religion will be satisfied with the Church, only if the Church proves to be a practical aid to holy living. It is when the Church is obviously promoting the health of the soul that she is seen in her proper light. When her authority is plainly being exercised for the enlightening of the mind and the strengthening of the will, then she may confidently appeal for recognition as the divinely commissioned guide of souls. One is a true Catholic, not through loyalty to family traditions or national customs; not because of mental agreement with an ancient and wise philosophy; but only because one uses the Church's assistance to shun sin and to seek holiness. Teachings that convince the logician are illustrated and confirmed by the sight of a long line of Catholic saints who have recognized the unique value of the Church as a guide towards the highest—

which are also by far the costliest—spiritual ideals.

Hecker returned again and again to the Catholic doctrine of the Holy Spirit dwelling in the soul of the just man. Both in writing and in speaking he stressed this ancient teaching that had been in many quarters temporarily obscured; and he thus brought vividly to the attention of Protestant observers the profound faith of Catholics in the invisible element of religion. For the doctrine of the indwelling Holy Spirit implies that the actual effectiveness of external religion may be measured by the degree of interior union attained. The Church impresses this upon us by recalling the words in which our Lord foretold the coming of the Holy Ghost: "It is expedient for you that I go. For if I go not, the Spirit will not come to you; but if I go, I will send Him to you." (John XVI, 7) It would be hardly possible to say more plainly that the sacraments, the Church, the crucifixion, even the Incarnation itself, are means to an end. The external, visible is for the sake of what is internal, invisible.

The Catholic doctrine of the Indwelling of the Holy Ghost in the soul was not commonly discussed in English books and sermons during the early and middle nineteenth century. Cardinal Manning, who felt that ignorance of this important doctrine had been a major cause of England's loss of faith in Reformation days, wrote *The Internal Mission of the Holy Ghost* in 1875; and his book remained the one widely circulated English treatise on the subject until after the publication of Pope Leo XIII's great encyclical letter on the Holy Ghost in 1899. That papal letter formulated the Catholic teaching clearly and authoritatively. It affirmed that devotion to the Holy Spirit is especially suited for our modern age. It proclaimed, at least equivalently, that this devotion should appeal strongly to souls of the type most honored in the United States—persons highly individual, of fine initiative, resentful of excessive interference with their liberty, yet willing to adjust themselves to the directions of legitimate authority, human or divine. The Holy Father emphasized the need of cultivating devotion to the Holy Spirit, if we wish to acquire the habit of loyal response to the inner promptings of grace. He put the final stamp of approval on a devotion already declared timely by priests and bishops throughout the English-speaking world; and after the pope's message was published, writers and preachers became even more active than before in promoting the spread of devotion to the Holy Ghost among the faithful.

In addition to writing and speaking of devotion to the Holy Ghost, Hecker diligently circulated books which helped toward an appreciation of that devotion—for example, the Jesuit Father Louis Lallemant's *Spiritual Teaching,* written in 1694, and published for the first time in English at the suggestion of Father Faber in 1855; and also the well known seventeenth century treatise, *Holy Wisdom,* by the Benedictine, Augustine Baker, republished in the middle of the nineteenth century. At Father Hecker's suggestion Ella McMahon, in 1887, translated into English the wonderful little book, *Abandonment*, written by the Jesuit Father Jean Pierre de Caussade in 1681.

* * *

As Hecker was in perfect accord with the Holy See in his devotion to the Holy Spirit, so he was in his notion of the Church. In a properly developed Catholic mind, the mystical ideal element is combined with practical appreciation of the visible society. If we are to fulfill our whole duty as followers of Christ, we must not only share Catholic ideals and principles; we must also become members of the visible body. For, as Hecker himself put it, "The Holy Spirit, in the external authority of the Church acts as the infallible interpreter and criterion of divine revelation. . . . The action of the Holy Spirit embodied visibly in the authority of the Church, and the action of the Holy Spirit dwelling invisibly in the soul, form one inseparable synthesis . . ." He also said, "In case of obscurity or doubt concerning what is the divinely revealed truth, or whether what prompts the soul is or is not an inspiration of the Holy Spirit, recourse must be had to the Divine Teacher or criterion, the authority of the Church. For it must be borne in mind that to the Church, as represented in the first instance by St. Peter, and subsequently by his successors, was made the promise of her Divine Founder, that 'the gates of hell should never prevail against her.' No such promise was ever made by Christ to each individual believer." To believe in the action of the Holy Spirit on the soul and yet ignore the Church's authority, would as Hecker said, "only open the door to delusions, errors, and heresies of every description, and would be in effect only another form of Protestantism." [1]

When these fundamental doctrines are set in order, there comes into view a vision of the Church which should be almost irresistibly persuasive to the type of listener that Hecker had in mind; for such a one would understand that the longed-for union with our Lord is to be achieved through membership in His mystical body, the Church. And this accords with the fundamental principle of the Incarnation, which is essentially a manifesting of the unseen through the seen, an expression of the invisible in the terms of the visible, a linking of the spiritual with the material.

Indeed the Catholic doctrine on the Church should commend itself to any thinking Christian. For if Christ came from the heavenly Father to teach a way of life, to lay down rules for the guidance of mind and will, He must of course have provided for the preservation of His teaching. And His teaching could be preserved only by some sort of court divinely guided, to which men may turn when tormented by doubt as to the interpretation of that teaching. This is in harmony with our human way of acting. Social and political institutions have to be built on something more solid than oral tradition or written documents. There must be also a living court to interpret and define the meaning of bequests and laws and constitutions. Otherwise men get involved in disorder and endless strife.

No reader of Hecker's writings could be unaware of his definite summons to persons outside the Catholic fold to enter in. Repeatedly he pointed out the costly error of Protestantism in rejecting the living authority of the Church and thus condemning itself to walk the fatal road of subjectivism. He displayed a typically Catholic characteristic, in showing a sense of the Church's reality so acute as to be almost incomprehensible to the agnostic and to the Protestant.

We might attempt to describe Hecker's vision of the Church by saying that when Christ's earthly life was nearing its end, God formed in the womb of humanity a Mystical Body for his Son—a heart to throb with sympathy for the afflicted to the end of time; a brow to wear the glory of Thabor and the shame of Calvary while the world should last; feet to tread the mountains of all the world, carrying the messengers of the good tidings of peace; lips to pronounce the pardon of every truly repentant sinner; hands to stretch to all nations, bearing gifts for every child of Adam; and fingers to break the bread of life to every famishing soul.

The Church's mission was to redeem countless millions from vice, to heal the soul-sick and the conscience-dead, to preach the Gospel of the homeless

Christ to the poor of all the world, to tame the savage and sanctify the barbarian, to defy monarchs in the cause of justice, to convert woman into an angel of peace and a symbol of purity, to strike the shackles from the slave, to be a sign of contradiction to the world until the last hour of its wicked existence. Out of the weak things and the ignoble and the base, the Church would form heroes and Christians and saints.

This Visible Church, this Mystical Body of Christ, has drawn to herself what was best in old times and in new, in East and in West, in all places and all ages; and she has given it out again to men as their needs demanded. To her the world has gone to school for nearly 2,000 years and from her has learned the highest and best it knows. Through her each of us shares in the fruits of the collective life of Christendom; to her we owe it that we are born not into a spiritual wilderness, but into a flourishing civilization. Raised in her arms to wider outlook than is possible to even the wisest of individuals or the oldest of nations, we discern an infinite horizon, we see things as it were, with the eternal eyes of Christ, we appropriate His divine enthusiasms, the noblest heritage of the race. Stimulated by her inspiration and guided by her age-old wisdom, we go out of our selfish littleness to become great in devotedness and generosity; and we are carried along by the crowds of her saints where he that walks alone must faint and lie down.

She names us, nourishes us, weans us, teaches us. She holds up the Crucifix before our childish eyes to win our young hearts' love for Christ. She reconciles us with God after we have strayed away. Home from our wanderings, we sit down at the heavenly banquet and are cheered with Christ's Sacred Body and His Precious Blood. At Baptism, Confirmation, Marriage, and Ordination she ministers to us the graces we need. She watches over and soothes our dying moments; and under her benediction we descend into the grave. She is literally the sacrament of sacraments, the Mystical Body of Jesus.

* * *

Hecker was optimistic about the progress of the Church in the United States. He wrote in 1879, "Let it once be shown that the Catholic interpretation of Christianity is consonant with the dictates of human reason, in accordance with man's normal feelings, favorable to the highest conceptions of man's dignity which awakens the uttermost action and devotion of all his powers, and you have opened the door to the American people for the reception of the complete evidence of the claims of the Catholic Church, and prepared the way for the universal acceptance of her divine character."

Hecker felt that Europe "under the lead of the religious revolution of the sixteenth century, turned its back on Catholicity and entered upon the downward road that ends in death; the republic of the United States, in affirming man's natural rights, started in the eighteenth century with its face to

Catholicity, and is in the ascending way of life to God." Again he wrote, "When the nature of the American republic is better understood, and the exposition of Christianity is shaped in the light of its universal principles so as to suit the peculiarities of the American mind, the Catholic Church will not only keep her baptized American children in her fold, but will at the same time remove the prejudice existing in the minds of a large class of non-Catholics, and the dangers apprehended from the influence of republicanism will be turned into fresh evidences of the church's divine character." [2]

Hecker's habit of stressing the aspects of Catholicism just mentioned developed out of his knowledge of the needs of his non-Catholic fellow Americans; and his enthusiasm for American institutions sprang from the fact that the Church and its members here enjoyed a degree of liberty denied them in many nominally Catholic countries. Later pronouncements of bishops and popes have made Catholic praise of the United States commonplace. Nowadays readers ask, Why all the excitement fifty years ago, just because Bishop John L. Spalding in the presence of the apostolic delegate voiced the rhetorical question: "What sacredness in Europe more than in America?" But the sad fact was that in the nineteenth century many a Catholic assumed that in order to think with the Church it was necessary to accept not only the ancient faith, but also a legacy of social and political traditions inherited from Europe. They cherished a sort of subconscious lurking disloyalty, born of the notion that Catholic ideals and American traditions were mutually exclusive; and this sentiment persisted even after the outspoken pronouncement of the Pastoral Letter issued by the bishops at the Third Plenary Council of Baltimore in December, 1884:

We think, the bishops said, "we can claim to be acquainted both with the laws, institutions and spirit of the Catholic Church; and with the laws, institutions and spirit of our country; and we emphatically declare that there is no antagonism between them. A Catholic finds himself at home in the United States; for the influence of his Church has constantly been exercised in behalf of individual rights and popular liberties. And the right-minded American nowhere finds himself more at home than in the Catholic Church, for nowhere else can he breathe more freely that atmosphere of Divine truth, which alone can make him free. We repudiate with equal earnestness the assertion that we need to lay aside any of our devotedness to our Church, to be true Americans; the insinuation that we need to abate any of our love for our country's principles and institutions, to be faithful Catholics."

The pronouncement was timely in other countries too, where some Catholics showed suspicion of modern political institutions—in France, for example, where consternation overwhelmed conservative Catholics when Leo XIII bade them accept the republican form of government. Catholicism had been associated with the monarchy so long and so closely that they thought the Holy Father must have lost the faith. But in France and in other nations, progressive thinkers Catholic, and non-Catholic alike, shared Hecker's view of the religious value of liberty; and we find him admired enthusiastically by eminent Europeans, many of whom have been quoted at length in Abbé Félix Klein's *L'Américanisme*.[3]

It must not be thought that Hecker was nationalistic or insular; he was ready to praise any country which guaranteed political freedom and liberty of conscience to all. One who understands Hecker can well imagine he would have given a shout of joy had he lived to read that most Chestertonian essay, "If Don John of Austria had Married Mary Queen of Scots." For the essay presents a thrilling description of what western civilization might have become had the wedding of those two symbolic personalities brought about the indissoluble union of age-old Catholicism and modern political freedom.

Among the more notable tributes to Hecker was one given by Canon William Barry of Dorchester, England. After referring to the profound impression made upon the French by Châteaubriand, their compatriot, Barry speaks of the influence exerted upon "the reserved and stubborn yet loyal English race" by "John Henry Newman, the teacher of conscience, acquainted with every fold of their hearts, and so entirely of this island-make." He then refers to the exquisite adaptation of personal gifts in the apostolate of Father Hecker who could make the Catholic Church intelligible to Unitarians, Methodists and Democrats. Barry goes on to say, "How impossible would it not have been for an alien to enter into their thoughts, or to convince them that by submitting to Catholicism they were not yielding up their native-American privileges and falling back into the worn-out ideas of the Old World? But Isaac Hecker had travelled every step of the journey; from them he had sprung, and their principles had been his principles. . . . He could say in the very neighborhood of Emerson, and on the same platform, that only in the Catholic teaching was there adequate justification of the principles on which he had ever acted." [4]

To the American reader, probably no interpretation of Hecker will be more intelligible and impressive than Archbishop Ireland's:

Hecker "looked on America as the fairest conquest for divine truth, and he girded himself with arms shaped and tempered to the American pattern. I think that it may be said that the American current, so plain for the last quarter of a century in the flow of Catholic affairs, is, largely at least, to be traced back to Father Hecker and his early co-workers. It used to be said of them in reproach that they were the 'Yankee' Catholic Church; the reproach was their praise. . . . His favorite topic in book and lecture was, that the constitution of the United States requires, as its necessary basis, the truths of Catholic teaching regarding man's natural state, as opposed to the errors of Luther and Calvin. The republic, he taught, presupposes the Church's doctrine, and the church ought to love a polity which is the offspring of her own spirit. He understood and loved the people of America. He recognized in them splendid natural qualities. Was he not right? Not minimizing in the least, the dreadful evil of the absence of the supernatural, I am not afraid to give as my belief, that there is among Americans as high an appreciation and as lively a realization of natural truth and goodness as has been seen in any people, and it seems as if almighty God, intending a great age and a great people, has put here in America, a singular development of nature's powers and gifts, both in man and out of man—with the further will, I have the faith, of crowning all with the glory of the supernatural. Father Hecker perceived this, and his mission was to hold in his hands the natural, which Americans extol and cherish and trust in, and by properly directing its legitimate tendencies and growth to lead it to the term of its own instincts and aspirations—Catholic truth and Catholic grace. . . . Now comes the opportunity of the Catholic Church to show that she is from God who created nature, by opening before this people her treasures, amid which the soul revels in rational liberty and intelligence, and enjoys the gratification of its best and purest moral instincts. These convictions are the keynote of Father Hecker's controversial discourses and writings. . . . He assumed that the American people are naturally Catholic, and he labored with this proposition constantly before his mind. It is the assumption upon which all must labor who sincerely desire to make America Catholic.[5]

Had the men of the nineteenth century been able to foresee definitely the ascent of the United States to its present level of dominant global influence, they would have been even more emphatic in their endorsement of Hecker's view that the prospect of a Catholicized America is the best hope for the future of civilization. Hecker knew that what America needed more than anything else was the planting of the seeds of divine truth preserved so long and so carefully in the granary of the Church; and he knew that what religion needed more than anything else was freedom to grow, the kind of freedom favored by the Founding Fathers of the Republic, and guaranteed by the Constitution of the United States.

NOTES FOR PART II

Study VI (Text, pages 91–105)

1. PFA, Hecker Papers.
2. PFA, Hecker Letters. Some light is thrown on Hecker's views by the discussions he held in 1875 with Cardinal Dechamps, who had by then come to look on Hecker with new respect, and with Bishop (later cardinal) Herbert Vaughan of Salford, Hecker's warm friend. Both of them encouraged the idea of a Paulist foundation in Europe; Hecker thought there should be a new community similar to the Paulists, "but not the same." Ten years later, after consulting with Hewit who did not oppose the idea, Hecker came to the conclusion that several Paulists might be spared to found a house in Europe; and the project was placed before Cardinal Manning by Bishop Keane, who, on August 1, 1885, wrote as follows:

> Now I come, I hope as the instrument of Divine Providence, to lay before your Eminence a proposal, directly, as it seems to me, in the lines of your great work.
>
> You are well acquainted, I believe, with Father Hecker—whom you have met both in London and in Rome—and have heard of the Society of Priests of St. Paul established by him many years ago in New York. Their aim is, to be, like their holy Patron, truly Apostolic men, appreciating the Providence of the age, understanding its needs, entering into its mind and heart, and laboring, in the truly Catholic and Apostolic spirit of the Apostle to the Gentiles, to turn it to God. The Paulist Fathers have given missions in every part of our country, and have won the highest esteem of the Bishops, the clergy, and the faithful.
>
> Aiming at wide action, they desire to have but few local centres of their spiritual activity. They are cosmopolitan in spirit, and desire to be international in organization with, as a rule, but one house at the great centre in each country.
>
> Now the Providence of God turns their eyes towards England—and towards London. And I, who have been for several years their intimate friend and ardent admirer, gladly assume the office of

agent and advocate in the matter, and now ask your Eminence whether you have not place & work for them. They do not ask or desire a parish or church. Their work would be Apostolic,—missions, preaching, giving retreats, etc.

It might be a year, perhaps two, before they would feel ready to establish a house in London; but they thus make the first overtures at this time, that they may be able to make the better preparation for the undertaking, if your Eminence thinks fit to accept their services. Among the members of their Community there are at present three or four Englishmen, who might, on that account, be specially fit for the work.

I am convinced that the Paulists would be a comfort to the heart of your Eminence, congenial auxiliaries in your great work, a blessing to religion in your Diocese and in the whole country. For these reasons, and as their friend, I shall prayerfully hope for a favorable reply.

With profound sentiments of reverence and affection, I am
Your Eminence's humble sevt. in Xt.
John J. Keane,
Bp. of Richmond.

As Cardinal Manning did not welcome the suggestion, the project of a European foundation was dropped.

For a transcript of Keane's letter now in their archives, the Paulist Fathers are indebted to Dr. John Tracy Ellis of the Catholic University of America.

3. Their founder, M. Jacques Olier, had limited the size of the congregation to seventy-two members, in addition to an administrative group of twelve assistants headed by a superior general—a limitation abolished in later years by Father Emery.

4. Founded in Rome by St. Philip Neri in 1575, and attracting people by unconventional methods, the Oratorians were denounced as extravagant and unsound. But with the approval of the Holy See the Oratory spread rapidly throughout Italy and many other countries. Highly adaptable, it took on a superior general in France; after its suppression during the French Revolution, it was revived in 1852 by Père Auguste-Joseph-Alphonse Gratry, one of whose disciples was the brilliant scholar, Adolphe Cardinal Perraud. In 1847, a year after his ordination, John Henry Newman adapted the Oratorians to England's needs and opened the first English Oratory.

5. *op. cit.*, 174.

6. Manning's feeling towards religious orders is explained in part by Cardinal Wiseman's extraordinary letter to Father Frederick William Faber in 1852, which reproached all the communities of priests in his archdiocese with giving him little aid in bearing his burdens. Manning visited Rome in 1857 and obtained permission to adapt the rule of the Oblates of St. Charles (founded by St. Charles Borromeo in the sixteenth century) for use by a new community of priests. The Oblates, established at Bayswater in 1857, gave strong support to Wiseman and to Manning, his successor. Manning's lifelong attitude is reflected in a memorandum made after a talk with one of the two Karslake brothers—converts to the faith, who left the Oblates to enter the Jesuits: "Poor Charles Karslake said bitterly to me, 'If the religious Orders were founded to keep priests from becoming religious, I wish they were abolished.' Again I thought to myself, 'If the religious Orders were founded to prevent the priests from believing that they are bound to perfection, I also wish they were abolished.'" Edward Sheridan Purcell. *Life of Cardinal Manning* (New York, 1896), II, 766.

7. "Programme of the Rule & Constitution of the Congregation of Miss. Priests of S. Paul the Apostle:

The undersigned agree to unite together to form a Congregation under Episcopal approbation with the intention of drawing up at the proper time a Rule to be submitted to the Holy See for approval and sanction.

Meanwhile they agree to adopt the following articles as expressing the essential features of their institute; according to which they will live together in a community and carry on the work of the missions and other accessory labors.

In the first place they will endeavor to promote their own sanctification by leading a life in all essential respects similar to that which is observed in a religious Congregation.

They will practice the three religious virtues of chastity, poverty and obedience. The first of these virtues they will practice in accordance with their sacerdotal vows, by endeavoring to preserve a spotless purity of soul and body.

The second they will practice by leading a life perfectly in common and in all things uniform. No member can dispose of his property or revenue (otherwise than by will) except for his relations or in favor of the congregation. Each one must receive those things that are necessary for him from the congregation. The living must be plain, the rooms small and furnished in accordance with

NOTES FOR PART II

the spirit of poverty, and the dress plain and simple but neat and suitable for respectable priests.

The virtue of obedience they will practice by paying a ready and prompt obedience to the Vicar of Jesus Christ, to the Bishops under whose jurisdiction they live or labor and to their own superior in accordance with this Rule.

The members of the Institute will moreover practice those religious exercises in community and in private which are the necessary means of their sanctification. Those who are priests will endeavor to live in such a way that they may celebrate Mass daily and as one of the chief means of preserving that purity of conscience which is requisite in one who approaches the Altar of God, they will go to confession every week. Those who are not priests will likewise confess weekly and receive Holy Communion every eight days and on Feasts of precept. Each one will make a retreat of eight days in the year and a day of recollection every month.

The following exercises shall be observed every day in community:

1. Two meditations of half an hour each, one in the morning and one in the evening.

2. A particular examination of conscience with the Litany of the Blessed Virgin before dinner and a general examination of conscience followed by night prayers in the evening.

Morning and evening the Superior will give his benediction to each one.

In addition to these the following daily exercises are prescribed to be performed in private:

1. A spiritual reading of half an hour.

2. A visit to the Blessed Sacrament and to the Blessed Virgin Mary.

3. One chaplet of the Rosary.

Besides the daily exercises the following exercises shall be observed in community each week:

1. A chapter of faults.

2. A conference relating to some subject of theology, rubrics, the manner of giving missions or some similar topic of common utility.

Since the spirit of mortification is absolutely essential to solid Christian and Religious virtue, the members of the Institute will sedulously endeavor to acquire and practice it.

Although no special corporal penances are enjoined, yet it is permitted to everyone to take discipline in private on Wednesday and Friday evenings, unless for particular reasons he is specially prohibited by the Superior.

Public penances and acts of humility will also be practiced in the Refectory. Silence will be observed during the afternoon and a more profound silence from the time of night prayers until the morning meditation.

At all times silence will be observed in the choir, oratory, sacristy, refectory, kitchen and corridors. The members of the community will endeavor to practice a continual recollection, a constant and exact vigilance over themselves, an accurate observance of their spiritual exercises, a fervent and laborious zeal in performing the duties of their ministry and supporting the fatigue and hardships of the Apostolic life.

In fine they will endeavor to imitate the example and follow the counsels of our Lord Jesus Christ according to the model furnished them by their great Patron, St. Paul the Apostle.

The members of the congregation unite themselves together not only for their own sanctification but also to carry on common labors for the salvation of others.

First of all they will carry on the missions in the spirit of St. Alphonsus and will avoid engaging themselves in works which will hinder or impede them in their missionary labors.

For this end they will avoid engaging in secular education and in making new foundations, they will be careful that each one shall have a community sufficiently numerous, and they will have but one parish with one church in any locality.

Whenever a parish is accepted all the duties and obligations connected with it shall be fulfilled in the most exact and conscientious manner according to the agreement made with the Bishop of the Diocese.

Until such time as a permanent organization having the approbation of the Holy See can be made the Congregation will be governed by a superior chosen for a term of three years. The original members who formed this Congregation shall constitute a provisional Chapter to continue until the Rule is approved by the Holy See, or until some other regulation is made on the subject. But in any case it shall continue for five years unless the Rule is approved before the expiration of that time.

This Chapter shall elect the Superior by secret ballot, a majority of two-thirds being necessary to a choice; it shall have power to decide on every question and to prepare the Rule which is finally to be presented to the Holy Father.

If any new house is founded before the rule is approved it shall remain subject to the Superior of the original foundation and its Superior shall be appointed by him with a concurrence of a majority of the Chapter.

The Superior shall have full power of governing where he is not limited by the statutes of the Chapter. If the Chapter thinks proper, it may assign him two consultors and define their powers.

NOTES FOR PART II

The superior may appoint such subordinate officers as may be necessary to aid him in his duties.

Dated July 7, 1858. (Signed) I. Th. Hecker
Augustine Hewit
George Deshon
Francis A. Baker

8. The agreement provides that the members of the Congregation will fulfill

all the duties and obligations annexed to a parochial charge, the Superior being ex-officio Pastor and responsible to the Archbishop. The church with all its fixtures and the ground it covers shall be deeded to the Archbishop. In case the care of the parish should ever be relinquished by the Congregation, the Archbishop shall have the right of purchasing at the original price, one or two lots, at his option, of the property belonging to the Congregation and adjoining the church for a parochial residence. The church grounds should include space for a parish school.

His Grace the Archbishop agrees to concede to the Superior duly elected and confirmed by him the ordinary jurisdiction of a Superior of a Religious Family.

He will exact from the priests of the Congregation no other duties besides the care of the above mentioned parish and he will leave them at liberty to carry on the missions and other apostolic works of their Institute under the direction of their Superior, subject to his own ordinary jurisdiction.

He will also permit them to retain the title to their own Religious house and the ground attached to it and will grant them the use in perpetuity of the aforesaid parish church. The same in all other respects to be administered as other parochial churches of the city and diocese.

Approved by me, 10th day of July 1858,
✠ John Archbishop of New York.

See PFA.

9. From a letter to his brother George. PFA, Hecker Letters.

Study VII (Text, pages 106–118)

1. Letter from Father Walworth to Bishop Francis Patrick McFarland. (The original of this letter is in the archives of the University of Notre Dame.)

St. Peter's Church, Troy,
July 19.

Monsignor.

The note which you addressed me requesting a mission for your Cathedral, I have forwarded to Rev. F. Hecker, as being the responsible person to accept the invitation. It appears from the note being addressed to me that your Lordship is not aware of my having separated myself from my former companions in missionary labor. Such however is the case; and the great kindness which you have manifested, Monsignor, to myself as well as the rest, and a desire not to be misunderstood by one whose regard I prize so highly, prompts me to address you a few lines in explanation of my motives. In accepting a dispensation from my vows, I had never any thought of changing my vocation as a Religious missionary. I looked upon it as a necessary but only temporary step, intending all the while, as I supposed all the others intended, to resume the vows again and our former rule of religious observance. It was therefore a great surprise and shock to me, when at our first conference together after F. Hecker's return, I found that my companions contemplated not only a very extensive change and relaxation of our former Rule, but even *the abandoning of the vows*. According to the plainest definition, nevertheless, of the Canon Law, *the perpetual vows of poverty, chastity, and obedience*, constitute an essential element of the Religious state, and that as the Canonists with St. Thomas say, *jure divino*, so that not even the Pope can dispense a Religious from his vows, in such way as to leave him the Religious character. I told them therefore, at the outset, that I felt my vocation to be to the Religious state and the vows, and that I could have no confidence in an organization for a missionary life, depending upon the voluntary principle, which would be too weak to furnish the society with the necessary energy, and unity; that moreover we occupied a certain position already in the country, before the Bishops and the people, which we were still *morally* bound to maintain; and that moreover we had in our memorial to the Pope declared our attachment to our Rule and vows, and our anxious desire to be relieved by Him if possible, without dispensation from our vows. If therefore they persisted in their purpose, I told them at once, we must separate. They afterwards consented to take *annual vows*, and for a time I endeavored to reconcile my mind to this, but I *could not*. Besides that annual vows do not constitute a Religious, the whole spirit of innovation and relaxation which manifested itself more and more at every interview was so destructive of all my confidence in the affair, that after long consultation with the Bishops of Albany and Newark, and with their full approbation I finally parted with them. It has been an awful blow to my dearest hopes on earth, for I have always cherished as my heart's blood, both my Religious character, and my missionary vocation; but I trust that God will not forsake me, for this thing is not my doing, nor done by my will, but by His own gracious permission.

You will understand, Monsignor, that I write these lines, merely to set myself right before you, but not to prejudice in any way the prospects of the others. We have parted as brothers part, without the least breach of charity, and they are to me personally the same dear friends as ever. They are most estimable, talented and energetic Priests, and will be certainly a valuable accession to the diocese where they locate, and a help to every Bishop who employs them, while they hold together as they are, and I shall not cease to pray for the establishment they form even beyond the extent of my hopes. With regard to the missions you have asked for, I have no doubt they will give you satisfaction.

May I request, Monsignor, your kind and pious prayers for me, that God may soften to me the present affliction which weighs upon me, and make me in this Parish where I am stationed, to do his holy will always, preserving in me his holy grace, and giving me both the zeal, and the ability to labor ever for his own greater glory and the good of souls.

Requesting also your benediction
I remain Monsignor
Your faithful Son and Servant
C. A. Walworth.

The Rt. Rev. the }
Bishop of Hartford }

2. Cardinal Farley tells the story. Forbes, a native New Yorker, graduate of Columbia College, after completing his divinity course at the General Theological Seminary, became rector of St. Luke's Episcopal Church, New York, and professor of pastoral theology in the seminary. He entered the Catholic Church in 1849 and was ordained to the priesthood in 1850, together with a fellow convert, Thomas Scott Preston, later vicar general of New York. In 1852 Forbes became pastor of St. Ann's, a former Protestant church, purchased to make a place for him. On October 17, 1859, in an open letter to the press, he renounced his communion with the Church. John Cardinal Farley. *The Life of John Cardinal McCloskey* (New York, 1918) 195 ff.

3. See Walworth's long letter, January 3–January 15, 1858. PFA, Hecker Letters.

4. Onderdonk, a friend of the High Church party to which Walworth had belonged, was accused of immorality; and the

trial, held in 1844, resulted in the bishop's suspension. See Clarence A. Walworth, *The Oxford Movement in America; or, Glimpses of Life in an Anglican Seminary.* (New York, 1895), Chapter IX.

5. Years later, when Elliott's *Life of Father Hecker* was appearing as a serial in the *Catholic World,* Walworth's niece, Ellen Walworth, used to read the installments to her uncle month by month. Father Walworth's most frequent comments were first, "That's Hecker's Hecker"; and then, from time to time, as the reading proceeded, "That's Elliott's Hecker." The comments are generally interpreted to mean that Walworth believed Hecker was not so great a man in reality as he was in Elliott's picture. Ellen Walworth, *Life Sketches of Father Walworth.* (Albany, 1907), 155.

6. New York, 1863.

7. Ellen Walworth, *op. cit.,* 149.

Study VIII (Text, pages 119–130)

1. Charles O'Conor, son of an Irish patriot, and himself devoted to the cause of Irish freedom, was the celebrated attorney who defended Jefferson Davis, broke the Tweed Ring, and—despite his refusal—was nominated for the office of president of the United States by the anti-Greeley Democratic convention in Louisiana in 1872. His gift to the Paulist Fathers of a tract of land on French Mountain, Lake George, for a summer home was a great boon to the community; and the donor is commemorated in a tablet on the wall of the house there. The Fathers built a little village church which stands near the terminus of the railroad at Lake George.

2. See Proceedings of the Board of Aldermen, vol. 79, 7, September 3, 1860. The famous draft riots of July 1863, caused widespread excitement and many deaths. The most serious incidents occurred in quarters distant from the Paulist church; but the mobs that gathered near Central Park before moving south and east, contributed their share of violence and bloodshed. The story may be read in detail in Joel Tyler Headley's *The Great Riots of New York.* (New York, 1873.)

3. The northern boundary of the parish moved down to 65th Street, when the Church of the Blessed Sacrament was founded on West 71st Street—an event which Father George

Searle, then acting superior, welcomed as a diminishing of territory and a lightening of burdens. Among the fine dwellings erected in former parish territory, none was quite so famous as Charles M. Schwab's French château, where in later years, the Paulist Choristers sang on special occasions —such as the reception given to Marshal Ferdinand Foch. When eventually the unsightly tracks of the New York Central Railroad were covered and landscaped, the old western boundary of the parish became a beautiful shoreline.

4. The builder of these houses, Buddenseik, already notorious for crooked work in the construction of tenements on the lower east side, was convicted of manslaughter and sent to Sing Sing for ten years.

5. John Talbot Smith, *op. cit.* II, 350.

6. James Kent Stone, born in Boston in 1840, son of the Episcopal rector of Christ's Church, Brooklyn, grandson of Chancellor Kent of New York, was educated at Harvard, studied two years in Germany, and became president of Kenyon College, Ohio. After having been ordained in the Protestant Episcopal Church, he was made president of Hobart College, Geneva, New York, in 1868. He became a convert in 1869, entered the Paulist Congregation and was ordained in 1872. He left the Paulists and took vows as a Passionist in 1877.

Francis Aloysius Spencer, born in 1845, son of an Episcopal clergyman, became a convert in 1866, joined the Paulists and was ordained in 1869. In 1871 he entered the Dominican Order.

7. (Buffalo, 1883.)

Study IX (Text, pages 131–153)

1. Robert Beverly Tillotson—having been prevented by illness from joining earlier—entered Newman's Oratory on August 14, 1852, and was ordained in September, 1856. Under date of February 2, 1860, the Oratory records state:

Whereas Fr. Robert Tillotson last Sept. 9th asked leave of absence from the Congregation in order to visit his father in the State of New York, and leave was granted him for that purpose up to Christmas day next following, according to the paper in his handwriting still posted in the Congregation Room, and whereas he wrote to us on October 25 to say that he did not mean to return, as he had offered himself as a subject to a religious community in his own country, and asked his release from this Congregation, and then, on our prolonging his leave of absence to this day of Purification, in order to his reconsidering his determination, wrote again to say in stronger terms that he has left this House forever; and whereas the Purification has come and he has not returned, we taking the whole case into consideration, hereby decree unanimously that he is no longer a member of the Congregation.

Decreed also unanimously that the Secretary shall send to Fr. Robert Tillotson the foregoing Decree.

Through the kindness of Father Henry Tristram of the Birmingham Oratory a transcript of the foregoing Decree is in the Archives of the Paulist Fathers.

2. Father Elliott wrote:

On the thirty-first of August, 1868, the present writer presented himself at St. Paul's, New York, for entrance into the Novitiate. I had already arranged, by letter, with Father Hecker to join the Community. This was a Monday morning; and as I entered the door, Father Hecker came in immediately after, having been absent over Sunday. Shaking hands with me, he pointed to a parlor, bade me welcome, and said to Mr. Patrick Clark, who was our clerk at that time, that he should call Father Deshon to attend to me, and immediately added, 'Mr. Clark, how is Father Robert?' Mr. Clark answered 'Very low, he passed a bad night.' Father Hecker immediately went up to Father Tillotson's room. Father Tillotson died that day. Meantime my brother James was with me in New York, and Father Deshon allowed me to spend the day with him, seeing the sights of the great city. Next day I was regularly enrolled in the Novitiate. The following Thursday Father Tillotson was buried. Father Hewit preached the funeral sermon. It was the first sermon I ever heard in our Church. It was my first appearance in our Sanctuary. I borrowed a habit from one of the novices and listened to that sermon with emotion altogether indescribable. There was Father Tillotson in his coffin, emaciated almost to a skeleton. That sermon was a masterpiece, exceedingly simple, but brimming full of emotion far beyond anyone's power to express. The Sunday after that I listened to another sermon at the High Mass on the same topic, preached by Father Deshon. He repeated nothing that Father Hewit had said but added many details of the character and incidents, making with Father Hewit's sermon a sort of biographical sketch of Father Tillotson giving altogether a sort of memorial biography. He told of his preaching that after the death of Father Baker, three years before, it was

NOTES FOR PART II

the favorite preaching among the people of the parish. He spoke of his undertaking to join in Mission work, and of his failure to do so at all extensively, on account of his feeble health. Then he told of his beautiful qualities as a Father Confessor, how patient, sympathetic, wise and well informed in guiding souls. He spoke again of his attendance upon the sick, for whom his sympathies were profoundly moved, being himself never a well man. He was also described in his convertmaking, his private interviews with inquirers, his wisdom, prudence, persistent zeal and uniform success. It is a sad thing that none of his family, or relatives even distant ones, entered the Church. The family was of the old New York Beverlys, staunch Episcopalians.

Among the Paulist sermons published in early days by the Appletons in several volumes, Father Tillotson's rank on a footing of entire equality from all points of view, with those of the other Paulists, Fathers Hecker, Walworth, Hewit, Deshon and Baker. I remember vividly that at the entrance to our Community Oratory there was a picture of St. Philip Neri, an engraving of an original portrait, and at the base of it was a spiritual motto of St. Philip signed with Father Tillotson's initials, R.B.T. He had brought this as a sort of Oratorian relic when he left the English Oratorians and joined our Community. See PFA, Hecker Papers, memorandum by Elliott.

3. Alfred Young, in the *Catholic World*, XLVI (December, 1887), 321.
4. New York, 1895.
5. William and Mary Lamers of Milwaukee, Wis., are writing a life of General Rosecrans, rebutting charges against him. On his maternal ancestors, see Timothy Hopkins, *John Hopkins of Cambridge* (San Francisco, 1932).
6. PFA, Rosecrans Papers.
7. George Searle, *Elements of Geometry* (Wiley, publisher 1877).
8. George Searle, *Plain Facts for Fair Minds* (New York, 1895); *How to Become a Catholic* (New York, 1905).
9. The *Confederate Veteran*, II (September 1903), 416.

FATHER HECKER AND HIS FRIENDS

Study X (Text, pages 154–168)

1. PFA, Hecker Papers.
2. Elliott, *op. cit.*, 341.
3. *op. cit.*, 344.
4. The first of these two sermons was published in the *Catholic World*, X (December, 1869), 289; the other, in the third volume of the series entitled *Paulist Sermons* (New York, 1865).
5. PFA, Hecker Papers.
6. Elliott, *op. cit.*, xiv.
7. Proceedings of the Catholic Total Abstinence Union in America XII (1882), 31, quoted by Sister Joan Bland, *Hibernian Crusade; The Story of the Catholic Total Abstinence Union of America* (Washington, 1951), 107.
8. Elliott, *op. cit.*, 348 f. A memorandum of Hecker's on the possibilities of the press outlines what may be called his vision: numbers of Catholic men and women finding their vocation as printers, typesetters, illustrators; the Church recognizing this vocation; work in the printing house sanctified in our days, as the work of copyists was in a former age; agricultural laborers organized in religious congregations. Why could the spirit of self sacrifice not be turned into these channels, so that men and women would set type, run presses, publish and illustrate daily and weekly papers? PFA, Hecker mss.
9. Elliott, *op. cit.*, 349.
10. Robert Gorman, *Catholic Apologetical Literature in the United States (1784–1858)*. (Washington, D.C., 1939), 146.
11. PFA, Hecker Papers.
12. Among Catholic enterprises which failed were: *The United States Catholic Monthly Magazine,* founded in 1843, and after six years converted into a Catholic weekly paper; Brownson's *Quarterly Review*, founded in 1844, which suspended publication after twenty years; the *Metropolitan of Baltimore*—alone in its field during its short life, from 1857 to 1859. The situation is well described by Father Richard Walsh, C.S.P. in his "Father Hecker and the Catholic Press," an unpublished master's thesis at the Catholic University of America (1945).
13. *op. cit.*, 99.

14. Elliott, *op. cit.*, xv.
15. *A History of the Councils of Baltimore, 1791–1884.* (New York, 1932), 219.
16. *op. cit.*, 121.

STUDY XI (Text, pages 169–187)

1. Isaac T. Hecker, *The Church and the Age: An Exposition of the Catholic Church in View of the Needs and Aspirations of the Present Age.* (New York, 1887), 33 ff. This volume is the principal source of the quotations that appear in Study XI.
2. *op. cit.*, 96 ff.
3. Paris, 1949.
4. "Father Hecker, Founder of the Paulists," in the *Dublin Review,* (July, 1892). Reprinted in pamphlet form by the Paulist Press, New York, 71 f.
5. Introduction to Elliott's *Life of Father Hecker,* xi.

PART III
The Latter Nineteenth Century

XII. THE AMERICAN SCENE
XIII. HECKER AND BROWNSON
XIV. HECKER AND ELLIOTT
XV. HEWIT, GLORIFIED YANKEE
XVI. DESHON, THE WEST POINTER

XII

The American Scene

(Notes, p. 289)

THE office of superior general was held by Father Hewit from 1889 to 1897; and by Father Deshon from 1897 until 1903. But Hewit, as vicar, had been in charge of the community during Hecker's frequent absences and protracted illness; and Deshon had been vicar under Hewit. So the last two of the founders had a large share of the government of the Paulists during the closing decades of the nineteenth century.

In this period the United States came to be recognized as a global power of the first rank; and the world began to appreciate the enormous resources and the unique vitality of American Catholicism which at the end of the century had nearly twelve million people, about 12,000 priests, and over eighty sees. Unhappily, our nation did not make the best use of its opportunities, political and religious. Forgetting the need of eternal vigilance, neglecting to set proper qualifications for citizenship, we permitted our old pioneer traditions of individual liberty to lapse; and we allowed secularism to dominate education. These were dangers against which Hecker had repeatedly warned the country; and the history of the twentieth century would later show how correctly he had forecast the future when he affirmed that America's chances of a happy maturity would be proportioned to America's acceptance of Catholic principles.

Hecker labored valiantly to spread the vital truths taught by the Catholic Church in the hope that his fellow citizens would assimilate them within a reasonably short time. Knowing that it would not be possible to convert America unless the Catholic people as a whole co-operated energetically, he kept urging the use of every means available—platform, pulpit, printing press, organized distribution of magazines and books and tracts through nationwide organizations, directed by competent, zealous men.

This campaign never quite achieved the expected success, partly because the bishops were harassed by so many other demands upon their resources, and partly because they did not attain the unity of purpose and the concentration of effort indispensable for victory. Unfortunately for both Church and nation, the hierarchy was divided on various issues, educational, political, even theological. At times the factions overlapped, so that in a new dispute an individual prelate would become the ally of a former antagonist. Thus, for example, in the German vs. Irish controversy, Archbishop Michael A. Corrigan of New York was on the same side as Archbishop Ireland of St. Paul; whereas in the dispute about fitting state schools into the Catholic educational system the two prelates were on opposite sides.

The sympathetic appreciation of the American way of life characteristic of Hecker and his associates was shared whole-heartedly by some bishops, not so whole-heartedly by others. Generally speaking, Gibbons, Ireland and John J. Keane were on the same side as the Paulists—a position not wholly free of embarrassment when the Archbishop of New York was on the other side. This was illustrated by Bishop Bernard J. McQuaid's message to Archbishop Corrigan during the controversy over Americanism, that the Paulists "should not be made scapegoats to cover up Ireland, Keane and Co." [1] It was illustrated too, by Corrigan's saying to Elliott in the course of the same controversy, that the main disagreement between the Paulists and himself was due to their connection with Ireland and Keane; "If you will repudiate them all will go well." [2]

In the secular field, individual Paulists, like other good citizens, supported various policies—even during the era when in New York many persons thought that every Catholic ought to be a Democrat. The present writer remembers his amazement when in the nineties, he heard that Father Elliott was "actually a Republican!"

Imagine the resentment then, when in 1894 Archbishop Ireland invaded the East to speak publicly in favor of the Republican Party. Archbishop Corrigan sent an indignant protest to Cardinal Gibbons; Bishop McQuaid, in his own cathedral of Rochester, declared that Archbishop Ireland "deserved a rebuke as public as the offense committed." The apostolic delegate took notice of the situation and Mariano Cardinal Rampolla, papal Secretary of State, addressed a reproof to Bishop McQuaid; and at the same time the Congregation of Propaganda commissioned Archbishop Corrigan to attempt to reconcile the disputants.[3]

Here it may be mentioned that the (Republican) commissioner of police in New York, Theodore Roosevelt, developed a great respect for the Paulist Fathers and carried it with him to the White House, where as president he repeatedly demonstrated his friendship for Father Alexander Doyle. Doyle, by the way, described the boyish glee of Roosevelt when told that his victorious splitting of the Catholic vote at the presidential election of 1904 took place "on the vigil of the feast of St. Theodore, Soldier."

A comparatively unnoticed but really significant feature of the period under consideration was the strong emotional current set in motion by the Catholic Total Abstinence Union. In this movement, Ireland, Keane, Spalding were on the same side as the Paulists, with Corrigan, McQuaid, several of the German bishops and at least one religious order on the other. Intense excitement was aroused by the declaration of Ireland and Spalding that the evils involved in cheap saloons and excessive drinking—particularly widespread among the Irish—should be checked by legal restraints, such as local option, high license or even prohibition. This deviation from the original policy of using only moral suasion was partly responsible for alienating the conservative Archbishop of New York.

An exciting dispute concerned the brewery operated by the Benedictine monastery at Latrobe. The historian of the movement writes, "It was not unusual for the temperance prelates changing trains at the railroad station to be grieved by the sight of beer barrels plainly marked, 'St. Vincent's.'" Bishop Michael O'Connor of Pittsburgh had objected to the brewery in vain, since the community had the necessary permission from Rome; and Archbishop Elder and Bishops Keane, Spalding and Richard Gilmour, who tried to have the permission withdrawn, were opposed by Bishops Joseph Dwenger of Fort Wayne and Francis S. Chatard of Vincennes.

Another clashing of views occurred when the C.T.U. of A. in a friendly gesture to the Women's Christian Temperance Union—an organization regarded by many Catholics as fanatical—made the celebrated Frances Willard a fraternal delegate at the convention of 1891.

The relationship between the promoters of total abstinence and the Catholic University of America, was emphasized by the Union's gift of $50,000. to endow the Father Mathew Chair. But, we are told "It is altogether possible that the University lost almost as much as it gained by the support of the Temperance people. Opposition of the German Catholics which plagued the institution for many years, was certainly augmented by this, to them, ridiculous project for the furtherance of temperance."

The temperance movement reached its peak at the New York convention of 1895, organized by the Paulist Father Alexander Doyle, and skilfully steered by the president of the Union, Father James M. Cleary, who had moved from the jurisdiction of Archbishop Frederick X. Katzer of Milwaukee to that of Archbishop Ireland in St. Paul, with the common agreement of all concerned. The convention made a profound impression upon the public. The New York *Times* and the New York *Evening Post* commented at length on the revolution in the political sentiment of Catholics, now in large numbers throwing their weight on the side of temperance and ready at election time to vote in favor of reform, irrespective of political platforms.[4]

Another episode in the tangled background of those years was the dispute which was occasioned by Archbishop Ireland's plan of leasing parish schools to the state, which paid the salary of the nuns teaching therein—known as the Faribault plan. Dr. Thomas Bouquillon, professor of moral theology at the Catholic University of America, wrote in defense of Ireland's plan, crossing swords with Father René I. Holaind, S.J. The quarrel raged until the Holy See terminated it in 1893 by means of the celebrated decision *Tolerari potest* (May 31, 1893) which both sides claimed as a vindication.

Thus the various controversies of the time developed antagonisms among the bishops on several points: the relations of Church and State; the preference for American over European customs; the limits of lawful co-operation with non-Catholics.

Omens of trouble multiplied. Archbishop Francesco Satolli, the apostolic delegate, began to show less sympathy for the progressive and more sympathy for the conservative ecclesiastics. In 1895 he published a letter from the Holy Father, written on September 18, 1895, disapproving of the participation of Catholics in Congresses of religion—an obvious reference to Bishop Keane's activity at the Parliament of Religions in Chicago, during the World's Fair two years earlier. However, the letter at the same time commended the practice of the Paulist Fathers in preaching to "dissenting brethren," both to enlighten them on Catholic doctrine and to answer their objections.[5]

Very serious was the "Americanism" controversy. The roots of it ran back to the situation of the Church in France in the late sixties, when French Catholics had begun to study religious conditions in America. The Comte de Chabrol—friend of the great lay apostle, Montalembert—and other writers took up the question of winning for Catholics in France the freedom enjoyed by their co-religionists in the new world. The idea spread that the Latin races had lost their old pre-eminence in religious affairs; that many of their traditional customs were outmoded; that world history was altering its course; that Hecker and his associates were the type of leaders who could affect a highly desirable "peaceful revolution." In 1897 at Chabrol's suggestion, the *Life of Father Hecker* was published in French, with a long enthusiastic preface by the progressive Abbé Félix Klein. Reviewing this book in the *National Review* of March, 1899, Canon William Barry of Dorchester, England, asserted that drastic action must be taken to keep the French Church from being "an ecclesiastical barracks," and the clergy from being serfs of an atheistic republic. Barry gave high praise to Hecker and his methods.

Thus it came about that the figure of Hecker, the Paulist leader, was—soon after his death—converted into a symbol in the bitter struggle that divided the "reactionaries" and the "progressives" of the French Church. The noise of the battling reverberated around the world. The controversy produced abundant literature, notably one book in which Abbé Maignen charged that Hecker was more like a heretic than a saint; and another book, in which Canon Delassus accused members of the American hierarchy of conspiring with Paulists, Freemasons, and Jews to destroy Catholicism and organize the new religion of "Universal Democracy." [6]

It is in the light of these contemporary domestic and foreign quarrels that we must look at the activities of Hecker's two successors during the closing years of the nineteenth century.

XIII

Hecker and Brownson[1]

(Notes, p. 289 ff.)

ORESTES BROWNSON was a many-sided personality—profound thinker, tireless writer, bold and fluent public speaker. The evidence for this is at hand in the twenty volumes of his collected writings; and the verdict of his contemporaries was echoed by the distinguished editor of the *American Catholic Quarterly Review*, Dr. James A. Corcoran, who called Brownson's writings "a rich mine, that will never lose its value for the student of controversial theology, of Christian philosophy, and of Christian politics." The second founder of the French Oratory, Père Auguste Gratry, named Brownson "the keenest critic of the nineteenth century, an indomitable logician, a disinterested lover of the truth, more than a philosopher, a sage, as sharp as Aristotle, as lofty as Plato, the real Newman of America"; and the German Jesuit, Otto Pfulf, classed Brownson as the greatest Catholic in the United States up to the end of the nineteenth century.[2] Tributes like these make us wonder why anyone so gifted, so prolific, so widely recognized, has completely lost the prestige he enjoyed less than a century ago.

The explanation is perhaps to be found, at least partly, in the scrupulous, almost fantastic, honesty which led him to alter his convictions with dismaying frequency and indeed, to trumpet each new conclusion loudly in challenging and sometimes offensive tones. "To one who once asked him how it was that he felt so sure of his final decision, he replied: 'When I was a Presbyterian, or a Universalist, or a Unitarian, or whatever I may have been, I was sure each time that I was right; but now I know that I *cannot* be wrong.'" [3]

Father Wilfrid Parsons, S.J., has thus summarized Brownson's characteristics:

Rarely has a man of his intellectual capacity been so thoroughly inconsistent.... He was fiercely proud, it is true, but he was also abjectly humble; boldly self-confident, and easily discouraged; a great boaster, and as great a self-doubter; selfish and generous, secretive and candid, a rough bear and a meek lamb. Where he felt himself superior, nobody could be more overbearing; where inferiority gnawed at him he was cowed.[4]

But Father Hecker, who knew Brownson longer and more intimately than any other of his friends, offered this not discreditable interpretation: "What native trait of Dr. Brownson marks him off from other men? I answer, Love of truth, devotion to principle. . . . His predominant passion was love of truth. This was all his glory and all his trouble; all his quarrels, friendships, aversions, perplexities, triumphs, labors —all to be traced to love of truth." [5]

* * *

During childhood on a Vermont farm, Brownson received early lessons in religion from Congregationalists; at nineteen he was a Presbyterian; a little later he exchanged the harsh Calvinist teachings for the more liberal Universalist creed and became a minister; then he renounced all belief in revelation and strove to improve social conditions. We find him getting out a new periodical, *The Philanthropist;* serving as a Unitarian clergyman in New Hampshire; publishing *New Views of Christianity, Society and the Church* (Boston, 1836), which was to be "the last word of the non-Catholic world"; organizing the Society for Christian Union and Progress, which was to be a new species of Catholicism; writing *Charles Elwood* (Boston, 1840), a heavy philosophico-religious novel; founding the *Boston Quarterly Review* (January, 1838), to which he contributed most of the material.

When Brownson visited New York to lecture there, he came into close association with the Hecker family and made their house his temporary residence; and between him and young Isaac there developed a strong affection, the older man acting as guide and teacher of the younger. Brought together first in an effort to better the lot of their fellowmen, they found they had other common interests too: a strong love of their native country, with its traditions of liberty and independence; passionate devotion to truth; a longing for spiritual development.

Brownson, who had a great esteem for the young colony of social enthusiasts at Brook Farm, "the most romantic incident of New England Transcendentalism," urged Hecker to go there in 1843; and the historian of Brook Farm reports the colony's reactions to the two men. Hecker "made a favorable impression by reason of his candor and amiability." Brownson, the gifted intellectual, was not popular; for he was disputatious, overbearing, inconsiderate in debate.[6]

Although Brownson married early in life and became the father of eight children, whereas Hecker followed the career of a missionary priest, the friendship between the two men was lifelong. They were intimately associated in their approach to Catholicism, in the planning of the apostolate which led ultimately to the founding of the Paulists, in frequently interlaced activities as writers and editors. The story of their relationship covers three periods: the ten years during which they were groping towards the Church; the twenty years in which Brownson was writing and publishing in Boston and in New York, while Hecker was preparing for the priesthood and then exercising his ministry; the ten years that followed the founding of the *Catholic World* in 1865.

In their pursuit of truth the two men from time to time exchanged the roles of leader and of follower. The phases of their religious growth were later described by Brownson in his book, *The Convert,* and by Hecker in the pages of the *Catholic World*. Each of them finally came to the conclusion that the Catholic Church is divine; and each presented himself to Bishop Fitzpatrick of Boston—Hecker in August, 1844, Brownson two months later. Fitzpatrick referred Hecker to his own bishop in New York, but he took Brownson in hand, instructed him, received him into the Church and began to direct his activity.

A few of Brownson's former friends followed him into the fold; and Father Hewit mentions that he himself was aided in his progress towards the Church by one of Brownson's articles. But, on the whole, Brownson seems to have persuaded very few of the truth of Catholicism. When he set forth on his career as a Catholic writer, he adopted a policy which, as he subsequently affirmed, had been chosen under the influence of Bishop Fitzpatrick. His comparative failure as an apologist was, according to Hecker, due to the fact that he had not used his own native gifts:

He could have cleared away passion, prejudice, ignorance in the minds of his fellow countrymen, especially in New England, and brought them to a decision in a multitude of cases as correct and inevitable as his own. What Dr. Brownson was best able to do he was not called to do enough of. . . . He was switched off the main line of his career, by the influence of Bishop Fitzpatrick, who induced him to enter upon the traditional line of controversy against Protestantism at a time when the best minds of New England had long given up belief in the distinctive errors of that heresy . . . When shortly after my conversion, I went to Europe, all the letters I wrote to him were filled with complaints that he had given up his first principles, or at any rate ignored them. ... It was only years afterwards, when he wrote *The Convert,* one of his greatest works, that he brought them out prominently, and then it was too late for much effect: he had become too closely identified with very different lines of controversy.[7]

Hecker's verdict seems to be confirmed in some measure by Lindsay Swift's description of Brownson as a forgotten man, who at one time had

> stood between contending forces a seemingly powerful figure. But against the subtle individualism of the Protestant mind he contended with singularly little result. So doughty a champion probably inspired his new friends [Catholics] with a measure of dismay, while it may fairly be doubted if he ever succeeded in winning a notable convert to his own way of thinking. In this respect the contrast between him and Father Hecker is striking.[8]

At the time of his conversion, Brownson was editor of his own magazine and a public figure of more than ordinary importance.[9] He planned at first to discontinue the *Review,* but Bishop Fitzpatrick persuaded him to retain it; for he saw in Brownson a powerful champion, and in the *Review* a promising weapon, for the fight in behalf of the Church. So he conducted the new convert through a systematic study of Catholic theology and then sent him forth to carry the war into Protestant territory and give battle to anti-Catholic writers. For ten years Brownson crusaded under Fitzpatrick's guidance.[10]

Trained to avoid novelty, not only in doctrine but even in the method of teaching and defending truth, Brownson went to extremes—aggressive both in the form and in the substance of his argumentation, and stirring up resentment among converts to the faith as well as those outside the fold. In a forty-page review of a book by John B. Morris, an Oxford convert,[11] he made this sweeping statement:

> Works written in a proper spirit against Protestants, for the purpose of showing them the utter untenableness of any form of Protestantism, cannot be reasonably objected to; but works written for Protestants, for the purpose of vindicating to them particular dogmas or practices of our church, can hardly be of much use. . . . Our proper method is to attack, and compel them to act on the defensive. . . . There is no Catholic dogma, taken apart from the authority of the Church, that is defensible.

Brownson spoke often of John Henry Newman as "a man of a sharp rather than a broad and comprehensive intellect. He has little faculty of grasping a subject in its unity and integrity, and he never masters a subject by first seizing it in its central principles and thence descending to its several details. . . . Whenever he attempts to mold his particular views into a systematic whole, he becomes confused, obscure, vague, and vacillating." As summarized by Henry Brownson, his son, the indictments charge Newman with teaching "that the infallibility of the Church is only probably established"; "that Christianity is a matter of opinion"; "that infallibility resides in the Church believing, not in the Church teaching"; "that Christian doctrine is an idea which the mind forms of truth." By way of climax comes the charge that Newman's theory "is a denial of all Christian doctrine."

Newman, said Brownson, suffers "from the common complaint of his whole school."

In reviewing a book by Rev. J. M. Capes,[12] "a Minister of the Anglican Establishment," who was received into the Church some five or six years earlier, Brownson said, "We have, unhappily, been forced to find fault with nearly all the works that have reached us from the Oxford converts." "Mr. Faber is the only one of the converts we are aware of having seen, whom we have had no occasion to criticize." Elsewhere Brownson wrote "We cannot expect that all we have said will be acceptable to the Oxford converts and their friends . . . but in reality we believe the writings of the school in question are doing great harm even in England." [13]

Theodore Maynard, after having quoted some rough sentences, declared that, in effect, Brownson's message to those outside the faith was: "This is what the Church holds. I will now demonstrate it so clearly that even your thick wits will be able to grasp it. But if you do not accept it to the last iota, you must understand that you are headed straight for hell." [14] We are not surprised to find Hecker passing this judgment on Brownson's method: "He defeats, but will never convince an opponent."

Nevertheless, Hecker's first book, *Questions of the Soul*, won high praise from Brownson who, in his *Review* (April, 1855), called it a remarkable work which "could have been written only by an American, 'to the manner born,' and is destined, in our judgment, to have a marked influence on American thought and American literature." He spoke of the author as one "to whom Almighty God has given a mission of vital importance to our country. Few men really know him, few even suspect what is in him; but no one can commune with him for half an hour and ever be again precisely what he was before." Brownson went on praising Hecker at length and speaking of their partnership in the search for truth. He added that the author "has done what we ourselves have often attempted to do, and would have done had Almighty God given us the genius and ability to do it. We can now throw the manuscript of our partially completed work on the same subject into the fire."

* * *

In 1855 Brownson began to consider the advisability of moving from Boston to New York and his friends there encouraged him. After discussing the matter with Archbishop Hughes, Father Hecker reported to Brownson that the archbishop "would be quite pleased at your coming, and said that if I wrote I should tell you so." [15] As soon as work on the October issue of the *Review* was completed, Brownson and his family moved to New York where he published his magazine for the next nine years.

To this period, says Henry Brownson, "we owe the profoundest and sublimest of his writings." He attributes the new tone of his father's work to association with friends of broader views. The first New York issue of the *Review* announced a change in its general character and undertook to mollify one group of critics by explaining that the editor's protest against regarding the Catholic Church as an Irish institution had been motivated not by dislike of the Irish but by a desire to let Americans realize they could embrace the Catholic religion without becoming Irishmen.

In New York Brownson had an enthusiastic following among the clergy and the laity. One of his best friends was Dr. Jeremiah Cummings, the scholarly pastor of St. Stephen's, who had earlier helped to arrange Brownson's lectures in New York. Another friend was Dr. John McCaffrey, president of Mount Saint Mary's College, Emmitsburg. Brownson's lectures in the Broadway Tabernacle and in the Academy of Music drew enormous crowds. Men like Charles O'Conor, the distinguished lawyer, saw in him the type of representative needed by the Church —"courteous but firm"; and he was recognized as the leader of Catholic controversialists. His friends in the hierarchy included Bishops Bayley of Newark, Martin J. Spalding of Louisville, and Archbishop Francis Patrick Kenrick of Baltimore. In September, 1857, he published *The Convert,* the story of "my entire religious life from my earliest recollection down to my admission to the bosom of the Catholic

Church." According to a student of the period, by the late fifties everybody in the United States knew the name of Orestes Brownson.

Invitations to lecture poured in from Savannah, Charleston, St. Louis, Chicago, and other cities. At the end of one tour he gathered his ideas into an article, "The Church and the Republic" or, "The Church Necessary to the Republic and the Republic Compatible to the Church." When it appeared in March, Judge George H. Hilton of Cincinnati wrote "I would be glad to see this lecture published in cheap pamphlet form for universal distribution throughout the length of the Republic." Hewit, when planning a lecture on the papacy, submitted an outline of the proposed address to Brownson and asked for suggestions. On March 17, 1856, Brownson answered "My own conviction is that our true policy in dealing with the American mind is to study first to ascertain, not its errors, but the truth it still maintains, and to show it that truth can find its unity and its integrity only in the Catholic Church. . . . I think Father Hecker has the right view on this subject, and after his, the next best is Father Walworth's, that of direct appeal to conscience. My own method, I believe, is the worst of all, that of logic." All this indicated a change from Brownson's previous approach to controversial problems.

On April 12, 1856, Hecker wrote from Richmond to express his joy at the news of Brownson's success on the platform: "You stand before our people as an

American, and the champion of Catholicity. The reconciliation which has taken place in your own heart between these is to take place also in the nation." Hecker then described the tentative "mission to non-Catholics" which he and Hewit had just given at Norfolk; spoke of his own lecture on "Popular Objections against Catholicity"; and added "F. Walworth was present. He was delighted and declared it was the best lecture he had heard in the U.S."

Archbishop Hughes, pleased to have so conspicuous a figure in his archdiocese, had greeted Brownson most cordially at his coming. But before long the two men began to feel ill at ease with each other. Brownson believed that Hughes was not playing fair. Hughes publicly found fault with several opinions that Brownson held, notably with his views on the shortcomings of the Irish in the United States, and on the relationship between Church and State. Years later, Brownson wrote: "The archbishop once said to us 'I will suffer no man in my diocese that I cannot control. I will either put him down or he shall put me down.' " [16]

In the summer of 1856, at the commencement exercises of St. John's College, Fordham, the archbishop made objections to parts of the address which Brownson had just delivered; and the incident was played up in Thomas Darcy McGee's newspaper, the *American Celt*. Thereupon the archbishop wrote to Brownson to say that he had never deliberately uttered a word or entertained a thought disrespectful to him;

but he did wish to submit respectfully, three points for consideration, namely that Brownson should (1) avoid every censorious allusion to the nationality of any of our Catholic brethren; (2) avoid writing or saying anything calculated to represent Catholic religion as especially adapted to the genius of the American people as such; (3) avoid noticing or resenting unkind articles in small Catholic papers.

Brownson answered promptly,

> I never for one moment entertained the thought that you intended in your remarks at Fordham anything unkind or disrespectful to me personally. But I was surprised to hear you make those objections in public to my address, after having just assured me they were only for my private ear. I regretted that, as I had said nothing against faith or morals or which I had not as a Catholic and an American citizen a perfect right to say, you should have felt it your duty to oppose me thus strenuously in public. It was taking an unfair advantage of me. It was opposing to me, a layman, the opinions of an archbishop and that archbishop, of New York. There was no equality in the case. It was crushing me with the weight of authority, in a matter of simple opinion. You must not blame me, if I did feel that I was hardly treated, and an ungenerous advantage given to my enemies over me. You and I cannot debate a question on equal terms before the public, for you cannot address the public in your own name against me without opposing to me the mitre. Your remarks, however intended by you, were an episcopal censure upon me, and I can see no reason why the American Celt had not the right so to consider them.

In reply Hughes formally repeated his disavowal—he had never said anything "ironical or disrespectful to Brownson."

A month later, in an article "Mission of America," Brownson gave serious displeasure to the archbishop by saying "If Catholics choose to separate themselves from the great current of American nationality, and to assume the position in political and social life of an inferior, a distinct, or an alien people, or of a foreign colony planted in the midst of a people with whom they have no sympathies, they will be permitted to do so, and will be treated by the country at large according to their own estimates of themselves." He then referred to young men as the hope of the future, and said "O, for the love of God and man, do not discourage them, force them to be mute and inactive, or suffer them, in the name of Catholicity to separate themselves in their affections, from the country and her glorious mission. Let them feel and act as American citizens; let them feel that this country is their country, its institutions their institutions, its mission their mission, its glory their glory." [17]

Hewit told Brownson on October 13, 1856, "I cannot refrain from writing to express my delight and heart-felt thanks for the article on the 'Mission of America. . . . I look forward to the conversion of a vast number of the best part of our American fellow-citizens with confidence, and I see in such movements as the one in which you are taking so distinguished a part, the beginning of this great work. I even hope for the conversion of the nation as such, though not so confidently. And if God spares my life, I wish to devote it and all my energies to this noble end of the conversion of America. I trust Almighty God will soon give to the American Redemptorists the opportunity of acting more directly on the American people and laboring for their conversion."

Archbishop Hughes, far from sharing Father Hewit's enthusiasm, published "Reflections and Suggestions in regard to what is called the Catholic Press in the United States." [18] After praising Brownson, he drew attention to three of his defects: first, that he was too hopeful of America's conversion; second, that he thought the progress of the Church in this country would be greater when immigration should cease, or at least sensibly diminish; third, that his appeal in behalf of young men was uncalled for.

Answering the archbishop, Brownson defended his right to publish his opinion on such matters as those under discussion, and declared that authority had no right to inflict censure unless for offenses against faith, morals and discipline. He continued "If the bishop or archbishop who judges in the first instance does us wrong, our remedy is not in disobedience, resistance, or public discussion, but in appeal to Rome, to the highest tribunal of the Church. The law that governs journalists is, we take it, the same law that governs Catholics in all lawful secular pursuits." [19]

Another source of disturbance was Brownson's connection with a club, composed of priests and laymen, who were agitating against the "europeanizing" of American students in Catholic colleges and seminaries. Brownson, himself, never joined the club, but his intimate friends, Dr. Jeremiah Cummings and Dr. Ambrose Manahan, were active in it; and Brownson's *Review* (1858–1859) devoted more than 260 pages to "Conversations of Our Club," a serial, which seemed to echo actual discussions—discussions presenting more than one opinion unacceptable to the archbishop. The series aimed to prove that in this country "we can be devout Catholics and at the same time enlightened and unflinching friends of both civil and religious liberty, even in the American sense of the terms." [20]

Then there was the case of the convert pastor of St. Ann's, Dr. Forbes, who in 1859, abandoned the Catholic Church and returned to the Episcopal ministry. Upon hearing news of this, Brownson wrote the archbishop a letter of condolence and added an expression of regret for having perhaps made Archbishop Hughes' burden heavier by things he himself had said or written. In replying on November 2, 1859, Hughes conveyed his thanks and said that Brownson's letter was more than sufficient reparation for anything he might have said at any time against the archbishop; and he added "The fall of Dr. Forbes was the heaviest blow that was ever inflicted on my heart." [21]

Brownson regarded the dwindling of his subscriptions about this time as due in large measure to the archbishop's attitude. Financial loss was, however, more than balanced by highly successful lectures, one of which, delivered in the Academy of Music, netted over a thousand dollars. Yet some two years later,

Brownson decided to move to New Jersey, partly in order to reduce his living expenses, partly to be a little farther away from Hughes, and partly to have a better opportunity to cultivate his friendship with Bishop Bayley.

During the period when Hecker and his companions were pressing for the establishment of an English-speaking Redemptorist house, Brownson was in close touch with them; and—as already narrated in the present volume—he gave Hecker a letter of recommendation to carry to Rome. They kept in communication with each other, and the news of Hecker's dismissal reached Brownson even before it reached the American Fathers.[22] Brownson sent a characteristic reply, saying that "No American Catholic who cares for the interest of religion will acquiesce in his [the General's] course."

It was after Hecker's dismissal and while he was still in Rome that Brownson reviewed *Aspirations of Nature*. He called the book a model of controversial writing and one of the most important contributions ever made by a native-born Catholic. He praised the independent thought, the broad and deep views, the enthusiasm of the author, who "had demolished forever the claims of modern Protestantism to be the friend of reason." Then came reservations. The reviewer disassociated himself from the school of theologians followed by the author, commented on the author's lack of technical precision, spoke of the risk he ran of seeming to assign to reason and to nature more than belonged to them. Much more dangerous criticism would have been made, but for the intervention of Father Deshon, who visited Brownson before the article went to press and persuaded him to revise and amend certain statements.[23]

Hecker showed his disappointment in a letter dated October 24, 1857, saying it was most unfortunate that Brownson's criticisms had been published at this particular moment.

About this same time Hecker spoke of having Brownson's pamphlet, *Mission of America,* translated into Italian; but on second thought he decided he could handle the situation better by writing an article with his own hand and getting it published in the *Civiltà Cattolica.*

For Brownson, 1861 was a distressing year. At the Fordham commencement he had another most unpleasant encounter with Archbishop Hughes, who pointed some critical remarks at him immediately after the doctor had given the address to the graduates. When Brownson rose to defend himself, he was told to sit down, and he obeyed. His advocacy of abolition also created antagonism in various quarters. One old admirer, a Jesuit Father, declared that Brownson's admirable passages were mixed up with statements "that grate terribly on the ears of friends." Some persons criticized his views on the temporal power of the pope; others found fault with his idea of eternal punishment. His friend, Dr. Cummings, told him "there are parties at work to injure you with the authorities at Rome." However, to official inquiries sent from the Propaganda, Archbishop Hughes replied that he entertained not the least doubt of Brownson's orthodoxy.

Brownson's burdens increased. Two of his sons and his brother died during the Civil War. Illness, financial trouble, mental depression made it necessary to suspend publication of the *Review* in 1864. Friends who discussed the possibility of financing a revival reached the conclusion that they could help Brownson more effectively by raising an annuity. Hecker took charge of the project which brought Brownson an income of $1,000. per annum for life.

* * *

When the *Catholic World* made its appearance in the following April, 1865, Brownson became a major contributor. He wrote for practically every issue, gave the new magazine weight and value and came into close, but not always pleasant, contact with Hecker and Hewit. Frequent misunderstandings occurred. In addition to the normal friction between a sensitive writer and his editor, there were particular circumstances which caused conflict. The *Catholic World,* having begun as principally a vehicle for translations and reprints, had adopted the practice of attaching no signatures to its few original articles; and this policy was continued even after the magazine was almost entirely filled with original contributions. Hecker's refusal to change the editorial policy angered Brownson who was under attack from many quarters and badly needed the prestige that he would acquire if allowed to sign the splendid essays which he was consistently producing. Brownson had grievances against Hewit too. Priding himself both on his orthodoxy and on his mastery of English style, he resented alterations of his manuscripts, whether the alleged motive was prudence or clarity; and his correspondence with the office in these days reveals annoyance which is made even clearer in his letters to his son. There were also disputes over technical matters of theology: the soul's first idea of God; the relation between nature and grace; the possibility of salvation for those not in visible communion with the Church.

In addition to writing for the *Catholic World,* which cost him, he said, more time than the *Quarterly* ever did, Brownson had also the task of editing the Catholic weekly, *The Tablet.* Burdened with the weight of years, and illness, and depression over financial problems and family debts, he experienced increasing bitterness. His visits to the Paulist house involved stormy debates. In June, 1866, he suggested to his son, an officer in the army, the idea of reviving the *Quarterly* if the son would edit it; but this was relinquished as an impossible plan.

The next year, after Hecker returned from Europe, Brownson said "He has improved . . . I trust we will be able to jog again together without much mutual snarling and growling." There were soon new disturbances however; for in February, 1868, he wrote to Henry "Father Hecker and I have had a fight, but it is over. It grew out of his rejecting one article, and mutilating another, because my views conflicted with some views on original sin, published by Father Hewit in *The Problems of the Age*. . . . As I expressed my view in the words of the Council of Trent, I trusted it would pass. But no, Father Hewit might contradict the Council of Trent, but nobody in the Catholic World must contradict Father Hewit, whose orthodoxy on more than one point is more than suspected. But after firing off several letters at Father Hecker I feel better. . . . Father Hecker was sick for a week from the scolding I gave him, and we're good friends again."

A little later we find him complaining to his son, "Father Hewit holds that Protestants may be saved by invincible ignorance. . . . Father Hecker agrees with him." Brownson kept returning to the idea of separating from the *Catholic World* and Hecker kept urging him not to abandon a field where he was doing so much good for which he was praised on all sides.

A really serious outbreak came at the close of 1871. Writing to his son (January 17, 1872) Brownson says "I have broken off my connection with the C.W. The immediate occasion of my doing it was the rejection of my article on Ontologism and Ontology, and another on Reason and Revelation. Both my theology and philosophy being under the ban of the C.W. I thought it best to have nothing more to do with it, and leave the Paulists to themselves. I shall hereafter devote my time to the Tablet and the preparation of my contemplated works." Hecker continued his efforts to dissuade Brownson from breaking away but in vain.[24] In March Brownson wrote to his son, "I have finally resolved to revive my review." [25] He was doing this, he said, because it was in accord with one of the last requests of his wife who had just died, and also because he wished to set himself right before the Catholic public and vindicate his honor as a loyal though unworthy son of the Church.

The first issue of the new *Review* appeared January, 1873; and the response was more favorable than Brownson had anticipated. Archbishops McCloskey and Bayley wrote warmly encouraging letters; but the burden proved too heavy. The *Review* closed in October, 1875; and Brownson moved to his son's house in Detroit. He wrote one more article for the *American Catholic Quarterly Review*—intended to be the first of a series; but he died in April, 1876, at the age of seventy-two. When news of Brownson's death came, Hecker wrote at once to Henry Brownson, saying "I owe more perhaps to your father than to any other man in my early life. My friendship and sense of gratitude to him has never been affected by any event during the last forty years."

Father Hewit stated in the *Catholic World* of April, 1876:

"The lion is dead; his thunderous voice is forever hushed. The farewell utterance which closed his career as an editor with so much dignity and pathos was his valedictory to life and to the world. It is pleasant to think that, before he died, a response full of veneration and affection came back to him from the organs of Catholic opinion and feeling in America and Europe, and that he has gone to his grave in honor and peace, where his works will be his monument, and his repose be asked for by countless prayers offered up throughout all parts of the Catholic Church, in whose battles he had been a tried warrior and valiant leader for thirty years."

Some ten years later, Father Hecker wrote a series of studies in the *Catholic World* on Brownson's character and career, making clear his lasting affection and profound respect for the man of towering intellect who had been also the oldest and most famous of his friends. Said Hecker: "Heartily, deeply did I ever reciprocate Dr. Brownson's affection, and the long and eventful years have but strengthened more and more my love for him and my admiration for his genius—my feeble attempt to estimate his providential mission and to introduce my countrymen to the study of his works." He quoted from *The Convert* these words of Brownson: "I had one principle, and only one, to which since throwing up Universalism I had been faithful, a principle for which I had perhaps made some sacrifices—that of following my own honest convictions whithersoever they should lead me." Hecker added, "This sentence should be put on his monument."

XIV

Hecker and Elliott

(Notes, p. 294 f.)

NO one of the Paulists now living came under Father Hecker's immediate influence. By way of compensation however, many had personal contact with Father Elliott, a highly forceful individual in his own right, but also an embodiment of Hecker's spirit. It was fortunate for this new generation of Paulists to have the opportunity to learn from Elliott; as indeed, it had been fortunate for Hecker to have so extraordinary a man as Elliott for his beloved companion and faithful disciple. Hecker once said it was difficult to set limits to what might be achieved by twelve men filled with the love of God and working together; and he may have been thinking of deeds that could be done if he had under his own leadership a dozen men of Elliott's type. But men of Elliott's type do not come by the dozen.

Born in Detroit on the Feast of the Epiphany, 1842, four months after his father's death, Walter Elliott was the seventh son and ninth child of Robert Elliott and his wife, immigrants to the United States from Tipperary, by way of Canada. He went to a school conducted by the Christian Brothers, and then to Notre Dame for three years. Here he seems to have been interested chiefly in music, playing in the band and singing in the choir; and a letter of his written many years later recalls the impression made upon him by the saintly Brother Basil:

> Basil was exceedingly humble. He was really (so I have ever thought) a much superior musician to any of our "big professors," but he never felt so. . . . For understanding and rendering what is beautiful in sound, true and touching, Basil had few equals. And I have known many fine musicians. . . . During all my stay at Notre Dame I was at music all the time, in the choir and band, and while we had it, the orchestra. . . . How plainly we wild young creatures, even we, could see Basil's deep religion. That man that made the violin sing angelic anthems, we would notice by times absorbed alone in prayer in the church.[1]

When the Civil War broke out, Walter followed his two brothers into the Union Army. As he was under age, his family got him back; but he ran away again, joined the Fifth Ohio Regiment, and served until the end of the war. His two brothers, attached to the Michigan troops, (Robert, major of infantry, and William, captain of cavalry) were killed in battle; and Walter was taken prisoner. All through the war he carried a golden crucifix given to him by the young woman chosen as his future wife. Her untimely death shattered the romance and ended his desire for marriage.

The war remained vivid in his memory. He read much about it in later years, revisited battlefields, spun many a yarn—some of them historical, some of them humorous tall tales. Having attained the rank of sergeant, he never quite abandoned the attitude and tone that traditionally go with chevrons, observing strict discipline himself and exacting it from others.

Home again in Detroit, having fulfilled the sketchy requirements of those early days, he was admitted to the bar, acquired a partner and an office, developed the habit of serious reading and became surprisingly familiar with the Anglo-American literary heritage. At the age of twenty-five he had become an earnest young man with a good sense of values, but uncertain of his future. Then he heard Father Hecker lecturing in Detroit. Years later, Elliott affirmed that he never could forget the impression made upon him by the personality of Hecker, at that time in the full tide of success, making the most of an exceptional opportunity to spread the faith. Elliott had listened to the nation's finest lecturers; and he perceived that here was a man "equal to the greatest then alive," able to deal with them on their own level, and—what was unique in a Catholic lecturer—putting the American stamp on every religious argument he proposed. It took Elliott little time to decide that he would rather follow in Hecker's footsteps than pursue any other career in the world. Leaving Detroit without a word to anybody, he traveled to the Paulist house in West 59th Street, New York, and asked to be received as a novice—climbing the steps of the rectory three times before he found courage to face the man of whom he was already in spirit an enthusiastic disciple. On the day that Elliott entered the novitiate, Father Tillotson, the community's first recruit, lay dying; and Elliott in a memorandum recorded the deep impression made upon him by the circumstances of this young priest's death and funeral.

For twenty years, first as a student and then as missionary, Elliott lived in the motherhouse of the community, close to Father Hecker, although each of them would be frequently away on missions or lecture tours. All this time Elliott was following Hecker's pattern of life, with the pursuit of holiness as his supreme interest and apostolic zeal as his dominating motive in the external order. The relationship between the two men is set forth in Elliott's preface to his biography of Hecker:

> The reader must indulge me with what I cannot help saying, that I have felt the joy of a son in telling the achievements and chronicling the virtues of Father Hecker. I loved him with the sacred fire of holy kinship, and love him still—only the more that lapse of time has deepened by experience, inner and outer, the sense of truth and of purity he ever communicated to me in life, and courage and fidelity to conscience. I feel it to be honor enough and joy enough for a life-time that I am his first biographer, though but a late born child and of merit entirely insignificant. The literary work is, indeed, but of homemade quality, yet it serves to hold together what is the heaven-made wisdom of a great teacher of men. It will be found that Father Hecker has three words in this book to my one, though all my words I tried to make his. His journals, letters, and recorded sayings are the edifice into which I introduce the reader, and my

words are the hinges and latchets of its doors. I am glad to do this, for it pleases me to dedicate my good will and my poor work to swinging open the doors of that new House of God that Isaac Hecker was to me, and that I trust he will be to many.

As a priest, Elliott was first assigned to parish work and then, five months afterward, to the mission band. He preached his first mission sermon at St. Peter's Cathedral in Wilmington, in October, 1872, five months after ordination. His ability was recognized at once; and for the next quarter century he labored strenuously on missions in practically every part of the United States, meanwhile striving with typical energy to develop his natural endowments which were of a very high order. He read, observed, questioned, adopted suggestions—notably those received from Father Walworth—and came to be classed as one of the most effective missionaries of his day. His voice, comparable to an organ in tone and power and range, was used with unstudied, but intensely dramatic, effect; and he threw himself into his preaching so whole-heartedly that he may well have had his own experience in mind when years later he spoke of a brain "fatigued and superheated in the fires of mission preaching." His volume of *Mission Sermons* [2] contains the substance of what he said, but conveys little notion of the terrifying force with which he delivered his message from the mission platform; for, when at his impassioned best, he seemed to be echoing the very voice of God.

As a lecturer he stood out a truly impressive figure, six feet three in height, fired with the consciousness of being champion of a great cause, restless to carry his message into every city or town where he could secure a hearing. He regarded himself as especially fortunate when he had as hearers a picked group of persons who might be depended upon to echo and re-echo what he said, if he said it with sufficient drive. On one such occasion, in the year 1898, when he lectured on the apostolate to non-Catholics to the seminarians of Boston—among whom was the future Paulist, James M. Gillis—the young men left the hall at the end of the lecture in unaccustomed silence, and walked over to the supper room feeling as if they had been listening to an Old Testament prophet.

Probably the most striking feature of Father Elliott's personality was his dominant will. Although a man of marked individuality and deep feeling, he attained a degree of self-control which seemed quite perfect. Thoroughly obedient to the voice of conscience within his soul and to the commands of legitimate authority, he would disregard the obstacles which discourage most men, and hold his resolute way, undeterred by the pleading of friends, the arguments or ridicule of critics.

He stood out from the crowd also by his moral superiority, a giant in stature. He had a characteristic disregard of the unpleasant consequences of doing his duty. Once when there was a question of the use to which a trust fund should be put, he made clear that no power on earth could make him endorse an application of the fund to any purpose but that specified by the original donors. On another occasion he refused to sign a declaration of loyalty which he regarded as merely politic and partisan, scorning the suggestion that the refusal might do irreparable damage to his career.

He displayed a rather disconcerting attitude toward the conventions; for he liked to make his democratic sympathies unmistakably plain. His family had good social standing; and relatives were occasionally mortified by his conduct, as, for instance, when he entered a public assembly late, clad plainly, wearing rough shoes, carrying a carpet bag, and equipped with a blue bandana handkerchief which he used not inconspicuously.

Elliott—in this respect resembling Hecker—lacked certain characteristics highly prized in this day of self-advertising, which dwells fondly on such words as "commercials," "salestalks," "press releases." Like many another holy person, including canonized saints, these two men had a distaste for self-advertising—the kind of distaste which is honorable indeed, but yet may limit the range of one's appeal and may even exasperate persons reasonably seeking information about a writer or a speaker. The problem is solved most happily, no doubt, by following a middle course between offensive publicizing of one's own work and maintaining a provokingly complete silence. Elliott, however, with his instinctive dread of being egotistical, habitually leaned backwards. At the Catholic Summer School at Cliff Haven, New York, listeners at his lectures complained that he used to depart immediately after his public appearances, giving his admirers no opportunity for closer acquaintance. Yet even those who were annoyed at this "anti-social" trait, probably in their secret hearts honored him all the more for it.[3]

Elliott often disclosed a poetic vein in his use of striking imagery. Frequently, too, we come upon a moving revelation of what perhaps can be best described as fervent, manly, priestly sentiment—for example in this passage apostrophizing the Blessed Mother: "I implore thee to witness my sincerity when I say to thee and proclaim to the whole world, that I will do thy bidding and be subject to thee in all things, as did thy Son Jesus, trusting that thou wilt, with a mother's affection, obtain for me the graces necessary to make this promise an efficacious one unto salvation."

These words—from Elliott's conference on the Blessed Virgin Mary in his volume, *The Spiritual Life*,—may seem commonplace enough to the reader; but, as spoken by Elliott, they would leave many a hearer stunned into silence.

During the four last years of Hecker's life, Elliott spent as much time as he could with his enfeebled leader, bringing him constant consolation in the long months of inactivity and depression. Meanwhile, he was steadily growing in knowledge of his hero's inner life; and when Hecker died, Elliott at once began work on his *Life of Father Hecker*. Then he turned again to field work, entering whole-heartedly into the temperance crusade, becoming an outstanding leader of the Catholic Total Abstinence Union, and winning a high place in the esteem of bishops, priests and people throughout the country. The historian of the movement, writing of the convention of 1890 says: "Father Elliott gave, as he usually did at this time, the ablest of the addresses." [4]

In 1892 at the Missionary Congress in Chicago, he aroused Catholics to fresh zeal for the conversion of their non-Catholic brethren. His next enterprise was the building up of missionary bands of diocesan priests in many areas—Detroit, Cleveland, Toledo, Pittsburgh, Buffalo, New York, Hartford. Then came the founding of the Apostolic Mission House, a school to train diocesan priests in mission work especially among non-Catholics; and then the organizing of the Catholic Missionary Union with its monthly organ, *The Missionary*. In all these undertakings Elliott enjoyed the complete sympathy and the valuable co-operation of his younger fellow Paulist, Alexander P. Doyle.

Appointed master of novices in 1899, Elliott moved to the novitiate on the campus of the Catholic University of America; and the two years spent with the novices vastly extended the ultimate range of his influence both in time and in space. If not all those who came close to him responded with equal enthusiasm, at least none could be unaware of his greatness and none could wholly forget the experience.

Elliott's active life had embraced the decades that transformed pre-Civil War America into the nation that emerged from the Spanish War. He had by turns been soldier, lawyer, student, missionary, lecturer, teacher. Now he was to train young men for the religious life and the priesthood in a world, superficially very different from that in which he had played his conspicuous part, yet essentially the same. This was the harvest season of his own priestly experience; and his enthusiasm for the apostolate remained as strong as ever in the quasi-monastic atmosphere of the novitiate.

At the beginning of his term as master of novices he adopted a new device in the form of a textbook, *An Introduction to the Devout Life,* by St. Francis de Sales. He made this the basis of his conferences, requiring every novice each week to select and memorize a brief, significant sentence—a "pithy," Elliott called it. His conferences were informal, arranged only in a rough sort of order; but he rarely failed to put across the message he wished to convey. A phrase that has come into common use in recent years applies neatly to his type of humor—it was "dead pan." With solemn voice and unsmiling features he would throw out phrases of sentiments that sent listeners into gales of laughter; and while they were thus off balance there would come, like a sledge-hammer blow, a spiritual principle, or a practical rule which, thus conveyed, would be remembered forever. Elliott belonged to the type of teacher whose instruction cannot be separated from his personality—like two facets of the same stone; and the impact of his "extra-curricular" speech and behavior was one of the strongest influences that played upon the novices. We who at that time listened to him reverently and gratefully still say to one another, "He was the greatest man we ever knew."

Father Elliott's declining years were spent in the Apostolic Mission House at Washington surrounded by students and young clerics, whom he daily inspired towards personal holiness and priestly zeal, both by word and example. Even after four score years had begun to tell on physical frame and mental vigor, there was never any change in the iron will, the steadfast affection, the loyalty to chosen ideals which had always characterized him. His scrupulously exact observance of poverty, his love of austerity, his good-natured, half-playful humility, his unswerving devotion to every detail of religious rule made observers feel as if the ways of a saint were being illustrated before their eyes. More and more his interest was concentrated on the things of eternity; more and more every aim but that of holiness was excluded; more and more each thought and word and heartbeat seemed an echo of the will of God. Serious by nature, he appeared to be more impressed each passing year with an acute consciousness of his approaching end. A vivid sense of the majesty of God colored each word of his that had to do with death.

He said his early morning Mass, he made his mental prayer, he followed the routine of daily spiritual exercises, he thumbed his beloved volumes, he toiled at the writing of books and articles practically until the last. He had declared himself in favor of being taken away quickly, rather than by means of a protracted illness which would involve anxiety and trouble on the part of others. And so the end came—increasing feebleness, a slight fall, a few weeks of enforced inactivity, a brief immediate preparation, and then the closing of his earthly life. Those who knew him best, felt that all was much as he would have wished it. Few, if any, could fail to be stirred with a sort of holy envy. A life generously consecrated to God in youth, and never in any sense withdrawn, visible gifts of grace, abounding faith, unchanging hope, and limitless charity—these seem to constitute the sufficient conditions for a peaceful, contented passing into eternity.

Decades later former novices, secular priests, old students of his who had become bishops would often communicate their impressions of Elliott. Bishop Thomas J. Shahan, Rector of the Catholic University of America, spoke of him as of one who "occupied a niche apart in the love and esteem of the American people. . . . Intense conviction shone from all his works, in his very features and speech, the living conviction that only the Catholic religion could satisfy the spiritual needs of this most wonderful of peoples." Bishop John J. Swint, of Wheeling, described Elliott as one of those persons who in some mysterious way grip and hold us, to whom we look up with profound reverence, to whom we feel that we largely owe what we are. "The really precious thing about the Mission House training was personal contact with Father Elliott. He was the Mission House." [5]

Elliott's writing was less distinguished than his public speaking. On the platform or in the pulpit he radiated his personality through his words—whether giving an informal conference or delivering a sermon or lecture. With a pen he was less effective. As he was no more a literary craftsman than he was a cabinet-maker, he would put a book together in the same rough and ready fashion that he employed when building a wooden bridge in the summer season at Lake George. This fact accounts for the obsolescence of volumes which, if edited carefully, would make a fairly complete course of practical theology and spiritual science.

In addition to his scattered articles in the *Catholic World* and elsewhere and his contributions to *The Missionary* which appeared in every issue for thirty years, Elliott published ten books: *The Life of Father Hecker;* two books on the life and passion of Our Lord; five volumes of sermons and conferences; a *Manual of Missions to Catholics and non-Catholics;*

and a translation of the sermons of the Dominican, John Tauler.

First and most important of his books was the biography of Father Hecker. Immediately after Hecker's death, he set to work to sift a vast amount of material, working from morning until night for the better part of two years. Elliott made no pretense of conducting original research or of gathering material from scattered sources. He was content to outline Hecker's life and to use this as a frame for Hecker's message to his age. After appearing first in the form of articles in the *Catholic World,* the biography was published as a volume in 1891. It remains a valuable source book which will not be displaced until considerable new intensive work has been finished. The great trial of Elliott's life came in connection with this biography. Translated into French in 1897, it was acclaimed by a number of prominent Frenchman as a vindication of their progressive policies; and it occasioned violent controversy. The quarrel grew so bitter that the book was—without prejudice—withdrawn from circulation; and Pope Leo XIII wrote a quieting letter. The episode was a distressing experience for Elliott who felt "as if he had been beaten from head to foot." He could not but fear that in some way he had been responsible for the reflections cast upon Hecker and his teaching.

Unlike Hecker, who was a lifelong diarist, Elliott set down practically nothing in writing about his own inner life, his hopes, his aspirations; with regard to these things we depend upon the reminiscences of those who knew him and upon unconscious revelations made in his books. In the biography we find little or nothing about the author, except that he was the devoted follower and the conscientious interpreter of Hecker. *The Life of Christ,* however, which from the popular point of view was his most important book, enables us to catch him unaware, while at worship.[6]

Elliott set about writing the life of Our Lord as if he were preaching the Gospel by means of his pen. It was a boon to the reading public to have the Gospel teachings summarized by a man possessing such keen powers of observation and so vast an experience. He drew upon years of meditation, upon wide-ranging familiarity with the writings of spiritual masters, upon intimate acquaintance with the consciences of sinners and of saints. He knew the needs of the multitude and the adequacy of the Gospel to satisfy these needs; and his book might be described as the story of Our Lord's life and teaching broken into fragments and distributed for the daily nourishment of wayfarers.

Elliott, like Hecker, was deeply interested in mystical prayer. Both these men held that ordinary Christians should be encouraged to pursue holiness; and that they were entitled to be given literature which would convey inspiration and adequate instruction. Both of them, therefore, were actively interested in reviving and circulating Catholic books which had remained comparatively unknown for long periods—books like Walter Hilton's *Scale of Perfection,* Father Baker's *Sancta Sophia,* the writings of Blosius. We find Elliott towards the end of his life undertaking a translation of John Tauler's sermons.[7] Anyone who looks over the almost forbidding volume of nearly 800 pages will have at least a slight appreciation of the labor involved in the translator's attempt to make it "a perfect reflex of the German original." Yet to Elliott the finished product was "the result of many delightful hours of labor."

Keenly aware of the gradual fading of physical powers, referring to himself as a train, "slowing down for the station," but rather reminding one of a giant oak yielding to nature's inevitable law, Elliott remained an impressive figure to the end, cared for affectionately by Father Lewis O'Hern, once his novice, now his superior. He died in April, 1928; and, after a funeral Mass in the National Shrine of the Immaculate Conception at the University and a second Mass in St. Paul's, New York, he was buried in the crypt of the church near the leader whose ideals he had so faithfully embodied.

Monsignor William J. Kerby of the University, a keen observer, who had studied Elliott at close quarters for years, made this comment on his character:

> I do not believe that Father Elliott ever calculated the effect upon himself, of anything that he did. He possessed a measure of humility which fitted easily into his unselfish outlook. It was the humility of strength, not of weakness; a

humility rooted in love of justice and truth. I could not imagine him hesitating to correct a mistake of judgment if he made one or counting the cost to his feeling if occasion for such correction arose.

The superior general of the Paulists, in Elliott's funeral sermon, said:

> We Paulists are under no illusion as to our claim on him. We understand that the spiritual ideals he embodied are not the private possession of our community; they are part of the common Catholic heritage. In another age, there might have been contention as to who would gain possession of his body. In this present day, if we should presume to appropriate his spirit, there might well be strife. For his spirit belongs to the Catholic Church; if to anyone in particular measure, then to the whole priesthood of America, since, especially during his latter years, nothing seemed closer to the heart of Father Elliott than the cause of priestly perfection, and surely no class was dearer to him than his fellow priests.

XV

Hewit, Glorified Yankee

(Notes, p. 295 ff.)

FATHER HEWIT'S family tree contains names that stimulate the imagination. On his mother's side we find John Mason, Captain of the Dorchester Militia at the massacre of the Pequot Indians on the Mystic River. John's grandson, William Hillhouse, was a member of the Continental Congress; William's great-granddaughter, Rebecca, married Nathaniel Hewitt, graduate of Yale, Presbyterian minister of Plattsburg, New York, temperance crusader, one of whose ancestors, an English Puritan minister, had come to Connecticut after having been expelled from his parish by William Laud, Archbishop of Canterbury. Nathaniel was a seventh generation descendant of John Alden and "Priscilla, the Puritan maiden." Nathaniel's son, Nathaniel Augustus, dropped the final "t" from his surname and changed his baptismal name to Augustine Francis. He became second superior general of the Paulists.[1]

Father Hewit might be described as a thoroughbred Yankee, glorified by Catholicism—the unglorified type being exemplified by a spinster who, after her brother had passed a lifetime as a Catholic priest, bequeathed him a legacy on condition that he would return to the Protestantism of his fathers.

In the *Catholic World* (October, 1887) Father Hewit, impelled by the hope of aiding others, sketched the steps which led him to the Church. He described his progress from Evangelical Protestantism, through the middle ground of High Church and Anglo-Catholic Episcopalianism, to the integral Christianity of the Catholic Apostolic Roman Church—not undertaking to prove the validity of premisses nor the inference drawn from them, but merely to narrate the process that went on in his own mind.

Bred in the strictest Calvinism and a New Englander at heart as well as by birth and descent, Hewit yet repudiated his father's "narrow, harsh and dreary system of religion" as soon as he began to have ideas of his own. This trend away from his inherited religion was promoted by contact with relatives and friends who themselves were affected by the more human beliefs of Episcopalianism, and also by his reading in history and general literature. Solid grounding in natural theology, in the evidences of Christianity and in the Bible kept him from being seriously disturbed by the passing currents of skepticism and rationalism. Yet, apart from sporadic emotional impulses, he never took religion seriously enough to make an outward profession of his belief until after his graduation from Amherst College, which he had entered at the age of fourteen upon completing his course in Phillips Academy, Andover.

While engaged in the study of law, he experienced a sort of spiritual crisis which terminated in a resolution to spend his life in complete obedience to the law of God as revealed through conscience and the Gospel. That resolution, he says—in the *Catholic World* article mentioned above—"I have never retracted. In virtue of it, I became and I remain a Catholic. I began at once to fulfill my part of the baptismal compact. I think that probably I did recover at that time the grace which I had received in baptism, and that from this time forward I was united to the soul of the Catholic Church, by faith, hope, and charity, several years before I was received into her outward communion."

As his baptismal obligation seemed to involve allegiance to Calvinism, he began a thorough study of Calvinistic theology; but this study, undertaken out of love of truth and pursued with logical consistency, led him to reject Calvinistic teachings "as merely human and spurious additions to the faith." Before long he lost respect for the whole Reformation movement with its "travesties of genuine Christian doctrine"; and he felt drawn to the Church of the early Fathers. Although he had already passed nearly two years in the Theological Institute of Connecticut at East Windsor and had been licensed to preach in 1842, he decided to enter the Protestant Episcopal Church; and in March, 1843, in a letter to his father, he communicated his decision to leave Congregationalism. This made the relationship between father and son less cordial and intimate than before. The younger man, however, was following his conscience; and to the charge that he was moving towards Rome, he answered that he had no sympathy for "the corruptions and errors of Romanism"; and he even listed fifteen Catholic doctrines which he considered impossible to accept. Hewit wrote: "As I am not, and do not know what Romish doctrines you suppose me to have embraced, I will specify a few of the principal ones which I reject as novelties, and corruptions of the Catholic faith. 1. The supremacy of the bishop of Rome. 2. The authority of the Council of Trent. 3. Transubstantiation. 4. Repetition of Christ's one sacrifice in the communion. 5. Purgatory. 6. Indulgences. 7. Canonicity of the apocrypha. 8. Doctrine of intention.[2] 9. Denial of the cup to the laity. 10. That there are more than two proper sacraments. 11. That saints may be invoked. 12. Works of supererogation. 13. That the whole of the necessary faith of a Christian is not in the Scriptures. 14. Prayers in an unknown tongue. 15. That the indefectibility of the Catholic Church amounts to infallibility. Besides a vast quantity of loose, floating undefined error, which pervades that most fallen and unhappy branch of Christ's divided and sinful church."

After he decided to prepare for the Episcopal ministry, he was invited to make his studies in the house of Bishop William Rollinson Whittingham of Maryland, who had been a professor in the General Theological Seminary. Having no church of his own, the bishop, as a rule, used old St. Paul's, Baltimore. In the *Memoir* Hewit writes, "In this church the people all knelt with their backs to the altar and facing the great door, whereat a number of us, being scandalized, determined to face about on all occasions and kneel toward the altar, which we did rigidly and in the most impressive manner to the great annoyance of the rector, Dr. Wyatt."

The bishop, having only the status of a visitor, was not at liberty to perform the acts which would properly be the prerogative of the head of the diocese; and Hewit notes that the bishops of the Episcopal Church in this country were all in the same anomalous position, without cathedrals or strictly Episcopal churches. "Bishop Whittingham was determined to remedy this evil, as far as possible, by establishing a parish where his proper place would be conceded to him voluntarily by the rector and vestry. Accordingly the Mt. Calvary congregation was formed and began to worship in the old grain warehouse."

While in Baltimore, Hewit formed a close friendship with Francis Baker, whose family lived in Courtlandt Street, opposite the residence of Bishop Whittingham; and the two young men were in the habit of visiting churches together, Catholic as well as Protestant. Hewit dwells upon the conspicuous position occupied by the Church in Baltimore at that time, with many buildings devoted to worship and works of charity; homes of religious communities; churches possessing a particular dignity and a quiet charm, appreciated but not understood by the two friends until later they learned to attribute it to the Presence of the Blessed Sacrament. He speaks of the Sulpician College of St. Mary's, with its little cemetery and Calvary, as a favorite resort. The sight of these devout pilgrimages by two youths of twenty-three, made considerable impression on many of the Catholics who said prayers for the young men; and a Redemptorist, Father Chakert of St. Alphonsus, frequently said Mass for their conversion.

The Protestants of Baltimore at that time manifested intense dislike of Catholics—motivated, Hewit thought, by their sense that the Catholic religion was so conspicuous and powerful that it must be either battled with or accepted. Bishop Whittingham showed particular hatred of Catholicism. He spoke of "the defilements of the Romish Communion"; and, in one of his written addresses, he used language so violent that Baker declined to read it for him at a convention.[3] The bishop's mental confusion was quite obvious to the logical Hewit, who reduced Whittingham's theological views to the theory "that there is no outward visible unity, except that which is completed in a single bishop and congregation—which makes him practically a Congregationalist. . . . It leads to the bishop making himself as authoritative as the pope."

Unconsciously Hewit was moving towards the

Church, although he assured his father—just as Newman almost at the same time was assuring the British public—that there was no danger of his landing in the arms of Rome. But the principles he professed were Catholic; before long he discovered that they led logically to the faith taught by the Roman Catholic Church; and a distinctly Catholic impression was made upon him by the texts of the New Testament which teach the doctrine of the Real Presence and the apostolic primacy. Baffled for a while by the "Branch Theory," he came to believe that the Anglican communion "was a true branch of the one, holy, Catholic, apostolic church, of which the Roman Catholic Church and the Greek Church were also branches; that it was the real continuation of the old Catholic Church of England, although unfortunately estranged and separated, in respect to external communion, from its sister churches and from the somewhat haughty and unkind mother-church of Rome." "I traveled rapidly Romeward, following the path of Froude, Allies, Faber, and Newman; but I did not know where I was going until I suddenly came upon the gate of the city."

Hewit had read few Catholic books; and he had been in direct communication with hardly any Catholics. He had, however, gained a certain respect for the Catholic Church from reading Wiseman's *Lectures on Science and Revealed Religion;* he had discovered the answers to certain calumnies in the writings of "partly enlightened historians" such as

Von Ranke, Guizot, and Macaulay; most important of all, he had been following with sympathetic interest the Tractarian Movement in England and the theological development of John Henry Newman. The first Catholic book of controversy he ever read was Dr. Constantine Pise's *Letter to Ada from Her Brother-in-Law*. Later he read *The Controversy between Dr. Hughes and Dr. Breckenridge*. A visit to St. Patrick's cathedral in New York led him to the conclusion "that the Mass was the most significant form of worship of Almighty God." He was questioned about his willingness to go to Constantinople and further the plan of effecting reunion between the Greek Church and the Protestant Episcopal Church; but this plan fell through. About this time a conversation with Dr. Seabury [4] led him to the conclusion that both the Greek Church and the Episcopal Church were in an anomalous condition; and he now retreated to the last "tenable" position outside Catholicism—the theory of "corporate reunion." This theory is based on the view that "certain Christian communities separated from the communion of the Roman Church are in a state of secession and revolt which is wrong and unjustifiable, but not destructive of their essential Catholic unity. Individuals however are not responsible for this. They may, and even ought to, remain where they are, desiring, promoting waiting for corporate reunion." It took much time and very hard blows for Hewit to rid himself of "this chimerical notion."

Hewit was ordained deacon by Bishop Whittingham in October, 1843. After a short period with a congregation at Westminster, Md., he resumed residence in the Whittingham family, without being attached to any parish; and he then organized a small congregation in a suburb of Baltimore, called Huntington. "Alarming symptoms of consumption" forced him to limit his activity and, upon the advice of his physician and the bishop, he decided to seek a warmer climate. In November, 1845 he went South, to pass the winter "at the plantation of an excellent and hospitable gentleman of Edenton, N.C., with the nominal office of chaplain to his numerous slaves. My ill health and the unfitness of the Episcopal service for slaves, prevented me from doing anything except for me to preach to them a few times."

The news that John Henry Newman had been received into the Church made a tremendous impression on Hewit who was living in the shadow of a possibly fatal illness, with much opportunity to reflect upon the conclusions indicated by the thought and study of the preceding two years. Early in 1846 he communicated to his father his decision to become a Catholic, writing at the same time to his brother Henry to say that Protestantism "can never satisfy those who have learned the deep capacities and deep wants of their own nature, and who seek for a real and a heroic, a true and a beautiful, a sincere and a cheerful religion."

So in March he left Edenton for Charleston where

he boarded with an Irishman named Preston. On his way he baptized a Negro child who was at the point of death from burns. Perhaps this incident was in his mind when on the morrow of his ordination to the priesthood—as he told us many years afterward—he walked the streets on the alert to use his priestly powers, ready, if a man should fall from a roof, to bestow conditional absolution "before the body hit the ground."

When Hewit presented himself to Bishop Reynolds—who had succeeded Bishop England in March, 1844—he received a cordial welcome. Within a few weeks he completed the course of instruction given him by Dr. Lynch (future bishop of Charleston). He made his profession of faith shortly before Easter Sunday, in April, 1846—without being conditionally baptized, as the baptism conferred on him in infancy by his father was valid.

The South still echoed with the praises of Bishop England, who had died four years earlier, and who through the medium of lectures and sermons and his weekly magazine, the *United States Catholic Miscellany,* had impressed the whole region with his learning, his eloquence, his sincere piety and his sympathy for non-Catholics. Hewit found himself in the enjoyable company of the Charleston priests. "All of them seemed to be very pious and excellent men, and some of them are very learned. The view I have had of the interior of that system of discipline under which the Catholic clergy and students live has pleased me very much. Here, at last, there is an actual strictness and poverty and self-denial which corresponds to their profession."

Applying himself to the study of theology privately under the direction of Dr. Lynch, Hewit was ordained to the Catholic priesthood in 1847. The next two years were devoted to work in the cathedral parish, to teaching in the classical school founded by Bishop England and then to preparing England's writings for publication in collaboration with Dr. Lynch and Dr. James A. Corcoran, both of whom were alumni of the College of the Propaganda. Hewit also published a small pamphlet, *A Few Thoughts Concerning the Theories of High-Churchmen and Tractarians*, "an able discussion on the intricate points of the Oxford Controversy."

While visiting Philadelphia in connection with the publication of England's writings and living in the house of the erudite Bishop Kenrick, he gained the reputation of being one of the brightest intellectual lights in the American priesthood; and obviously he was on a path that might well lead to the episcopate. But his thoughts were turned elsewhere; for he had formed a friendship with two Redemptorists, the sympathetic and zealous provincial, Father Hafkenscheid and the saintly Father John Nepomucene Neumann (declared venerable in 1902 and "heroic" in 1921). Impressed by their edifying lives and by their apostolic spirit, he decided—after consultation with Bishop Reynolds and with his confessor—to apply for admission into the order; although "Dr. Kenrick gave his advice to the contrary." Hewit wrote: "Probably his personal attachment and his wish to retain me in his own diocese has biased his judgment in this case. . . . Bishop Reynolds always expected that I would finally join a religious order, and I actually asked his leave to become a Jesuit nine months ago . . . but several reasons caused me to select the Redemptorists instead of the Jesuit Order."

After a year with the Redemptorists at Baltimore, Hewit was transferred to the mission field, joining Fathers Walworth and Hecker in New York City in April, 1851; and the band was later reinforced by Fathers Baker and Deshon. The *Memoir of Father Baker* describes the exhausting but happy labors of this unique group during the next seven years. Hewit's exceptional gifts led his superiors to give him the position of provincial consultor. Later came trials due to the financial troubles of his brother's family.

Still later he had to deal with his own growing sense of frustration; for he and his companions began to feel that the German wing of the community was reorganizing it on a system quite different from that of the founder; that the vision with which De Held and Bernard and Alexander had inspired the young Americans was fading away; that those now in control were opposed to working for the English-speaking people. Regarding this as a setback to the welfare of the Church, the country and the order, Hewit took a leading part in the plan to send Hecker as delegate to Rome to make an appeal to the superior general. Definite, outspoken, unafraid, Hewit showed himself to be the kind of comrade one likes to have in a struggle. He wrote to Hecker: "I wish you to understand that it is my undoubting opinion that you should go to Rome, and as soon as possible, and that I share with you in full the responsibility." And again, "I am perfectly certain you have the right to go, a right which the general himself cannot derogate from." To the superior general, Hewit wrote: "The Reverend Father Hecker undertakes this journey to Rome with my full approbation. The Very Reverend Father Provincial . . . thinks he has not the power to grant this permission. It is my judgment, however, that the gravity of the matters in question make it proper and advisable that Father Hecker should use the right given him by the constitutions and still go to Rome."

When a few months later the four Fathers in America sent the Holy See a memorial requesting, as a last alternative, separation from the Redemptorist Order, Father Hewit added a letter signed by himself as "secretary and consultor of the American province," addressing it to Cardinal Barnabò as "prefect of the Propaganda and as head of American ecclesiastical affairs." In this letter Hewit says that a new, despotic regime "has been fastened on us without the knowledge or consent of the greatest portion of our members"; that the Belgian Fathers "feel themselves crushed under the same system which threatens to crush us also." He adds that the American Redemptorists find themselves "under a yoke against which our souls revolt, and beneath which our true vocation is in peril of being totally destroyed." After referring to the leadership exercised by Walworth and Hecker, he continues:

> Of Father Hecker it is requisite that I should speak more fully, as his character is assailed and undeserved ignominy is inflicted on him by those who ought to honor and love him most. It would be difficult to convey to your Eminence a just idea of the veneration and affection which the Catholics of all classes, from the lowest to the highest, cherish towards this truly Apostolic man, who has thrown lustre on the Congregation, both by his writings and his labors. There was no Father in this Province who was a more devoted son of St. Alphonsus, a more ardent lover of the Congregation, or more completely animated with the religious spirit. Not only did he renounce great wealth to enter the Congregation, but he also made free use of the resources which have been placed at his disposal by generous and wealthy relatives, for the benefit of the Order, and was disposed to confer on it still greater benefits of the same kind.[5]

Once the new community has taken shape, Hewit entered on the venture with courage and with trust; and for close to forty years he contributed richly to the spiritual and intellectual life of the Paulists. Well-trained and well-balanced, he could always be relied upon for sound advice. He formulated the first rule of the young community in Latin; he labored in the parish; he taught the students; he preached missions; he served as theologian for Bishop Lynch at the Second Plenary Council of Baltimore; he often contributed articles to the *Catholic World,* to the *American Catholic Quarterly Review,* of which his old friend Dr. Corcoran, was editor, and to other periodicals. He acted as assistant editor of the *Catholic World* to Father Hecker from the beginning and became chief editor after Hecker's death; and the contents of the magazine during these years form a source quite indispensable to students of American Church history. In connection with Hewit's editorship, mention should be made of his relationship with Dr. Brownson, a frequent and most prominent contributor to the periodical. Differences that occurred between the two men have been distorted out of all proportion, for their fundamental friendship was not broken.[6]

In addition to several booklets, hardly more than brochures, Hewit published two volumes, *Problems of the Age,* and *Memoir of Father Baker.* He wrote many articles, chiefly in the two magazines already named, confining himself invariably to serious writing. He was in considerable demand as a reviewer, for he could be relied upon to weigh carefully, to judge honestly and to write without spleen. In his writing as in speaking, he would sometimes assume a gruffness of tone which did not deceive persons who knew him well, for under his superficial grimness was hidden a spirit of consistent kindness and humanity. His feigned outbursts of wrath over theological nonsense did not deter Father Searle from poking fun at him in an oft quoted intramural jingle:

HEWIT, GLORIFIED YANKEE

> There was an old scholar named Hewit,
> They sent him a book to review it.
> He read but a page, flew into a rage,
> And out of the window he threw it!

Among Hewit's articles was a little known piece of writing on the delicate topic of possible mitigation of the sufferings of Hell—a subject treated elsewhere unskillfully and even disastrously by the celebrated scientist, St. George Mivart.[7] These pages show Hewit at his best, possessing an easy familiarity with patristic and theological sources, both Greek and Latin; logical and courageous in his conclusions; discriminating carefully between dogma and opinion, between sound and unsound private teachings. From Père Emery, he quotes this piece of practical advice: "Would it not, then, be wiser for preachers at the present day, to be more careful to avoid exaggeration, and to confine themselves ordinarily to within the limits of the doctrine which is of faith."[8] Hewit's final words are, "I leave what I have written to have its due weight with sincere and considerate readers, hoping especially that it may help them to find the harmony which certainly exists between the revealed truth, and the dictates of reason and the moral sense."

Unable to attend the 1852 reunion of his Amherst classmates, he answered their request for an account of his activities since graduation by narrating the steps of his progress from Calvinism to Catholicism, adding by way of postscript, "I leave it entirely to yourselves to make use of this letter or not according to your own discretion; but if you wish to do it, I place it in your hands only on this condition, that it be published word for word, without abridgment or alteration." [9] His relationship with his Alma Mater remained always cordial. In fact this college, chartered by Congregationalists, made him a Doctor of Divinity—an honor that might have proved embarrassing, had not a Roman university come to the rescue by conferring the theological doctorate on him in 1885, so that he could use the title without being criticized.

A quarter century after his death Amherst honored him again by displaying a portrait of this distinguished alumnus and inviting one of the Paulist Fathers to make a public address on the occasion. The picture hangs on the south wall of the second floor of the library near the seminar rooms of the English and Romance Languages Department. A non-Catholic writes, "Father Hewit's face, as depicted by the artist, is one of the most beautiful I have ever seen. The crucifix is prominent upon his breast." Hewit was in truth a splendid figure of a man. He might have posed as a Roman proconsul. Six feet tall, broad shouldered, he had a well-shaped head, sharply chiseled features, a strong jaw hidden in old age by a white beard.

The idea of a national school of higher learning, long debated by the American bishops, began to take definite shape at the Third Plenary Council of Baltimore in 1884; and both Hecker and Hewit gave enthusiastic aid to the project.¹⁰ Probably more articles on this subject appeared in the *Catholic World* than in any other leading periodical.

Hewit, who had succeeded Hecker as superior early in 1889, transferred the responsibility of the local community and parish in New York to Father Deshon and the editorial duties of the *Catholic World* to Father Elliott; and when the University opened, he went to live on the campus at Washington, taking the chair of ecclesiastical history temporarily. He allowed Father Searle—formerly on the staff of the United States Naval Academy, and highly rated in scientific circles—to become a resident member of the faculty. He also moved the Paulist house of studies to the old Middleton Manor on the campus; and the Paulist students as auditors helped to swell attendance at the small classes of the early years.¹¹ The first Paulist student to matriculate at the University majored under the celebrated Dr. Bouquillon, professor of moral theology, intimate friend of the triumvirate, Gibbons, Ireland and Keane.

Hewit, then in his seventies, found walking increasingly difficult because of eczema that affected his legs; and the present writer, at that time a novice, had the privilege of wheeling his superior about the University campus in an invalid chair. Pleasant memories remain of talks with the venerable scholar and of fragments of conversation overheard, when visiting prelates or other dignitaries would stop to chat for a moment. To questions of the kind that occur to a young novice beginning to study philosophy, Father Hewit would listen patiently and reply kindly. Once, when asked "Does a charitable man run more risk than other men of being tricked?" Hewit gave the laconic answer, "Yes, but I'd rather run the risk." Commenting on the community rule which prohibited the use of gold in general, but made an exception in favor of pens, he said "When I was writing the Rule I remembered that a gold pen makes writing easier." Often in conversation the old missionary would refer to incidents of earlier years; and once he added a new feature to the tale of his adventure during the draft riots when one of the mob split his head open. He told us that he had kept the bloodstained shirt as a sort of relic for quite a while; and to the question what became of it finally, he answered with a sort of wry smile, "Sent it to the laundry."

While Father Hewit lived at Caldwell Hall the novices would go over to serve his Mass at 6:00 A.M.; and he in turn would come over to the Paulist novitiate for evening meditation. Sometimes while praying he would unconsciously give expression to his thought—dazing us all upon one occasion by breathing out in a sort of stage whisper, "Uneasy lies the head that wears a crown."

Hewit spent the final years of his life at the motherhouse in New York, dying there in July, 1897, four months after his golden jubilee. In a eulogy published in the following issue of the *Catholic World*, Father Michael Smith presented him as a man distinguished not only for external achievements, but also for simplicity, high sense of honor, industry, fine sense of humor, religious observance, love of the convent home and of his brethren, rare holiness. In that judgment all who knew Hewit would concur.

XVI

Deshon, the West Pointer

(Notes, p. 297)

LAST survivor of the four founders, Father Deshon spent forty-five years in the Paulist community, laboring in the parish, on the missions, as procurator, as master of novices, as instructor of students; and serving in the office of superior general from his election in 1897 until his death in 1903.

The Deshons of New London (originally Deschamps) are descended from Daniel Deshon, son of one of the thirty Huguenots who came from France to Massachusetts in 1686. Daniel's wife was descended from "the godly & religious" Elder William Brewster, who landed from the Mayflower in 1620. The Deshon family gained distinction in Washington's army during the Revolution. George Deshon, who was born January 20, 1823, entered West Point July 1, 1839. At the Academy he was room-mate of the future President Grant; and he ranked second in his class when he was graduated in 1843. He returned to the Academy to teach mathematics and ethics; and with his fellow instructor and lifelong friend, William S. Rosecrans, and a number of other army officers, entered the Catholic Church—partly through the influence of the Episcopal chaplain. It is said that Deshon and Rosecrans were together when they purchased their first Catholic book.

Deshon was received into the Church in 1851 by a Jesuit Father; and while still in uniform he visited the Redemptorist house in Baltimore to seek admittance to the community. Walworth related that he asked Deshon why he was not applying to the Jesuits instead of to the Redemptorists, and Deshon answered, "They have so many colleges they would put me to teaching the first thing. . . . I want to be a priest—not to teach students, but to preach the Gospel to the people; and that, as I understand it, is what you Redemptorists are doing all the time, isn't it?"

On the missions Deshon played a humble role, taking a lion's share of the hard work, especially in the confessional; and giving instructions with a simplicity free of rhetoric—the mark of an efficient teacher. He has left in print some published sermons and one book, *Guide for Catholic Young Women: Especially for Those Who Earn Their Own Living*, which was advertised as having a larger sale than any other Catholic volume published before 1860. It ran into twenty-five editions.

Deshon had certain characteristics that we associate with the military profession. One was loyalty. This quality comes out in a letter he wrote to Hecker as the latter was about to carry their appeal to the Redemptorist superior general in August, 1857: "I consider your going to Rome at this time, as my act as much as it is your own, since I coincided entirely with you as to the right, propriety and necessity of taking this step." Loyalty comes out again, in other letters written to Hecker in Rome during those trying seven months. Deshon was personally incapable of lying and seemingly unable to understand why some persons are afraid to tell the truth. He had also a characteristic which is often regarded as an occupational weakness of military commanders—he was disposed to take for granted that men under him would do what they were told, what they ought to do, what he himself would do if he were in their place. He was amazed when persons supposed to be collaborating in a common task did not get along together as well as they should.

Deshon retained the stamp of early military training until the end. When ordered to remain in bed during his last illness, although he thought this unnecessary, he answered, "I have to obey orders. I learned that at West Point." Some who had been his fellow cadets believed that he would have attained distinction in the Civil War had he remained in the army. Certainly he was always submissive to authority; and certainly he had the ability to stick to a decision once made—traits supposed to be typical of military men. He had something of the martinet in his manner too. Rigging or sailing a boat, building a shack, or making a campfire, he would bark out orders like a drill-master; although his sparkling, kindly eyes belied his superficial grimness. Once at Lake George, coming on a rattlesnake near where the Paulists were camping, he walked right up to it as a matter of course and killed it with his stick.

He was naturally reserved, undemonstrative. His brusqueness and seeming severity kept some people from perceiving that underneath lay deep affection for his brethren and kindly feeling for all men. He taught and observed a strict ideal of poverty; and he would only smile when intimate friends ventured to comment on the contrast between his shabby green overcoat and the uniform of the trim young officer, who years before had walked into the Redemptorist house in Baltimore, seeking for a commission to preach the Gospel. Once he told a newly ordained priest to return the smart-looking desk sent by the young man's relatives as an ordination gift; and when an umbrella came to one of the Fathers as a Christmas present, Father Deshon's decision was, "If you already have another umbrella, leave this here." One of Father Searle's celebrated jingles—composed when a novice sought permission for a new hat—immortalized Deshon's love of poverty and his aversion to unnecessary expenditure:

> There was an old man, named Deshon,
> Who considered the pro and the con.
> When asked for a hat, he looked terribly flat,
> And said, "Look at the one I have on!"

To a novice who excused his own lack of sympathy for a fellow novice by saying he did not wish to be hypocritical, Father Deshon suggested "at least it would do no harm to practice a little pious dissimulation." As novice master, he taught his young men an almost Carthusian detachment from the world. We get a striking picture of him in the article published by Father Searle in the *Catholic World*, February, 1904, a few weeks after Deshon's death:

> With him, and in his direction of us, the religious or community life was accentuated. We were, of course preparing for the priesthood and the mission or parish work . . . [but] he preferred to constantly call [our] attention to the one thing needful; the one thing without which no ability or zeal will accomplish great or permanent results in the work of a community, and with which, well grounded in a community and in its individual members, even the most ordinary talents will yield abundant fruit. . . . It was [to] the interior life of love of God and union with Him that he constantly directed our thoughts and efforts; detachment from the world, poverty, obedience and mutual charity were favorite subjects with him for conferences. . . . The Carthusians or the hermits or the coenobites of the desert, . . . were certainly his favorite saints. One would not have gathered from them that we were on the verge of an intensely active life, the greater part of which was necessarily to be occupied with people and things external to the community.

Deshon loved to cultivate flowers and vegetables and fruit trees, and here as elsewhere, he had an eye to the practical; for his famous and good-sized garden in front of the first Paulist church provided flowers for the sanctuary, vegetables and fruit for the community table, pleasant walks for visitors. At the Paulist country house on Lake George, in addition to

DESHON, THE WEST POINTER

constructing buildings, he laid out a truck-garden and orchard.

Man of affairs, clear-headed and prudent in business matters, skilled engineer, he was of immeasurable value to the community especially in its pioneer days. Much of his personality went into the great Paulist church in New York City. That church, by the way is a curiously symbolic edifice; embodying Hecker's ideas; given shape by Deshon; fitting into no definite architectural category; suggesting Seville to some observers, and Monreale to others; decorated by the great artist, John LaFarge, and revealing Gothic features Romanized, and European plans Americanized; and in many places displaying additions made by Deshon's protégé, the convert artist, William L. Harris.

Father Malloy's fine booklet on the church preserves for posterity various traditions, including the tale of Deshon's acquiring the stone of an old aqueduct to build the walls and of his victory over a professional architect in a dispute about the type of roof needed to span the wide nave.

Father Deshon, who before becoming a priest, had been an instructor in military engineering at West Point, designed a truss to meet the needs of the case, without the use of a tie-rod. When the architect saw the design he declared that the roof would collapse under the weight of the first heavy snowstorm. Father Hecker called in for consultation two experts, Professor Trowbridge of Columbia University and General Newton who was then in charge of dynamiting Hell Gate in the East River. Both pronounced Father Deshon's plan perfectly sound and thereafter Mr. O'Rourke decided to withdraw and Father Deshon became architect-in-chief for the building of this great church. He was the master-builder. His technical training at West Point made him well qualified for the task. As a former Army engineer he was not afraid of broad spans, the burden on trusses, the weight of the roof. He knew the strength of the buttresses.[1]

Even a casual observer notes the military aspect of the church. But the first to publicize this feature was a neighboring pastor who urged his congregation to attend services in their own parish church, instead of "rambling down to Deshon's fortress!"

A gratifying episode occurred near the beginning of Deshon's rule as superior. Father Wuest, C.SS.R., chronicler of his Congregation, was allowed at his own request to have access to letters and documents bearing upon the origin of the Paulists. When he came to return the material he stated that it had "swept away prejudices and misunderstandings and cleared the atmosphere." His old views, he said, "were completely changed"; he now believed that the departure of the five convert Americans from the Redemptorists in 1858 "had separated five noble brothers from the body of the Congregation, not from its heart."[2]

Among new activities began during Father Deshon's term was the founding of a Paulist parish in Winchester, Tenn., to serve thirteen counties sparsely settled by Catholics; the Apostolic Missionary Union; the Converts' Aid Society—organized to assist converts, especially former ministers, during the difficult period following entrance into the Catholic Church. Worthy of mention also, was the important step taken by Father Deshon when in 1899 he appointed Father Elliott, master of novices.

* * *

Deshon was a man of few words. His habit of laconic speech was well illustrated by a unique postcard, bearing the words: "All right. G.D."—his reply to a request. But he could write forcefully when he had something worth saying; and he was the author of two letters that were probably the most important —historically speaking—of any written by the founders. One was addressed to the American archbishops during the Americanism controversy; the other to his Holiness, Pope Leo XIII, who had closed that controversy with his encyclical *Testem Benevolentiae*.

Deshon had been superior general less than a year when he was called upon to face a grave situation involving the reputation of the community. The *Life of Father Hecker*, first published during Hewit's term of office, aroused no serious criticism; but its appearance in a French translation in 1897, with the addition of a challenging preface by the Abbé Klein, occasioned excitement on both sides of the Atlantic. In France, as explained in an earlier page of the present volume, Hecker's biography became an issue between progressives and conservatives. The conflict spread to the United States where the embattled forces were aligned much as they had been during the conflict over the Catholic University; and the quarrel grew so bitter that Deshon felt it necessary to write a letter which he requested Archbishop Corrigan, ecclesiastical superior of the comunity, to present to the American archbishops at their meeting in October, 1898. After referring to the attacks on the Paulists, Deshon said that he was led to notice the accusations only because they had apparently made considerable impression on many learned and devoted prelates of the Church in Europe. The original book had been submitted to the careful scrutiny of Hewit as censor; it carried the imprimatur of the archbishop of New York; and it had been circulating for years in English-speaking countries without encountering any challenge. It had been written in English for English readers and it expressed an adaptation of the conservative truths of Holy Church to new political and social conditions. The French translation contained some omissions and inaccuracies; it appeared when a bitter controversy inspired chiefly by political antagonism was dividing Catholics in France; and it had been attacked and defended with great violence. Abbé Maignen was one of "the bitterest and most prominent of the assailants." Father Deshon continued:

> We are in duty bound to protest emphatically against his attacks on the Paulists, which are utterly untruthful, and, seemingly, malicious. It may be said in all truth that the Paulists are known to their Archbishop as men who are faithful in duty, submissive to discipline, obedient to eccle-

siastical authority and zealous in the prosecution of apostolic labors.

After summarizing Abbé Maignen's accusations, Father Deshon concluded as follows:

> Such a bitter and calumnious attack on American Catholics deserves to be officially resented and the eminent Prelates and persons of Europe who already half believe that there is some truth in Abbé Maignen's affirmations should be disabused of any such delusions.
> In order to avoid strife the Paulist Fathers have hitherto abstained from taking any notice of this book.
> For the Paulist Fathers
> George Deshon, Superior.

In accord with Father Deshon's request, his letter was read at the meeting of the archbishops by Archbishop Corrigan, who then moved that in view of the recent reassuring message from Cardinal Rampolla, secretary of state, to Cardinal Gibbons, there was no need of any action on the part of the archbishops. The motion was carried.

On the last day of January, 1899, the cardinal secretary of state transmitted to Cardinal Gibbons a letter signed by Pope Leo XIII—the *Testem Benevolentiae*. It terminated the controversy that had raged around the alleged heresy. The pope did not accept drastic suggestions made by some of his advisers who regarded the Catholic Church in this country as in the throes of an aggressive, widespread heretical movement. The tone of his letter was kind and conciliatory. After having mentioned that the translation of a book on Hecker's life had aroused controversy, he proceeded to specify the various errors to which some persons had given the name "Americanism"; and he then declared that these erorrs are opposed to Catholic teaching. He drew a clear line between what was taught by the Church and what was in opposition to that teaching; and he took care to express his satisfaction at what had been done by the American hierarchy and the whole American people in safeguarding and promoting Catholic interests.

Replying to the papal letter, Cardinal Gibbons and other American bishops assured the holy Father that the errors in question were false conceptions of Americanism emanating from Europe and that they had no existence among the priests, prelates or Catholic laity in America. The writers testified that Father Hecker had never countenanced any deviation from orthodoxy and that the teaching of the Paulist Fathers was irreproachable. Archbishop Riordan of San Francisco, in an address at the seminary of St. Sulpice, Paris, declared the heresy known as Americanism "existed only in the imagination of three or four Frenchmen."

As superior of the Paulists, Father Deshon too felt bound to acknowledge the letter of the pope. He stated in the name of the community that all the Paulists, whole-heartedly and gladly embraced the Holy Father's teaching and that they were especially pleased because his Holiness stated "that the errors reproved are rather to be ascribed to interpretations of Father Hecker's opinions than to those opinions themselves." Father Deshon added that the Paulists gladly acquiesced in the judgment of the Holy Father, not only because the Roman Church is the pillar and ground of the truth, but also because the rule of the Paulist community commands "a prompt and cheerful religious submission to Holy Church and to every authority lawfully constituted in it."

Writing in a prominent English periodical, Canon William Barry made the comment that the "Americanism" controversy was really a phase in the battle between the advocates and the opponents of adaptation; and he foretold that despite all opposition the progressive movement would continue in France and outside France. After mentioning the contribution made by Newman's subtle and refined philosophy, by Hecker's flaming mysticism, by Gibbons's mild, wise leadership, by Keane's energy in the world of scholarship, Barry added: "He would not be far wrong who should say, with Joseph de Maistre, 'there is some great unity towards which we are moving with accelerated speed.' Of that unity, the Americans . . . are the appointed pioneers." [3]

There is no denying that the mention of Father Hecker's name in the papal letter did cast a temporary shadow on his memory and on the prestige of the Paulists. All sorts of suspicions, rumors and distortions came into circulation. But within a short time, events fell into perspective and the true significance of the whole affair became plain.

Father Deshon lived long enough to read the letter of Pope Leo's in 1902, which spoke with enthusiasm of the numerous consolations received from America during the twenty-five years of his reign, and of his joy in finding the progress of Catholicism in this country more and more splendid from day to day—although "almost all the nations which during a long series of centuries professed the Catholic faith have undergone change and suffered grievous vicissitudes." Adding a word of praise for the activities in which Hecker and his friends had been leaders, the Holy Father said that the American bishops had done well to undertake to solve the difficulties of non-Catholics by selecting wise and virtuous men to go about the land giving public addresses in churches and elsewhere, and conveying truth by familiar conversations in private. "This is a truly excellent work and we know that it has already produced good results."

In 1902 Father Deshon was elected for a second term as superior general. One of his last official acts was the arranging of a Paulist foundation in Chicago in the Fall of 1903; he died in December of that year.

Long after the last of the founders had gone to his reward, there came new proofs of the Holy See's confidence in the Paulists. In 1922 Benedict XV entrusted them with the care of the church of Santa Susanna for Americans in Rome; in 1929 Pius XI signed a decree commending the Paulist Society; in

1940 Pius XII gave definite approval to its rule. It was almost precisely a quarter century after Deshon's death that the Jesuit weekly *America* published a tribute which the Paulists value highly. On the occasion of Father Elliott's death, a writer—presumably the editor of *America*—spoke of the "characteristically Paulist phenomena" that at first had been considered novel and radical, but finally proved so practical that everyone took them for granted. He added that perhaps no better attempt can be made at valuing the retrospect of some seventy years than to ask: What would be the position of the Church today, if those men "had not banded themselves together, as they did under the patronage of the Apostle of the Gentiles?"

Reviewing the French original of a recent book by the Abbé Klein,[4] Father Gillis in the *Catholic World*, (July, 1949), drew this lesson:

> True Americanism would have been a "shot in the arm" to European Catholicism. If, fifty years ago, the Church in France had adopted some of the methods of the Church in the United States, we should not now in 1949 be reading such embarrassing documents as that of Father Godin's *France Pagan?* and the pastoral letter, *Growth or Decline?* by the late Cardinal Suhard, Archbishop of Paris. The state of affairs in which priests must become miners, factory hands, day laborers in order to obtain access to the people might not have happened if the Catholics of France had appropriated rather than repudiated American methods.... The happy condition of the Church in North America we may attribute to the use of ways and means and methods once characterized as "Americanism" and condemned as

heretical by critics, most of whom had never had so much as a "look-see" at the Church in the United States. For the progress of the faith among us we have to thank under God, Father Hecker and those members of the hierarchy, clergy, and laity, who upheld him and his ideals at the time when the going was hard, fifty years ago.

NOTES FOR PART III

Study XII (Text, pages 205–213)

1. Frederick J. Zwierlein, *Letters of Archbishop Corrigan to Bishop McQuaid and Allied Documents* (Rochester, New York, 1946) 195.
2. PFA, Hecker Papers, memorandum by Elliott.
3. Zwierlein, *op. cit.*, 178 f.
4. In connection with the preceding paragraphs, see Sister Joan Bland, *op. cit.*, 127, 179, 187.
5. See Zwierlein, *op. cit.*, 190.
6. See Charles Maignen, *Le Père Hecker: est-il un saint?* (Rome et Paris, 1898); Henri Delassus, *L'Américanisme et la Conjuration Antichrétienne* (Lille, 1910); Byrne, *op. cit.*, 304.

Study XIII (Text, pages 214–236)

1. The correspondence between Hecker and Brownson would fill a fair-sized volume. Letters to Hecker are in the Archives of the Paulist Fathers, New York; letters to Brownson are in the Archives of the University of Notre Dame. We have also Brownson's autobiographical memoir, *The Convert* (New York, 1857); the twenty-volume collection of Brownson's writings (Detroit, 1882–1887); and Henry Brownson's three-volume biography of his father, *Brownson's Early Life, 1803–1844* (Detroit, Michigan, 1896); *Brownson's Middle Life, 1845–1855* (Detroit, Michigan, 1899); *Brownson's Latter Life, 1856–1876* (Detroit, Michigan, 1900). In addition we have a series of five articles on Brownson published by Hecker in the *Catholic World*, XLV and XLVI (1887–1888). Of books which deal with Brownson's career, special mention should be made of Theodore Maynard's *Orestes Brownson* (New York, 1943).
2. Dr. Corcoran, Père Gratry and Father Pfulf, S.J. are cited

by Thomas F. Ryan, C.PP.S., *The Sailor's Snug Harbor, Studies in Brownson's Thought* (Westminster, Maryland, 1952) viii, x, 166.

3. Lindsay Swift, *op. cit.*, 250.
4. Wilfrid Parsons, S.J. *The Catholic World*, CLIII (July, 1941), 397.
5. *The Catholic World*, XLVI (November, 1887), 234.
6. Swift, *op. cit.*, 246–248.
7. *The Catholic World*, XLV (April, 1887), 7.
8. Swift, *op. cit.*, 246. However, a subscriber to the *Review* wrote to Brownson in January, 1857, saying

> I am now 19 years a subscriber to your *Review*. It is to you as the instrument in the providence of God to whom I owe the inestimable grace of faith. Two others who were members of the Congregational Society also owe their conversion to the same instrumentality.

Brownson's Latter Life, 91. Father Hecker, writing from Savannah, on January 31, 1857, speaks of Brownson's influence in winning converts to the Church in the South and makes the comment that, with this result "you should feel new hopes and labor with new zeal." PFA, Hecker Letters.

9. In 1842 the *Boston Quarterly Review* had merged with the monthly *United States Democratic Review of New York*. Largely because of a dispute over articles on "The American Republic" (published twenty years later in book form), Brownson began to issue his own *Review* again; and the first number appeared in January, 1844, with the title changed to *Brownson's Quarterly Review*.

10. In a letter to Bayley, future Bishop of Newark, Brownson (April 3, 1848) declined the offer to take charge of the *Freeman's Journal*, giving as his chief reason that he had been trained by the Bishop of Boston, without whose direction he dared not trust himself. See Sister M. Hildegarde Yeager, C.S.C., *op. cit.*, 86.

11. Rev. John B. Morris, *Jesus the Son of Mary, or the Doctrine of the Catholic Church upon the Incarnation of God the Son, considered in its Bearings upon the Reverence shown by Catholics to His Blessed Mother* (London, 1851). See *Brownson's Quarterly Review* (July, 1852).

12. J. M. Capes, Esq., *Four Years' Experience of the Catholic*

NOTES FOR PART III

Religion (Philadelphia, 1849). See *Brownson's Quarterly Review* (July, 1850).

13. In 1848 William George Ward wrote a reply to the attack on Newman. The forgiving Newman, when appointed rector of the new Catholic University of Ireland at Dublin, invited Brownson in 1853 to become a member of the faculty. Brownson was not unwilling, but he had excited too much opposition on both sides of the Atlantic and the pressure was so strong that the offer had to be withdrawn. See *Brownson's Middle Life*, 469 ff.

14. Maynard, *op. cit.*, 163, in the chapter, "No Salvation outside the Church."

15. In September, 1855, we find Hecker writing to Brownson to find out precisely when he would come to New York, how large a house he would require, what rent he would be ready to pay; and Hecker adds, "Your friends here intend to pay the first year rent of your house." In October, he suggests that Brownson might come to New York, and stay at George Hecker's home, look over the available houses and then make his choice.

16. *Reprinted from Brownson's Quarterly Review* (January, 1874), *Brownson's Works*, XIV, 492.

17. This is the article which Hecker, while in Rome, planned to translate into Italian.

18. The article first appeared in the diocesan paper, the *Metropolitan Record,* and later in pamphlet form.

19. For letters quoted in the preceding paragraphs, see *Latter Life,* 67–79.

20. Dr. Jeremiah Cummings (1814–1866), popular preacher and lecturer and a regular contributor to Brownson's *Review,* created much excitement in October, 1860, by calling seminaries, "cheap priest-factories". Dr. Ambrose Manahan, frequent visitor at Brownson's house, published a book *Triumph of the Church,* which was greeted as a masterly work in the Review in January, 1860. It is interesting to note that when on one occasion the public press reported that Archbishop Hughes' aspirations for the cardinalate were being promoted in Rome by two New York priests, the archbishop, denying the charge, declared that only two of his priests were in Rome and that if they never returned to the archdiocese he should not regret it. Cummings and Forbes were the two priests referred to. (*Latter Life,* 191n.).

21. According to Henry Brownson, Forbes frequently spoke to Brownson about the manner in which he was treated by Archbishop Hughes and when narrating what he had endured he would walk up and down the room in much excitement.

On the other hand, the archbishop in a letter to Brownson spoke as follows about Dr. Forbes: "I may have been hasty in admitting him to the priesthood—I may have been too kind in allowing him to have his own way in almost everything since that date—but he was an exceptional Priest and I have not been deceived or disappointed in anything except in the last page of his sacerdotal history." (*ibid.* 193) It speaks well for the archbishop's courage that in 1863 he bestowed the pastorate of St. Ann's on Thomas Scott Preston, a former professor in the General Theological Seminary, who had been received into the Church and ordained at the same time as Forbes.

22. On September 28, 1857, Brownson wrote Hecker: "I am neither surprised nor disheartened by the information conveyed in yours of the 4th inst. On Saturday your brother George and I communicated it to Fathers Walworth, Hewit & Deshon. They received it as you would wish. They will do all they can to save the usefulness of the Congregation. . . . Your good people at Rome seem to have a totally erroneous idea of us Americans. . . . There is not a more loyal people on earth than the American, or more ready to obey the law." PFA, Hecker Letters.

23. Toward the end of 1857, Deshon wrote to Hecker: "I objected to a number of very offensive expressions and ideas and the Dr. changed them or struck them out. . . . I battled it out for 3 hours with the Dr. and he declared that I had made him strike everything in the article that had any point in it." *Ibid.* This letter is undated.

24. The letters exchanged at this time give a partial but not complete picture of the state of mind of these two men at this critical—and as it proved a final—phase of their partnership. On January 30, 1872, Hecker wrote:

Dear Dr.

It seems to me that if you would continue to write such articles as you have done the last two years or more in refutation of the calumnies of the enemies of the Church, in applying Catholic principles to the social and political questions of the day, in directing the young Catholic mind how to judge and act in the midst of existing difficulties, which never were greater or more threatening, and in boldly confronting and silencing the leading advocates of heresy and error, you would promote to the greatest degree Catholic interests, give the highest satisfaction to the hierarchy, and interest most the readers of the Magazine.

Believe me Dear Dr. you can have no idea of the great good which you have done by your pen employed in this direction. I who am in more direct contact with the readers of the Catholic World hear the satisfaction expressed on all sides and by all classes for articles of this nature, all rejoicing that in you they have found a champion of their faith and a master who teaches them how to harmonize their duties as Catholics with the best interests of Society and the State.

Whatever value you may attach to my judgment, or sincerity, to my friendship for you, believe me that this is a matter of most serious consideration in the presence of God, before you leave this great field of doing good, and give up the privilege of leading and directing the Catholic minds of our country.

I have never known you to falter in what you considered to be your duty, and whatever may be your deliberate conclusion in this matter, the high esteem and sincere friendship which I have borne for you now nearly forty years, will be none the less or in no way affected.

As ever

Yours faithfully and affectionately,
I. T. Hecker

On January 31, 1872, Brownson answered:

Dear Father Hecker,

The rejection of my two articles may have been the occasion of my withdrawal from the Catholic World, but not the cause or reason. I was a little vexed I admit, but I could and should have soon got over that. But I found neither my head, nor my eyes, nor even my hand would allow me to write so much as I was writing. I was decidedly breaking down. If I continued to write for the Cath. W. I must abandon the works I had under way, which I might have consented to do, perhaps, if I could have published some things on which my heart was set, in the C.W., but that was henceforth out of the question, I therefore concluded to withhold my contributions.

The *Tablet* pays me more than I could make by writing for the C.W. and at one fourth of the labor. What it pays me so long as my connection with it lasts with my annuity enables me to support my family, and secures me three weeks, instead of one out of four, to devote to my work. Atheism refuted and Theism demonstrated, I judged it best therefore to drop the C.W. to which I had devoted upon an average about three weeks a month of hard labor.

I think you overrate the importance of my articles, and if you did not I could not be expected to keep up articles of equal merit, month after month, and year after year, at my age. Then you do not need me. You have better and far more popular writers than I am. The writer of the 1st article in the last number, the writer of the article on calumnies refuted, and Father Preston's article on the Episcopalian convention, as well as Col. Martin's far surpass mine in freshness and freedom of style. My withdrawing will also enable younger men and develop fresh genius and talent.

If I was convinced that it was my duty to continue my contributions, I would at once withdraw my resolution, but I think I can serve Catholic interests even more effectually in completing the series of work I have in contemplation than in any other way that I can employ the few days I may yet remain on the earth. At any rate it will be no disadvantage to you to let matters remain for the present year as they are.

I thank you for the many proofs of your friendship you have given me, and I assure you that my feelings towards you have undergone no change, and I trust our intercourse is not to be interrupted, but is to continue as cordial and friendly as ever.

Yours truly
O. A. Brownson

25. The situation described has been greatly exaggerated in the accounts given by some; but a balanced verdict was pronounced by Maynard; and Wilfrid Parsons wrote a good article on "Brownson, Hecker and Hewit" in the *Catholic World*, CLIII (July, 1941), 396.

STUDY XIV (Text, pages 237–253)

1. The original letter is in the Archives of the University of Notre Dame.
2. Walter Elliott, *Mission Sermons* (Washington, D.C., 1926).
3. An illustration of this characteristic may be found in the *American Catholic Who's Who* of 1911, a 700 page volume which contains good sized notices of hundreds of persons not comparable to Elliott in importance. The item on Elliott, utterly devoid of data on which to base a proper appraisal of the man, and looking suspiciously like his own work, follows:

ELLIOTT, REV. WALTER, C.S.P.: B. 1842, in Detroit, Michigan; ed. by the Christian Brothers and at Notre Dame University, Indiana; was a practising lawyer in Detroit before joining the Paulists; contributor to the *Catholic World* and other publications. Address: Brookland, Washington, D.C.

4. See Sister Joan Bland, *op. cit.*, 159.
5. *The Missionary*, XLII (June, 1928), 225.
6. *Life of Christ* (New York, 1901). Fifty thousand copies of this book were published between the time of its appearance, and the printing of the latest edition in 1925. The first edition contained numerous illustrations which a Paulist amateur artist skillfully adapted from Tissot's famous watercolors.
7. (Washington, D.C., 1910). This celebrated Dominican, known as the Illuminated Doctor, was one of a group of preachers who, in the middle of the fourteenth century, addressed themselves with vigor and success to raising the spiritual level of all classes of people. Tauler's reputation rests chiefly upon sermons translated into English—for the first time completely—by Elliott. True, Tauler has been looked upon with suspicion by some Catholics, partly because of his many Protestant admirers; but Newman's associate, J. B. Dalgairns, successfully vindicated Tauler's orthodoxy.

Study XV (Text, pages 254–273)

1. We have a good deal of detailed information with regard to Hewit: his correspondence; his own account of his conversion published in the *Catholic World* (October, 1887); an earlier booklet on the same subject; revealing pages that appear in his *Memoir of Father Baker;* also a letter from Hewit to his Amherst classmates at their reunion in 1852. These and other supplementary sources have been studied by Paulist Father Joseph Flynn, who embodied the results in his scholarly unpublished Master's dissertation, "The Early Years of Augustine F. Hewit, C.S.P., 1820–1846." The Catholic University of America (1945).
2. Catholic theology teaches that in the case of adults an intention is required as a condition for the valid reception of sacraments. Presumably Hewit shared the Protestant misconception of this doctrine current at that time.

3. The spirit of that period among American Protestants was reflected in a poem written on the ordination of the convert, James Roosevelt Bayley, to the diaconate in Rome. The author, Rev. A. E. C. Knox, later an Episcopal bishop, entitled the verses *Hymn of the Priests,* and called it a lament for "one of their number who had been sacrilegiously ordained a deacon, after abjuring the Catholic communion at Rome." In 1843, an Episcopal periodical, the *True Catholic,* announcing the "conversion of a popish priest" referred to "the public admission of a clerical convert from the Church of Rome, into the bosom of the Catholic Church in this country." The "penitent," an Italian gentleman named Bignati, who had been two years a priest in the Romish communion, "stood outside the rails until the bishop of Chichester absolved him, took him by the hand and received him into the holy Communion of the Church of England."

4. Dr. Charles Seabury was rector of St. Luke's Church, later editor of *The Churchman.*

5. For letters in the preceding paragraphs, see PFA, Hecker Letters.

6. Theodore Maynard makes this plain in his fine biography. *op. cit.*

7. Father Hewit's article appeared in *That Unknown Country* or *What Living Men Believe Concerning Punishment After Death* (Springfield, Massachusetts, 1888). These essays by some fifty picked writers in Europe and America, represented all shades of belief. In one essay, Cardinal Manning pointed out that it is contrary to the Catholic faith to teach that grace is withheld from pagans, Jews and heretics.

8. Emery, practical leader of the French clergy during the French Revolution, left many writings, the best known of which is an essay on the mitigation of the sufferings of the damned.

9. Father Flynn, *op. cit.*, 87, gives a transcript of this letter taken from the *Statistical Catalogue of the Amherst College Class of 1839.*

10. John Tracy Ellis in *The Formative Years of the Catholic University of America* (Washington, D.C., 1946), cites numerous articles published at the time in the *Catholic World.* The same author mentions various disputes that occurred in connection with the founding of the university; and in some of these the Paulists were involved, partly because of

personal associations with members of the hierarchy—Cardinal Gibbons; Archbishop Ireland; Bishop Keane, who regarded himself as spiritual disciple of Father Hecker; Bishop John L. Spalding. Spalding, who secured the contribution of $300,000 that launched the University and who was at first put forward as candidate for the rectorship, had resided in the Paulist motherhouse, while writing a biography of his uncle, Martin J. Spalding, with the help of papers bequeathed to Father Hecker by the late archbishop. The part played by Hewit in the activity that preceded and followed the opening of the University is indicated by Father Ellis. The University began as an exclusively graduate school of theology. For the degree of licentiate it required two years of work, a written dissertation, and a public defense in Latin of printed theses. Bishop Keane, the first rector, toured Europe before the opening of the University, for the purpose of securing internationally distinguished professors, but failed in some of these attempts—as he failed later to secure from Archbishop Ryan a waiver on Dr. Denis Dougherty (later cardinal) at that time professor at Overbrook Seminary, but willing to go to the University if permitted.

11. The old Manor House was the College of St. Thomas Aquinas; and the Paulists remained there until 1910 when Father Gillis, then master of novices, selected a new site nearby on which the present St. Paul's College was erected.

Study XVI (Text, pages 274–288)

1. Joseph I. Malloy, C.S.P. *The Church of St. Paul the Apostle in New York* (New York, 1951), 5.
2. PFA, Hecker Papers, memorandum by Elliott.
3. The *National Review* (London), No. 193 (March, 1899).
4. Abbé Félix Klein. English translation, *Americanism: A Phantom Heresy*. The Aquin Book Shop (Atchison, Kansas, 1952).

Index*

Alden, John and Priscilla, 254
Alexander, Father, *see* Czvitkovicz
Alphonsus Liguori, St., 15-16, 27-28, 57, 74 n, 75 n, 85 n, 86 n, 102, 192 n, 267
Antonelli, Giacomo Cardinal, 81 n

Badin, Stephen, 73 n
Baker, Augustine, O.S.B., 94, 177, 252
Baker, Francis A., C.S.P., 27, 29, 33, 35-36, 38, 46, 62, 87 n, 97-98, 111, 116, 127, 132-138, 141, 193 n, 258-259, 265
Barnabò, Alessandro Cardinal, 49, 55-58, 60-67, 80 n, 81 n, 84 n, 101, 155, 266
Barry, Bishop John, 52, 58, 78 n
Barry, Canon William, 185, 212, 285
Bassi, Ugo, 72 n
Bayley, Archbishop James Roosevelt, 45-46, 48, 52, 57, 74 n, 80 n, 81 n, 96, 98-99, 107-110, 140-141, 223, 230, 235, 290 n, 296 n
Becker, Bishop Thomas Albert, 74 n
Bedini, Archbishop Gaetano, 12, 55-56, 64-65, 72 n, 73 n, 81 n, 96
Benedict XIV, 87 n
Benedict XV, 286
Bernard, Father, *see* Hafkenscheid
Bizzarri, Giuseppe-Andrea Cardinal, 59, 61, 64-65, 84 n
Blanchet, Archbishop Francis N., 73 n
Blosius, François-Louis, 252
Borgess, Bishop Caspar H., 78 n

Bouquillon, Dr. Thomas, 210, 271
Brady, Edward, C.S.P., 130
Brann, Henry A., 130
Brown, Algernon, C.S.P., 130
Brown, George Loring, 63, 86 n
Brown, Louis, C.S.P., 130
Brownson, Henry, 220, 222, 234-235, 289 n, 292 n
Brownson, Orestes A.: 214-236; as apologist, 218-221, 224; *Catholic World* and, 232-236; characteristics, 214-218; Fitzpatrick and, 218-219; Hughes and, 222-223, 225-229, 232
— verdicts on: by Maynard, 215-216, 221; by Parsons, 215; by Swift, 219; by Hewit, 235-236; by Hecker, 215, 218, 236
— writings, 216-223, 227, 230-235; letters, 224, 226-230, 233-234, 292 n, 294 n
— *see also*, 11, 18, 75 n, 86 n, 106, 165, 268, 289 n, 290 n, 291 n, 293 n
Buggenoms, Louis de, C.SS.R., 79 n
Burke, Edmund, 6
Byrne, John F., C.SS.R., 75 n, 78 n, 79 n

Carroll, Archbishop John, 5, 69 n, 73 n
Carroll, Charles, 73 n
Caussade, Jean Pierre de, S.J., 94, 178
Chabrol, Count Guillaume de, 211-212
Channing, William Ellery, 78 n, 171

* *Index* made by Josephine D. Casgrain, B.A., formerly editorial assistant, Mid-European Studies Center, New York, N.Y.

INDEX

Charles Borromeo, St., 190 n
Chatard, Bishop Francis S., 209
Chateaubriand, François-René de, 185
Cheverus, Bishop John, 10
Church in the U.S.: 3-14; Americanism, 207, 211; Catholic Total Abstinence Union, 208-209; Catholic University, 209-210; clergy, 5, 73 n; councils, 13-14; disputes, 206; Germans, 6, 45, 50, 71 n, 206, 208-209; growth, 3-14, 205-213; Irish, 5-11, 39-40, 71 n, 101, 206, 209; laity, 5, 73 n; Parliament of Religions, 211; school question, 207, 210-211; Vatican and, 5-6, 12, 72 n
Civiltà Cattolica, 62, 86 n
Clement Hofbauer, St., 16, 75 n, 78 n, 79 n
Coffin, Bishop Robert, 76 n
Connolly, Archbishop Thomas L., 58, 65, 83 n
Corcoran, Dr. James A., 34, 214, 264, 268, 289 n
Corrigan, Archbishop Michael A., 206-209, 282-283
Cummings, Dr. Jeremiah, 223, 229, 231, 291 n
Curci, Carlo Maria, S.J., 62, 86 n
Curtis, George William, 76 n
Czvitkovicz, Alexander, C.SS.R., 23, 26-27, 30, 33, 265

Dechamps, Victor Cardinal, C.SS.R., 21, 48, 76 n, 79 n, 82 n, 188 n
Delassus, Canon Henri, 212, 289 n
Deshon, Daniel, 274
Deshon, George, C.S.P.: 274-288; characteristics, 275-279; letters, 59-62, 275, 281-285, 292 n; see also, 27, 29-30, 34, 36, 46, 87 n, 98, 108-109, 122, 127, 141, 144-145, 151, 168, 192 n, 198 n, 199 n, 205, 231, 265, 271
Dold, Louis, C.SS.R., 78 n, 79 n
Dougherty, Denis Cardinal, 297 n
Douglas, Edward, C.SS.R., 51, 60, 77 n, 85 n
Doyle, Alexander P., C.S.P., 146, 161, 208, 210, 245
Druelle, Father, C.S.C., 59, 84 n

Dudley, Thomas, 147
Dwight, Theodore, 11

Early, Father, S.J., 121
Eccleston, Archbishop Samuel, 16, 74 n
Elder, Archbishop William, 209
Elliott, Walter, C.S.P.: 237-253; characteristics, 241-244, 294 n; declining years, 18-23, 247-248, 251; Hecker and, 240-241, 244-245, 250-251; missionary career, 241; spiritual teaching, 251-252; tributes to, 252-253; writings, 249-251, 295 n; letters, 238; see also, 28-29, 76 n, 91, 106, 115, 127-128, 139, 144-146, 152, 156-158, 161, 196 n, 199 n, 200 n, 201 n, 207, 271, 281, 287, 289 n, 297 n
Ellis, Dr. John Tracy, 189 n, 296 n
Emerson, Ralph Waldo, 75 n, 78 n, 155, 171, 186
Emery, Jacques-André, 269, 296 n
England, Bishop John, 6, 34, 37, 69 n, 73 n, 77, 98, 162, 263-264
Errington, Archbishop George, 82 n, 83 n
Ewing family, 73 n, 74 n

Faber, Frederick William, 177, 190 n, 221, 260
Farley, John Cardinal, 108, 195 n
Fenwick, Bishop Benedict, 18
Fenwick, Edward, 73 n
Fitzpatrick, Bishop John, 10, 18, 25, 76 n, 218-219
Fitzralph, Archbishop Richard, 102
Flynn, Joseph, C.S.P., 295 n, 296 n
Forbes, Dr. John Murray, 111, 195, 229, 291 n, 292 n
Francis of St. Lawrence, C.P., 59, 83 n
Francis of Sales, St., 246

Gallitzin, Demetrius, 24, 73 n
Gartland, Bishop Francis, 77 n
Gaston, William, 12, 74 n
Gavazzi, Alessandro, 72 n
Gibbons, James Cardinal, 27, 101, 207-208, 271, 283-285, 297 n
Gillis, James M., C.S.P., 242, 287

INDEX

Gilmour, Bishop Richard, 74 n, 209
Godin, Henri, 287
Gratry, Auguste, 189 n, 214, 289 n
Greeley, Horace, 72 n
Gregorio, Father, Carmelite, 58, 83 n
Gregory XVI, 70 n
Guilday, Peter, 34-35, 70 n, 71 n, 77 n, 167

Hafkenscheid, Bernard, C.SS.R., 17, 22-23, 25-27, 33, 42, 45, 62, 264-265
Harold, William V., O.P., 5
Hecker, George V., 48, 66, 68, 97-98, 121, 168, 291 n, 292 n
Hecker, Mrs. George V., 166
Hecker, Isaac T., C.S.P.: bishops friendly to, 47, 52, 57-58, 65, 80 n, 81 n, 96-97, 99; Catechism of Trent, 18, 148, 171
— characteristics: 17, 42-43, 53, 80-81, 169, 221-222, 240, 267; as editor and publisher, 154-168; as speaker, 24, 29, 42, 154-168; as writer, 43, 62-63, 170
— expulsion, 53-68, 81 n; first missions, 23-40, 97; influence in community, 93, 105, 125, 128-129; spiritual authors favored by, 94, 177-178
— tributes to: by Barry, 185; by Bayley, 80; by Elliott, 240; by Ireland, 186; by Keane, Spalding and Walworth, 80; at Council of Baltimore, 168
— views: on Church authority, 167, 171-173, 175, 178, 188; on conversions, 29, 32, 43, 64, 66; on Holy Ghost, 176-177; on ideal community; on religious vows, 25-26, 95-96, 99, 102-104, 190 n; on total abstinence, 161-162
— vocation, 18-20, 43; letters, 51, 58, 60-61, 63-68, 81 n, 85 n, 93, 95, 140, 156
— see also, 11, 21-22, 46, 48-51, 73 n, 76 n, 79 n, 82 n, 83 n, 86 n, 106-107, 110, 113-117, 124, 126-127, 129, 141, 151, 172-174, 179-184, 187, 193 n, 194 n, 196 n,

Hecker, Isaac T. (*continued*)
198 n-201 n, 205-207, 212, 214-220, 223-236, 237-239, 241-253, 265-266, 268, 270-271, 275-276, 279, 281, 283-286, 288, 289 n-295 n, 297 n
Held, Frederick de, C.SS.R., 17, 19-21, 48-50, 57, 79 n, 81 n, 82 n, 265
Hewit, Augustine F., C.S.P.: 254-288; Catholic University and, 270-271; family tree, 254; Hecker and, 265-266; progress towards the Church, 254-264; writings, 264, 268-269; letters, 227-228, 262, 264, 266-267, 269-270; *see also*, 23-24, 26, 29, 32, 34-39, 46-47, 60, 62, 77 n, 81 n, 87 n, 98, 103, 106, 109, 116, 122, 127, 132-137, 165, 188 n, 193 n, 198 n, 199 n, 205, 218, 224-225, 227-228, 232-235, 281-282, 292 n, 295 n, 296 n, 297 n
Hewit, Henry, 262
Hewitt, Nathaniel, 254
Holden, Vincent, C.S.P., 75 n
Hughes, Archbishop John, 18, 52, 57, 72 n, 73 n, 80 n, 99, 104, 110, 119, 127, 193 n, 225-226, 228-231, 291 n, 292 n
Hurley, Edmund, 129, 144

Ireland, Archbishop John, 7, 101, 128, 130, 164, 167, 186-187, 206-208, 210, 271, 297 n
Ives, Dr. Silliman, 81 n, 113

Joseph, St., sermon on, 160

Karslake brothers, 190 n
Katzer, Archbishop Frederick X., 210
Keane, Bishop John J.: Parliament of Religions and, 211; *see also*, 93, 188 n, 189 n, 207-209, 271, 285, 297 n
Kenrick, Archbishop Francis P., 52, 57, 65, 70 n, 73 n, 110, 134, 136, 223, 264-265
Kerby, Msgr. William J., 252
Klein, Félix, 185, 212, 281, 287, 297 n

INDEX

LaFarge, John, 279
Lallemant, Louis, S.J., 94, 177
Lambert, Louis A., 130
Lambruschini, Luigi Cardinal, 75 n
Lamers, William and Mary, 199 n
Lecky, William, 6
Lefevre, Bishop Peter P., 78 n
Leo XIII, 176, 184, 250, 281, 283, 285-286
Leslie, Shane, 76 n
Letters:
— *Part I:* Bayley, 80 n, 81 n; Dechamps, 82 n; Deshon, 61-62; Hecker, 51, 58, 61, 63-68, 81 n, 82 n, 85 n; De Held, 79 n, 80 n, 82 n; Hughes, 57-58, 80 n, 81 n; Ruland, 85 n; Walworth, 60
— *Part II:* Hecker, 83, 95, 104-105, 140, 156; Rosecrans, 144-145; Walworth, 108-109, 112, 115-117, 193 n; Young, 140
— *Part III:* Brownson, 224, 226, 234, 292 n-294 n; Deshon, 275, 282-285, 292 n; Elliott, 238; Hecker, 224-225, 235, 292 n, 293 n; Hewit, 227-228, 257, 265-267; Leo XIII, 286
Lyman, Dwight, 132, 134
Lynch, Bishop Patrick N., 34, 37-38, 52, 58, 98, 263-264, 267

McCaffrey, Dr. John, 223
McCloskey, John Cardinal, 18-19, 107-108, 110, 116, 235
McFarland, Bishop Francis P., 108, 193 n
McGee, Thomas Darcy, 225
McMaster, James A., 17, 19, 21, 81 n
McQuaid, Bishop Bernard J., 207-208
Maignen, Charles, 212, 282-283, 289 n
Malloy, Joseph I., C.S.P., 279, 297 n
Manahan, Dr. Ambrose, 229, 291 n
Manning, Henry Edward Cardinal, 76 n, 82 n, 83 n, 103, 176, 188 n, 189 n, 190 n, 296 n
Maréchal, Archbishop Ambrose, S.S., 5, 70 n
Martin, Jacob L., 72 n

Mauron, Nicholas, C.SS.R., 44, 50, 79 n, 80 n, 82 n
Maynard, Theodore, 221, 289 n, 291 n, 294 n, 296 n
Meulemeester, Maurice de, C.SS.R., 76 n, 80 n, 82 n
Missions, early: 15-40; in Charleston, 34; chronicle of, 77 n; in Georgia, 35; in New York (St. Joseph's), 24; in Norfolk (St. Patrick's), 30-33; *see also,* 41, 97
Monk, Maria, 11-12
Morse, Samuel F. B., 11

Neumann, Ven. John Nepomucene, C.SS.R., 16, 111, 264
Newman, John Henry Cardinal, 83 n, 84 n, 132, 138, 151, 158, 185, 189 n, 214, 220-221, 260-262, 285, 291 n, 295 n

O'Connor, Bishop Michael, 209
O'Conor, Charles, 121, 196 n, 223
O'Gorman, Bishop Thomas, 130
O'Hern, Lewis, C.S.P., 252
Olier, Jacques, 189 n
Onderdonk, Dr. Benjamin T., 113, 195 n

Parsons, Wilfrid, S.J., 215, 290 n, 294 n
Passerat, Joseph, C.SS.R., 44, 78 n, 79 n
Paul, St., 41, 92, 188 n, 192 n, 297
Paulist parish, first: 119-130; development, 120-129, 196 n, 197 n; instruction of children, 129; liturgy, 127; music, 129, *see also* Young; sermons, 126-128; staff, 129-130, *see also* 131-153; topography, 119-121
Paulists: beginnings, 97-98; convert members, 131, 151-152; decision on vows, 102-103; decree of separation, 67; early missions, 15-40, 140-141, 145, *see also* Redemptorists; first parish, 104, 131-153, 161, 193 n; first rule, 99, 104, 190 n; first ten (racial and academic origins), 131; founding, 61, 63-68; growth, 91-93, 105, 107, 122, 131, 286; specialized aim, 100-102; tribute

INDEX

Paulists (*continued*)
  to (in *America*), 287; *see also* Hecker, Walworth
Perraud, Adolphe Cardinal, 189 n
Petersen, Theodore, C.S.P., 86 n
Philip Neri, St., 94-96, 189 n, 199 n
Pierce, Franklin, 33, 72 n
Pise, Dr. Constantine, 261
Pius IX: 53-68; comments on Americans, 55, 66; Italy under, 12, 54-55, 72 n; *see also* 50, 82 n, 83 n, 87 n, 92, 97, 101, 194 n
Pius XI, 286
Pius XII, 287
Pocahontas, 152
Poe, Edgar Allen, 121
Prendergast, John, 145
Preston, Msgr. Thomas Scott, 153, 195 n, 212 n, 294 n
Protestants: bigots, 4, 7-11, 69 n, 71 n, 72 n; converts, 12, 14, 17, 37, 40-41, 73 n, 74 n, 91-105, 126; sympathetic, 12, 70 n, 72 n; *see also* 18, 78 n
Purcell, Edward Sheridan, 190 n
Purcell, Archbishop John B., 25, 52, 58, 73 n

Quinn, William, 25

Rampolla, Mariano Cardinal, 208, 283
Redemptorists: 15-29, 74 n; Belgian, 49-50, 76 n, 81 n; changes in, 44-47, 78 n-79 n; converts among, 17, 19, 27; early missions, 22-29, 30-40, *see also* Paulists; Eastern rites and, 49; English-speaking house, 33, 44, 46; German, 15-16, 44-45; Neapolitan, 74 n, 83 n
Reed, Rebecca, 11
Reisach, Carl Cardinal von, 62
Religious communities: Holy Cross, 83 n, 84 n; Jesuits, 121; Oblates, 190 n; Oratory, 95-96, 189 n; Sulpicians, 96, 189 n; *see also* Paulists, Redemptorists
Repplier, Agnes, 166
Reynolds, Bishop Ignatius, 34, 263-265
Richard, Gabriel, 73 n

Riordan, Archbishop Patrick William, 284
Ripley, George, 43, 75 n
Robinson, Thomas V., C.S.P., 126, 152-153
Roman congregations: Bishops and regulars, 57, 59, 61, 81 n; Propaganda, 55-56
Roosevelt family, 74 n
Roosevelt, Theodore, 74 n, 155, 208
Rosecrans, Adrian, C.S.P., 93, 127, 131, 143-146, 152
Rosecrans, Bishop Sylvester, 74 n, 144
Rosecrans, Gen. William S., 143, 146, 199 n, 274
Ruland, George, C.SS.R., 45, 47, 81 n, 85 n, 266
Ryan, Archbishop Patrick J., 297 n

Santa Susanna, Church of, 81 n
Satolli, Francesco Cardinal, 210
Searle, George, C.S.P., 144, 147-152, 197 n, 199 n, 268, 271, 277-278
Smetana, Rudolf, C.SS.R., 50, 78 n, 79 n, 81 n
Smith, Bernard, O.S.B., 59, 84 n
Smith, John Talbot, 71 n, 197 n
Smith, Michael, C.S.P., 272
Spalding, Bishop John L., 7, 52, 97, 130, 183, 208-209, 297 n.
Spalding, Archbishop Martin J., 57, 73 n, 130, 167, 223, 297 n
Spencer, Francis A., O.P., 130, 197 n
Stone, James Kent, C.P., 130, 197 n
Suhard, Emmanuel Cardinal, 287

Talbot, Msgr. George, 58, 76 n, 83 n
Taney, Roger Brooke, 12, 74 n
Tauler, John, 250, 252, 295 n
Thoreau, Henry David, 9, 71 n, 76 n, 155
Tillotson, R. B., C.S.P., 122, 126-127, 138-139, 143, 197 n-199 n, 240

Vaughan, Cardinal Herbert, 188 n

INDEX

Wadhams, Bishop Edgar P., 74 n, 113
Walsh, Richard, C.S.P., 168, 200 n
Walworth, Clarence A.: 106-118; characteristics, 111-115; eloquence, 28, 112-113; separation from the founders, 106-118; views on founding of Paulists, 97, 102-103; writings, 113, 116; letters, 60, 62, 97, 109-110, 115, 117, 193 n; *see also* 17, 19, 21, 23-24, 27, 30-32, 34, 36, 42, 45-46, 85 n, 87 n, 101, 122, 127, 194 n-196 n, 199 n, 224-225, 241, 265, 267, 275, 292 n
Walworth, Ellen, 116, 196 n
Ward, Wilfrid, 83 n, 84 n

Ward, William G., 149, 151, 291 n
Whittingham, Dr. William R., 133, 257-259, 262
Willard, Frances, 209
William of St. Amour, 102
Wiseman, Nicholas Cardinal, 22, 76 n, 82 n, 190 n, 260
Wood, Archbishop James Frederick, 74 n
Wuest, Joseph, C.SS.R., 280
Wyman, Henry, C.S.P., 130

Young, Alfred, C.S.P., 107, 116, 122, 127, 129, 139-143, 199 n
Young, Bishop Josue Moody, 74 n

Zwierlein, Frederick J., 289 n